ENCYCLOPAEDIA OF HINDU CIVILIZATION, CUSTOMS AND TRADITIONS

ENCYCLOPAEDIA OF
HINDU CIVILIZATION, CUSTOMS AND TRADITIONS

Edited by

Shailendra Sengar

ANMOL PUBLICATIONS PVT. LTD.
NEW DELHI - 110 002 (INDIA)

ANMOL PUBLICATIONS PVT. LTD.
H.O.: 4374/4B, Ansari Road, Darya Ganj,
New Delhi-110 002 (India)
Ph.: 23278000, 23261597
B.O.: No. 1015, Ist Main Road, BSK IIIrd Stage
IIIrd Phase, IIIrd Block,
Bangalore - 560 085 (India)
Visit us at: www.anmolpublications.com

*Encyclopaedia of Hindu Civilization,
Customs and Traditions*

First Published, 2008

ISBN 978-81-261-3523-3

PRINTED IN INDIA

Printed at Mehra Offset Press, Delhi.

Contents

Preface

India is one of ancient civilization of the world. The underlying efficiency of the ancient Indus Valley civilization is remarkable. An efficient and technologically advanced urban culture is clearly evident in the Indus Valley civilization. Advanced Harappan art indicates that the people of the ancient Indus Valley had fine artistic sensibilities. Moreover, the underlying efficiency of this civilization is accurately reflected by the complex Harappan social structure, which integrated several different ethnic and religious groups and ensured enduring peace and prosperity. The ancient Indus Valley civilization was quite clearly advanced, to a great extent.

The Vedic civilization is the culture associated with the people who composed the religious texts called the Vedas, in the Indian subcontinent. It stretched from what is today Punjab in India and Pakistan, NWFP (Pakistan) and most of northern India. Mainstream scholarship places the Vedic civilization into the 2nd and 1st millennia BC. Hindu traditions suggest dates as early as the 6th millennium BC and a spread of the hyperpower-style Vedic culture.

One of the most controversial topic regarding the India's society and culture is its stringent caste system. The word "caste" is taken from the Portuguese word casta. It can be defined as a rigid social system in which a social hierarchy is maintained generation after generation and allows little mobility out of the position to which a person is born. This system dates almost 3000 years back and was formed based on the need to form a social order in ancient India. It is still very prevalent as part of India's society. Today, it occurs more in the rural villages than in big urban cities; and more in the social matters of kinship and marriages than in impersonal day-to-day

interaction, such as taking the bus. Having been around for centuries, it is highly doubtful that the caste system will die out completely. Its presence will still be felt in the near future.

Hinduism is the religion of the majority of the population of India. The holy books of the religion namely the Vedas and the Upanishads clearly explain the rituals and their mystical contents. They also explain in detail the observance of sacrificial and purification rituals Hinduism is another name for what is known as Sanatana Dharma or the Religious Prennis. The objective of this book to offer directly analysis of Indian Civilization, the great Indian traditions and the unique Indian customs.

Shailendra Sengar

Early Hindu Civilization

The Ancient Indus Valley Civilization

The underlying efficiency of the ancient Indus Valley civilization is remarkable. The Harappan government was very complex, and yet very efficient. An efficient and technologically advanced urban culture is clearly evident in the Indus Valley civilization.

Advanced Harappan art indicates that the people of the ancient Indus Valley had fine artistic sensibilities. Moreover, the underlying efficiency of this civilization is accurately reflected by the complex Harappan social structure, which integrated several different ethnic and religious groups and ensured enduring peace and prosperity. The ancient Indus Valley civilization was quite clearly advanced, to a great extent.

The quality of municipal town planning is an outstanding feature of the Harappan civilization. The uniform planning of towns and cities suggests the presence of efficient municipal governments which placed a high priority on hygiene. The streets of Harappan cities such as Mohenjodaro or Harappa were laid out in an efficient grid pattern, which ensured that houses were protected from noise, odours and thieves.

In addition, houses were safeguarded against floods by platforms, and, as an additional measure of precaution against inundation, rectangular salients or bastions were added to the peripheral brick walls of the towns, Lothal for example, in order to divert the current. Baked bricks, which were rare at this time in the Near East, were used by the Harappans to construct wells, building platforms and drains that provided the cities of the Indus Empire with excellent drainage for rainwater and sewage.

Most Harappan towns had adopted the standard Indus gridiron planning, including smaller towns such as Rangpur and Surkotada. One exception is the town of Banawali, according to the excavator, who commented that "the general principles of Indus planning as observed elsewhere were followed here also, yet there were some significant departures from the established norms. It therefore belies the general conception of a chessboard or gridiron pattern of planning... Systematic drainage is the exception rather than the rule." Regardless, the uniformity of town planning throughout the Indus Empire indicates that a strong centralized government must have functioned to standardize urban planning.

An efficient Harappan administration had many functions in the ancient Indus Valley civilization. There is evidence that town administrators enlisted the cooperation of the people in order to efficiently execute public works. The Harappans were highly disciplined people who were very conscious of their civic duties. The citizens kept their cities clean, and also had various other responsibilities. For example, residents would ensure that the underground drains were not choked by the solid waste carried by private drains from the baths. Moreover, the Harappans cooperated wholeheartedly when planning the towns and rebuilding damaged public buildings such as the docks, warehouses, fortification walls and platforms.

The Harappan administration also functioned to standardize industrial products such as metal tools and weapons, and even the units that were used to measure length. According to S. R. Rao, the "smooth flowing of trade channels can be attributed to strict vigilance by guilds or state agencies." In fact, an efficient system of distribution of agricultural and industrial products, and raw materials, indigenous as well as imported, is the high watermark of Harappan administration. The Harappans could grow surplus food to feed the various specialized workers through an efficient distributary channel which presupposes an equally efficient administration of towns and cities and regulation of trade. The high degree of homogeneity in Harappan products, the uniform planning of Indus towns, the rigorous enforcement of trade and municipal regulations and the efficient Harappan distribution system all confirm that there was a highly effective and efficient administration in the ancient Indus Valley civilization.

The Harappans had analytical minds. The great accuracy that they achieved in measuring the physical units of length, mass and time indicates the advanced level of scientific and technological development reached by them. Harappan measurements were extremely precise. Their smallest division, which is marked on an ivory scale of Lothal, was approximately 1.704 millimetres, the smallest division ever recorded on a scale of the Bronze Age. Harappan engineers followed the decimal division of measurement for all practical purposes, including the measurement of mass as revealed by their hexahedron weights. Consequently, Harappan measurements are very precise. The remarkable symmetry in the disposition of Harappan buildings is shown by the remaining rows of baths, drains and remnants of walls. The designing of the Lothal dock and warehouse and the provision of manholes and sewers in cities are other examples of the Harappan scientific approach to human problems. The scientific approach of the people of the Indus Valley is indicative of their technologically advanced and efficient lifestyle.

The Harappans were great lovers of the fine arts, and especially dancing, painting, and plastic arts. Various sculptures, seals, pottery, gold jewellery, terra-cotta figures and other interesting works of art indicate that the Harappans had fine artistic sensibilities. The art of the Harappans is highly realistic. The sheer anatomical details of much of Harappan art is unique, and terra-cotta art is also noted for its extremely careful modelling of animal figures. Sir John Marshall once reacted with surprise when he saw the famous Harappan bronze statuette of the slender-limbed "dancing girl" in Mohenjodaro:

When I first saw them I found it difficult to believe that they were prehistoric; they seemed so completely to upset all established ideas about early art. Modelling such as this was unknown in the ancient world up to the Hellenistic age of Greece, and I thought, therefore, that some mistake must surely have been made; that these figures had found their way into levels some 3000 years older than those to which they properly belonged.... Now, in these statuettes, it is just this anatomical truth which is so startling; that makes us wonder whether, in this all-important matter, Greek artistry could possibly have been anticipated by the sculptors of a far-off age on the banks of the Indus.

Bronze, terra-cotta and stone sculptures in dancing poses also reveal much about the Harappan art of dancing. Similarly, a harp-like instrument depicted on an Indus seal and two shell objects from Lothal confirm that stringed musical instruments were in use in the ancient Indus Valley civilization. Today, much of the Harappan art is considered advanced for their time period. The pictures that were carved into seals that were used for commercial purposes are regarded today as masterpieces in miniature art form. The fine brush work of the Harappans is attested to by various motifs drawn on the vessels of Micaceous Red Ware from Lothal. The finest examples of plastic art are the seals, known for their calligraphy and realistic rendering of animal figures. In fact, the Harappans were responsible for developing a new style of painting animal figures in their natural environments. It is generally accepted that Harappan art is much more advanced than any other art from this time period.

The crowning achievement of the Indus Empire was the cultural integration of different ethnic and religious groups, which ensured enduring peace and material prosperity. Although mythological scenes portrayed on seals suggest occasional skirmishes between the different socio-religious groups, the Proto-austioloids, Mediterraneans, Mongoloids and Alpines, many more seals suggest the integration of ideologically or socially different groups, which is symbolically shown by animals with several heads that represent a combination of different tribes or social groups. This integration of heterogeneous clans or tribes in the Harappan socio-politico-economic structure was secured by the free trade of different goods and commodities between different peoples of the Indus Valley, which resulted in mutual benefits for all Harappans. The central government could regulate trade and ensure the efficient and equitable distribution of agricultural and industrial products throughout the vast Empire, and to all socio-religious groups, by establishing a network of market towns.

Another approach of the Harappan peoples to the problem of religious differences was to form confederacies in order to convert other peoples to the Harappan ideology and way of life by offering the benefits of superior material culture and ensuring a more peaceful life. In addition, interethnic marriage was encouraged and was very common, as revealed by the examination of joint-burials of Lothal. This integration of different socio-ethnic groups in Harappan society closely resembles the integration of different cultures in the Greek Empire under Alexander the Great, who ruled over two thousand years after the prime years of the Indus Valley civilization.

Serious social inequalities existed in the Harappan civilization, most notably between the rulers and the ruled, and between men and women. The treatment of women by the Harappans indicates that this civilization, at least in some respects, was very primitive. The dichotomy of Harappan towns and cities into a citadel or Acropolis and a "Lower Town" was deliberately introduced in the Indus Valley in order to enhance the prestige of the ruler of the town, or rajah. These rulers and nobles lived on the Acropolis, which offered better protection from floods.

Although greater importance was clearly given to the rulers than the ruled, among the ruled the rich merchants and the poor craftsmen lived together in the "Lower Town," and, in contrast to ancient Mesopotamian and Egyptian traditions, Harappan rulers were treated as common men after their deaths. Within the Harappan family, the father had absolute authority. He would make all of the decisions in the house, and the children and wives were often treated unfairly. Girls were unwanted, and boys were treated much better, and with more respect. Undeniably, these social inequalities were a major problem for many of the peoples of the Indus Valley, and were likely among the many factors which led to the decline of Harappan civilization.

The Harappan society was indeed a "Complex Society" in the sense in which Gordon Childe first used the term. According to him, the criteria for considering a society as complex are: (1) cities (2) full-time craft and career specialists (3) taxation (4) monumental architecture (5) social stratification (6) exact and predictive sciences (7) writing (8) developed artistic styles (9) long distance trade in luxury items and (10) the state. Firstly, it is universally accepted that Indus cities such as Harappa, Mohenjodaro, Lothal and Rehman Dheri were extremely well planned. The knowledge that full-time specialists, such as bead-makers, ivory-carvers, metallurgists and seal-engravers, contributed to the efficiency of the Harappan economy satisfies the second criterion.

Although there is no evidence of taxation, the third requirement, the maintenance of public works must have necessitated the collection of a minimal amount of taxes, since the wages of workers would have to be paid. Monumental architecture, the fourth requirement, is evident in the massive Harappan dockyards, granaries, warehouses, brick platforms and protective walls which were utilitarian in character. The fifth requirement, social stratification, is obvious from the dichotomy of Harappan town planning which gave greater importance to the ruler than to the ruled. The contributions of the Indus civilization to exact and predictive sciences, which criterion number six requires, such as mathematics, astronomy, engineering and chemistry are noteworthy: they introduced the decimal division in measuring length and mass, studied the stars and invented an instrument to measure whole sections of the horizon, built tidal docks after studying tides, waves and currents, perfected the system of sewerage and evolved new techniques in metallurgy.

In addition, certain seal-inscriptions suggest great progress in conceptual thinking, especially in the field of cosmology. Harappan writing, the seventh requirement, was extremely advanced. The Harappans were the first to simplify a primitive logo-graphic-cum-syllabic writing into a phonetic script which was partially syllabic in the beginning, and then ultimately evolved into an alphabetic script. Indus script is currently being decoded, which is of crucial significance to ancient Indian history. Consequent of their fine artistic sensibilities, the Harappans did indeed have developed artistic styles, which satisfies the eighth requirement.

Long distance trade, the ninth requirement, with the other ancient civilizations of that time period, namely Egypt and Mesopotamia, was quite common, as indicated by the presence of foreign seals in the cities of these Empires. Finally, the uniformity of town planning in cities throughout the Indus Empire, from Surkotada to Mohenjodaro, indicates the existence of a strong centralized government, and satisfies the final requirement of Gordon Childe, the State. Undeniably, the Harappan civilization was very sophisticated and complex.

The Indus civilization has made several permanent contributions to the progress of humankind. Their simplified alphabetic system of writing which facilitated quick communication and recording of thought was the first of its kind. Harappan metrology laid the foundation of science and technology. The engineering skill of the Harappans, especially in building docks after a careful study of tides, waves and currents, is remarkable for their age. They not only followed modern principles in their building techniques, but also achieved advanced standards of construction.

The Indus decimal graduation of weights and length measures was the basis of later metrology. Another great achievement was the cultural integration of different religious and ethnic groups. As written by S.R. Rao, the eminent archaeologist and Indologist, "the Indus Valley civilization could not have survived for five centuries in its pristine form enforcing uniform laws and ensuring the proper distribution of goods over a vast territory of 1.5 million square kilometres had it not been a culturally and politically advanced society with a state that was effective, but not ruthless." Nevertheless, Harappan social inequalities indicate that the Indus Valley civilization was indeed a relatively primitive, ancient civilization.

The Indus Script and the Rongorongo Script have several things in common, apart from the fact that both are still regarded as undeciphered. The most striking parallel is that some pictograms look identical, as was pointed out already by G. de Hevesy, though he relied on insufficient renderings of the signs. Moreover, signs that look identical or nearly identical in its form must not have the same meaning. It cannot be denied, however, that both writing systems make use of a similar method of rendering words by pictograms and word sequences by ligatures and fusions. Moreover, the number of basic signs in both scripts is about 100. It is known that the Rongorongo script was not used for ornamental purposes, but that the inscribed tablets called kohau rongorongo were recited publicly on special occasions with a religious purport. Many of the inscriptions of the Indus seals and tablets look too short for a recitation, but since they have amulet function they served for a religious purpose, too. This is also evident from the motifs.

On the other hand, there are great differences. The Indus script was written on small seals, the average number of signs on a seal being only five, whereas the Rongorongo script was carved into wooden plates and sticks of considerable length in long lines of about 40, sometimes about 80 signs depending on the length of the tablet. The language that is expressed by the signs is known in the case of Rongorongo as being Rapanui, the language of Easter Island, called Rapa Nui nowadays, though not identical in grammar and words with the Rapanui that is presently spoken there.

It can only be surmised that the language of the Indus script is related to some of the languages spoken today in the Indus Valley or in the neighbouring areas. The Indus script is often applied as a legend to a motif, whereas the Rongorongo script has no relation to motifs, except that in a few cases the signs were carved on wooden figures like a breast ornament and a birdman.

Besides, the Indus script was used in big towns with a population of many thousands of people that had far reaching oversee and overland relations with other civilizations, the Rongorongo script was used by and known to a very small group of persons not exceeding five hundred, and it was developed in a tribal society that had very little and over several centuries no contact at all with other cultures.

Besides, the Indus script is one of the oldest writings that were conceived by the human mind going back to the era of the bull 3000 years before the beginning of our era. There are only the Sumerian and the Egyptian pictographic writings that are of equal age or even older. The Rongorongo writing is quite a new invention. It is certainly not older than 500 years. If the Easter Islanders had obtained any knowledge of a script in their former homeland, it can either be a derivative of Chinese or one of the many branches of the Brahmi script. Petroglyphs found in the Marquesas can be related to the Old Javanese Kawi script. The Kawi is based on the Brahmin script, that retains several features of the Indus script.

But even if there would be a closer relation between the Indus script and Rongorongo, it would not be helpful in the decipherment of each of the two, because we do only compare the unknown with the unknown. A decipherment of one or both of them can only be afforded by studying the two scripts in their own surroundings. This has been done here in the case of the Indus script by comparing it with verses of the Rig and Atharva Veda, the oldest books of the Indian tradition. They have been transmitted orally until our time, but nonetheless they contain several words that can be related to writing and writer. The word for 'sign' is well known in the Rigveda already and is once even used in connection with word (RV X.71.2). In the Atharva-Veda, charms in relation with amulets are common.

As in the case of the Vedas, the oral tradition of Easter Island is older and has survived the knowledge of writing. There exist, in particular, the readings of the islander Metoro of four tablets. They are not as incoherent as was thought hitherto by most of the ethnologists and linguists in this field. Several inscriptions and motifs of the Indus seals and tablets and the inscriptions of two Rongorongo artifacts as well as two lines of Metoro's reading of the tablet called Aruku Kurenga are presented here to the general public for information and further discussion.

A word script, with which we have to do in both cases, can be understood even by people who do not speak the same language, as is obvious from the Chinese script. It is not necessary to write grammatical forms, if the oral tradition is known to the writer and the reader alike. Even a letter script cannot dispense with the oral transmittance altogether, otherwise we could close our schools and universities. There is a great amount of disbelief and distrust, if somebody ventures to read these inscriptions as word scripts. In addition to those people who believe in the incomprehensiveness of all symbolic writings, there is another group who tries to mould them into a letter script under the influence of a way of thought that is associated for more than thousand years with letters.

We have heard in the Biblical tradition that the letter kills, but we do not care for this. I am myself no exception to this rule. So I tried to read the Indus signs as syllables. The results thereof have been published in 1997. Some of them have also appeared in the internet. Only after I was sure that the Rongorongo script can be read as a word script indeed, I came back to my former logo-graphic word readings of the Indus script published in 1992. Thus, the endeavour to read the Indus script syllabically was not entirely fruitless.

The author of the present paper does not pretend that his readings of each or of both the two writings are final, but after it has been in a process of more than 12 years most of the signs of the Indus script and a great number of inscriptions have been made readable in a way that it can be called a decipherment. The same can be said of the Rongorongo script. Not a decipherment in the narrow sense of the word, however, which is impossible in the case of word-scripts that do not consist of ciphers or letters, but of pictograms that can and must be read in various ways, but in the sense of making them understandable for the modern mind in spite of their inherent ambiguity.

If the word 'decipherment' could be altogether discarded in regard to these writings, he would do so. We do not possess a better word in our languages, however, and the newspapers want to have their headline. At any rate, this word should not be used by those who have nothing more to tell, but that symbolic writings are no writings at all. To use the word 'decipherment' in this sense is simply deceiving the public opinion. The reader who takes the time will find that a word script is very well readable and that it can even open new insights to a mind that is not only occupied with economics or technical problems.

The discussion of this issue should not be confined to the internet, but there should be held a symposium, where the protagonists of the different ways of deciphering can present the results of their investigations to each other and to an interested audience.

In the meantime, the rules that have been applied for the decipherment of the Indus script and the Easter Island script have also been proved successful in reading the Disk of Phaistos, which is incribed by another unknown symbolic writing, the Cretan hieroglyphs (cf. Egbert Richter-Ushanas, The Disk of Phaistos and the Sacred Marriage of Theseus and Ariadne).

The interpretation of the Indus script in relation to the Rig- and Atharva-Veda.

The Historical Setting of the Indus Script

Like the Sumero-Akkadian pictographic writing the Indus script has been engraved on seals. In Mesopotamia cylinder seals were used, whereas in the Indus Valley stamp seals prevail. Far more important for the reading is, however, that in case of the Indus Valley, there are only these seals and a few terra-cotta tablets and graffiti, there are no inscribed clay tablets of larger size as they have been found in Mesopotamia. Accordingly, the inscriptions on the Indus seals are very short, on an average they consist of only 5 signs.

On account of their pictographic character the signs of the inscriptions can and must be read in a symbolic way. That a symbolic interpretation is subjective, can only be maintained to a certain extent: Symbols have to be regarded subjectively like old and modern art. One has to consider the cultural environment, however. Nearest or even contemporaneous to the Indus civilization is the Vedic tradition, whose oldest and holiest book is the Rigveda. It consists of about 1000 hymns addressed to different gods and goddesses. The Atharva-Veda, that is said to be of a younger age, has many hymns in common with the Rigveda. Its main subject are charms which are to be expected to be found on seals, too. The language of the Vedas is an ancient type of Sanskrit. Western science dates the origin of the Rigveda between 1500 to 1200 BC, but since some of the Vedic gods are mentioned in a Hittite contract of 1350 ante, the Aryans, the people to whose tradition these gods belonged, must have lived in the area of the Indus Valley already at a much earlier time.

It is highly unlikely that the recollection of the Indus civilization and the script in particular was lost all of a sudden after the end of the Indus cities. Certainly, the production of seals stopped henceforward, but the Indus pictograms could be and were written or painted on pottery and bangles and also on perishable materials. Contrarily to the opinion of most of Western and Indian scholars, there are also words for to write and writer in Vedic times and in the Veda itself, they have only not been registered as such in the dictionaries.

Thus Rbhu, the name of three Vedic artisans, may mean writer, too. Its root rabh is related to Greek rhaptein, to knit together, and glyphein, to write, from which hieroglyph, sacred sign, is derived. Synonymous and homophonous with rabh is the Sanskrit root grabh corresponding to Greek graphein for to write. The root grabh is not used in this sense in the Veda, but we come across the roots ri, to let flow (the line of writing) and rsh, to pierce, which can mean to write, too. From the latter root rshi, seer, singer, is derived. It is synonymous with the root rad, to scratch, that was explained as to write by Geldner (Vedische Studien III, Stuttgart 1901, p. 26). Another root that is used for to write is pish, to carve (in stone). It can hence be supposed that the early Vedic poets could, if not write themselves, at least understand the pictographic meaning of the Indus signs.

The signs of the Indus script may have been called 'cups' after the most frequent pictogram that served as a marker for the end of a verse or a quarter (pada) of it. In the symbolical language of the Veda this sign may be compared to a cup or vessel. The grail of the Celtic mythology may have its origin here, too. In several hymns the Rbhus are said to have made the cup of the creator Tvashtr into four. This can be explained in relation to the quarters of the universe and the yugas, the cosmic periods, but it could also contain a hint to the development of the script that consisted of simple signs in the beginning as it is found on early Harappa graffiti and in neolithic cave paintings. In a second phase diacritic strokes were added to it. In fact, there exist cup-signs with one, two, three or four additional strokes.

Divine and urban origin is also ascribed to the modern Sanskrit script, the Devanagari, (the script) of the town of the gods, and the Brahmi script that comes chronologically between the Indus script and the modern Sanskrit script. The Brahmi is named after the daughter of the god Brahma, who is the creator of the world, whereas his daughter Brahmi has invented all the sciences. Brahma is the successor of Tvashtr in later Indian tradition. Many scholars believe that the Brahmi alphabet is based on the Old Semitic script going back to the Phoenicians who are said to have developed it from the Egyptian script at a time when it was still pictographic. It is more likely, however, that it is based on the Indus script, whose geometric signs have much more similarity with the Brahmi and the Greek and Latin alphabet than the Egyptian.

It can further be objected that it is not very likely that the Indus inscriptions or even some of them are contained in the Rigveda, since Sanskrit, its language, is Aryan, whereas the so-called priest-king illustrated at the left and other human figures excavated in the Indus towns have no Aryan features at all. The thick lips make the illustrated figure appear like a eunuch who had a leading function in the government and the army in Mesopotamia.

The functions of the priest and the king were separated there as in the Vedic tradition. The denomination priest-king cannot be correct hence. It may be an image of a leading priest, however, indicated by the ribbon with a third eye he wears round the head, which corresponds to the fish-sign with a stroke or eye. The language of the Veda that was transmitted orally for at least two thousand years, is an early type of Sanskrit, no doubt, but we do not know, whether the Veda was transmitted in this language from the very beginning. It is much more likely, that its original language was a Prakrit idiom. Certainly, the founders of a high civilization can also be credited with the ability of developing a refined language like Sanskrit, that was from the very beginning the language of a small group of people, for the common people a Prakrit language like Pali, that served this purpose for the Buddhists, is better suitable.

The Veda consists of an older and a younger part. It is possible that the older hymns were translated into Sanskrit from a Prakrit language, and that only the younger hymns were originally composed in Sanskrit. This would imply to give up the idea that Sanskrit is older than any other language and that the Aryans are the supreme race. Even if the elaboration of Sanskrit took place after the decline of the Indus civilization, as it is maintained by Western scholars, the reminiscences of its tradition may have been incorporated into the Vedic tradition in this language, as is maintained by the Vedic scholar J. Gonda (Orientalia Neerlandica, Leiden 1948, p. 348).

Though the feelings of the Aryan poets for the former tradition were inimical sometimes, as it can be deduced from the fight of their main god Indra with the snake-god Vrtra called a eunuch in RV I.32.7, they could not prevent or did not even want to prevent the infiltration of the ideas of the Indus lore in the Vedic tradition. This is also obvious from the method of etymology applied in the Brahmanas and the Upanishads. Sometimes an abstract word or name is explained there by a concrete homophone. The same method was applied by the priests and poets of the Indus civilization in respect to the pictograms of the Indus script.

The Testimony of a Bilingual

For any decipherment a working hypothesis is necessary to begin with. On the ground of the hypothesis that the Indus seals contain mantras of the Rigveda I was able to translate nearly all inscriptions logo-graphically already in 1992. There remained a great amount of ambiguity in regard to the pictographic as well as to the phonetic value of the signs, however. A bilingual could be helpful in finding out this value and it would also give us greater security in regard to the language spoken in the Indus Valley at that time. With regard to the shortness of the Indus inscriptions the discovering of a name written in two languages has the greatest probability. This has promoted already the deciphering of other ancient scripts like the Egyptian and the Mesopotamian.

The only name that is known in this field is Meluhhaki, the Akkadian name for the civilization at the Indus river. The name appears in old Sumerian picture writing on an Akkadian cylinder seal that has been published in the catalogue of the exhibition Vergessene Stadte am Indus (Forgotten Towns at the Indus River). From the Sumerian signs of the name written vertically on the seal we obtain when they are written from left to right. The syllable ha is rendered here by the sign, that originally meant a fish. In the same position a fish is found in the second line of the inscription of the Failaka seal 9702 that is reproduced here as a drawing.

The inscription of the first line that belongs to the Indus script is rendered as in the Finnish Concordance II (read in the direction from right to left of the impression). Since the position of the man-sign is at the end normally, particularly when it follows a cup-sign, we shall read the signs from left to right here or from right to left of the original as rendered under the figure. The triangle is part of the stroke-sign and the man-sign and the cup-sign form a ligature. The three pictograms of the lower line are most probably Sumerian. If they can be read as Meluhha, as is suggested by the fish-sign, the same name may be found in the upper line. Since the fish-sign renders ha, the first sign of the lower line should be read as me-luh or me-lah.

The equivalence of me on the Akkadian seal is a pictogram that is explained in A. Deimel's Sumerian Dictionary (sign 889) as a mouth with an outstretched tongue. The main part of the compound of the lower line may be interpreted as a mouth, but the Akkadian equivalence pu is too far away from me. The

Sumerian sign for lah is explained by Deimel as a yoke (sign 700). This could indeed be the meaning of the main part of the compound. An Akkadian reading for it is shabu, meaning people, men, worker. A worker in this context is a man going under a yoke, for instance a water-carrier, which is a sign of the Indus script, too. The extensions of the sign can be read as water because the 'teeth' indicate the waves. The Akkadian word for water is mu, with the genitive me. The genitive is appropriate here, because the water-carrier is a carrier of water, or, if lah is read as man, because the people of the Indus cities are closely related with water. It is known from the excavations that nearly every house in the Indus cities had a well. Since the two syllables form a ligature, they can also be read as mel-uh. Perhaps it is for this reason that on the Akkadian seal the sign for me has not been separated from the sign for luh. If read as me-luh, we would obtain to purify (luh) with water.

The fish-sign can be read logo-graphically as a synonym for the wise man, who is equal in the Veda to the kavi, the seer and author of the hymns. The root ku is identical with the second Sumerian reading for fish, the first being ha. On several Akkadian seals the god of wisdom, Ea, is surrounded by fishes. The fish-sign in the Indus script may have a similar connotation. This may be the reason why the fish is also related to the stars and to astrology.

The final triangle of this line can easily be read as ki, the Akkadian determinative for town, since it is similar to an Akkadian wedge which forms the main part of the related Akkadian sign. According to Deimel (sign 812) the Sumerian sign is derived from a lozenge, but when taken as it is, it can mean house. The whole line can then be read logo-graphically as from Meluhha, the land of the wise men, who venerate (the god of) water (Varuna).

Deimel's interpretation of a mouth with a tongue is well applicable for the second sign of the upper line, the first sign can even be interpreted as a row of teeth like the similar sign of the Indus script. Parpola regards it as a pictogram for a comb, but its real meaning is woman, because it is a symbol of the womb or the vagina dentata. In the ancient civilizations woman is not only regarded as giving life, but also as taking it. It has the same capacity as the ocean, which was also regarded as female.

The row of teeth can be interpreted here in two ways: As a symbol of smiling in the sense of being gracious or of being angry or disdainful. The first is called mrl in the Veda, with the stem mrla, the second mrdhra. The two words are related to each other, because graciousness can be caused through negligence. If the second sign of the first line is read as a mouth, it can also mean to speak, Sanskrit vac, with the stem uc and the noun vac, word, language, sound. The initial consonant can have been changed into u by the Akkadians or they may have taken the stem in place of the root. Perhaps there was a root uc originally, since the replacement of *w* through u in Akkadian is attested for only in the times of the Assyrians. In addition there was inserted a vowel between the initial double consonant according to the Akkadian rules of euphony. The Akkadian scribe did not care at all for the original meaning of the name of the Indus country.

The compound mrla-vac, speaking gracious, does not occur in the Veda, the compound mrdhra-vac, speaking disdainful, is found several times there as denomination of the language of the Asuras who became the enemies of the gods in the later portions of the Veda as the Dasyus became the enemies of the Aryans. In these times mrdhra-vac in the sense of language of the enemy must have replaced mrla-vac. The inhabitants of the Indus cities would not have called themselves enemies. The two words are related to each other, because graciousness can be caused through negligence (Mayrhofer 1963, sub marhati). As the Asuras were the earlier gods, they may have spoken with negligence or even disdain of the later gods.

The following compound could be a number-sign, but on account of the triangle at the bottom that has been omitted in the Finnish Concordance it can be read as grass growing on a hill. This is equal to Munja Dharo, which is in the form Mohenjodaro the name of one of the greatest towns of the Indus civilization. Munja is the name of a grass. The last compound can be read as a man carrying a filled vessel. This can be related to a worker, but also to a merchant. In those times many things were transported and kept in vessels. The contents may also have been soma. The whole line would then be equal to merchant from Munja Dharo in Mrla-vac (who speaks the language of the Asuras/who speaks friendly.

The merchant is called vanij in the Veda. The first letter can be changed into pa, then we obtain panij, which can be related to the Phoenicians. When the final ja is dropped we get Pani, a class of merchants described as mizers in the Veda. Such a merchant hides his treasures in pots and boxes.

But the merchant has also positive connotations in the Veda. A good merchant wins his customers through his friendly behaviour. Many Indian merchants are known till today for their religious commitment. This applies in particular to the Jainas, who mostly live in Gujarat, at the border of the former Indus country. In RV V.45.6 such a merchant is described as a man busy with prayers (*i.e.* friendly speaking) and it is said that he will obtain full vessels (purisham). This word is also an attribute of the creator in I.164.12. The word for busy, vanku, is interesting, too. The root vank, to roll (as a car or a ship), German wanken, with the derivation vankri, rib, is synonymous with parshu, which is a name of the wife of Manu meaning rib, too.

The Munja grass is mentioned in RV X.34.1, a hymn addressed to the dice:

The mobile (fruits) of the high (tree) intoxicate me, that born at an airy place, roll into the excavation; like a drink of soma from the hill Munjavat the always wakeful vibhidaka nuts appear to me.

With relation to the Failaka-seal we obtain: The dice (1) from an airy place (2) rolling into the excavation (3) are like a drink of soma (4) from the hill of Munjavat for me. The owner of the seal was not only a merchant, but also a dice-player. The name of the author of the hymn, Kavasha, (wearing) a shield, corresponds to the compound at the end. The dice were taken from the nuts of the vibhidaka tree in Vedic times. The bull that is found as motif on almost all seals found in Mesopotamia, is the animal of the merchants, too. The bull is also an attribute of the common people in general.

The Akkadian name Meluhha can also be related to Baluchistan, now the southern province of Pakistan. The letters M and B are interchangeable in this area as is obvious from the name Bombay, spelled Mbumbay originally. But the first syllable could also be derived from Sanskrit paras, on the other side, or para, other, enemy. This would either render parokshasthana, invisible (distant) land, or parocasthana, land of the other language/the language of the enemy. In later time meluhha changed into Sanskrit mleccha, barbarian. It can be explained as a reimport serving as retaliation for the disdain of the former enemy. Though not alive anymore his influence was still feared.

The reading of the name Meluhhaki is also warranted by the square seal 9000 found in Ur. It bears the three Akkadian signs separated from the bull-motif by a partly dotted line. The bull looks to the left in the impression, as it generally does on the Indus seals. In Sumerian, the signs render, when read in the Akkadian way from left to right, the reading sak-ku-si. This is equal to me luh-har in Akkadian. The arrow-sign that is explained by Deimel (No. 112) as a door-opener can be read as mrla or mrdhra, amical or inamical, because messages of both character can be transmitted in the same way as the shooting of an arrow. The second sign explained by Deimel (No. 893) as a texture can be a mouth or an ideogram for language. The last sign explained by Deimel (No. 563) as the head of a bull, is equal to Sanskrit vrshan, which means region in the form vrsha. Read in the direction of the Indus script from right to left this is equal to mrla-vac vrsha or region of Meluhha.

The most frequent motif of the Indus seals is not the bull, but the unicorn. It has the body of a bull and the head of a goat or horse. The lines on its neck look like the cloth that domesticated horses often wear. Recent finds confirm that the horse was extant in the Indus civilization, but probably it was not used for driving a car, but as a race-horse. In the Veda the unicorn is sometimes replaced by the horse, sometimes by the deer, sometimes by the bull.

The Vedic name of the goat is aja, whose second meaning unborn is equal to amrta, immortal, another name of the soma. In RV IV.58.3 the bull of Soma is said to have four horns, three feet, two heads and seven hands or parts. It can be compared to a composite animal with seven parts found on several Indus seals. On seal 8630 (Allahdino-8) it is associated with the standard that is normally found in front of the unicorn. There are also seals with a unicorn or a bull bearing two additional heads.

Hence it is likely that the single horn was attached to the animal from artistical or mythological reasons. This assumption is supported by Assyrian seals from the 8th century ante, where a winged unicorn with the body of a gazelle is depicted, a similar motif is found on the Hittite carvings at Karatepe dating from the same time. Some scholars believe that the unicorn is an urus that appears to have one horn only, because it is looked upon in profile as in the case of the bull on Sumerian seals of the Uruk period. Inspite of its one horn, the Sumerian animal is definitely a bull, however, whereas the unicorn is always a different animal, whether is has one horn or two horns, as it has in a few cases.

We have got only the values or some of the values of six signs through the reading of the Failaka seal, but the cup-sign is the most frequent sign of the Indus script and the fish-sign, the mouth-sign and the man-sign are also quite frequent. Though the unaccented cup-sign invariably appears at the end of the inscriptions, it seems to be difficult to affiliate it to a word in the list arranged after the final letter in Grassmann's Worterbuch zum Rigveda.

If we assume its reading as ha, the last letter of the Sanskrit alphabet and the suffix of the nominative form, we face the difficulty that this syllable has no word-meaning in Vedic Sanskrit as it has in Sumerian. There is, however, the related syllable hu meaning to pour in (the sacrificial beverage). This reading could be appropriate for the cup-sign. It also corresponds to the sign for god in the Hittite script. Besides, the cup-sign has a similar form as the last letter of the Greek alphabet W, when it is written upside down.

The cup-sign incorporates all letters and syllables like the chest incorporating the breath. The cup can represent abstract and concrete forms, male and female, subject and object, noun and verb, matter and spirit, but for the Indians and the Hittites it represented a die or the hand grasping the dies. The dies were treated like gods, because they ruled over the fate. The cup-signs are a further argument that the Indus script must be read logophonetical.

The Cosmic Principles of Duality and of Unity in Diversity

The method applied in reading the Failaka-seal on the ground of the Rigveda proved to be successful also in case of many other inscriptions. In the course of this study it was confirmed that not only the cup-sign, but also signs with lesser frequency can have several meanings. This cannot be otherwise in the case of a word script, since it is a feature already found with syllabic writings. Deimel mentions in the preface of his Sumerian Dictionary 26 signs for the syllable 'ge', 12 for 'gi'.

The ambivalence of the signs applies to a certain extent to sequences, too. On the other hand, their consistent meaning is a great help for the decipherment (cf. § 10). Sanskrit offers many possibilities in this respect, that are far from infinite, however. The greatest difficulty is to find the most appropriate verse for a certain inscription in the bulk of the 1000 Vedic hymns. Even with the help of the Veda not all inscriptions are readable till now. At least we need an 'indicator' to start with.

To illustrate that this method of reading the Indus inscriptions works and how it works we shall study at first several seals with one sign only. Apart from early Harappan graffiti and pot-marks, where the script is still in a rudimentary stage, inscriptions with a single sign are rare. It seems to be impossible to get more than a name from such an inscription, but we have to consider that generally the sign is a compound as in the case of elephant-seal 2058 (M-1162) and the five unicorn-seals 5131, 1292, 3089, 4678 (H-481) and 2704 (M-842) and the tiger-seal 3246 (H-94), where the man-sign is combined with a wheel-sign. On the unicorn-seal 2546 the wheel is written separately and the man-sign is replaced by the compound sign of the elephant-seal 2058. The compound consisting of a man with a girdle indicating his female aspect and hoofs indicating his animal aspect can be explained as a symbol of the Purusha, the cosmic man, who is androgyn and theriomorph and represents the principle of unity in diversity. This notion directs us to RV X.90.10:

> *Out of him (the Purusha) came forth the horses, those animals that have teeth on both sides (of the mouth), the cattle, the goats and the sheep. The animals with teeth on both sides are relatives of the horse like asses and mules. According to Baudayana II.2.2 they were merchandise like wool. Hence they cannot be beasts of prey or men. The owner of the seal can be identified with the principle of unity in diversity like the Purusha. From the elephant-motif it follows that he was a rich man or the king.*

The same principle is illustrated, when the owner of the seal is the writer. It is identical with dub-sar on many Akkadian seals and with rbhu in the Veda. This can be the meaning of the compound on seal 2704, since its elements are a stylus and a hand. The writer or carver stands for the male aspect of the Purusha, the material of the seal for the female.

The same sign is found on the round seal 3413 (H-342) with a wheel on the reverse, a symbol of carving, too. The triangle-sign can also denote the creative power of the gods, in particular of the mother-goddess who can be identified with the wheel, too, if it is identified with the womb or the heart. The heart is the inner wheel or motor of the body. On seal 2546 the female aspect is depicted by the wheel and the girdle of the compound sign to give it still more authority.

On seal 3089 the female principle is written by a thigh and two oblique strokes that form the step-sign, when they are elongated. The compound can be read as Uttanapad, elevating the feet or spreading the legs (for conceiving and giving birth). This is a name of the mother-goddess in RV X.72.4. By invoking this name the owner of the seal wanted to obtain a wife of similar qualities.

On seal 4678 the Purusha is rendered by the man-sign again, the staff denotes authority and the triangle at the left his female aspect like the girdle in the compound of seal 2058. The triangle-sign is a variant of the step-sign. The compound of seal 5131 occurs at the end of several other seals. The upper board can be read as above, the cross as all (directions). This is combined in the appellation best, vasishtha. Besides of being the name of a Vedic seer, it designates Indra, the king of the gods.

Accordingly, we read in RV X.86 at the end of all stanzas Indra is higher than everything. The sign is similar to the Hittite sign for table, but in the connection of the Veda it would be equal to altar, where the gods with Indra as their head take their dishes. In the compound of seal 1292 the male and the female aspect are formed by the seed and the field. The seed or drops belong to the humid father of the sky of UV I.164.12. In V.45.6 they are an epithet of the merchant.

The two aspects of creation are also illustrated by the initial compound of the inscription of the unicorn-seal 5030 that can be explained as a flower or plant and a hand. Its Vedic equivalence is found in X.101.3: The man shall sow the seed in the willing womb. The flower is identical to the womb, the hand renders to sow, the nose-sign is equal to the male member, the single stroke denotes the seed. In an abstract form this is contained in RV X.129.4: In the beginning it felt desire, this was the first seed of thought. The inclination of the male for the female is the first seed of thought.

The reading of all these inscriptions is based on the cosmic principle of duality and of unity in diversity. It can be expressed in various ways. Which sign or compound is used to express a certain word or idea is left to the seer or writer. The pictographic meaning had only to be in agreement somehow with the word it stood for. The Purusha can be represented by a bull, as we have seen in the foregoing chapter. It is related to the cosmic energy that can be conceived as male or female like the Purusha himself. In RV X.5.7 Agni is called a cow and a bull. On account of seal 4678 I have formerly affiliated the five unicorn-seals to the first verse of the Agni-hymn I. 1. The rule that different signs can have the same meaning can easily lead to a wrong affiliation.

A Markhor-seal as a Reference to the Sacred Marriage

We shall now study the inscription of the markhor-seal 2606 (M-1179) as an example for two signs. The markhor is a goat with spiral horns that lives until today in the Western Himalayas. Since the animal has a human face regularly, it may be a symbol of a god. For this reason, the two signs can be read as the streams of soma running in the cup, the soma being represented by the two curves. The Vedic name of the animal is avika, derived from avi, wool. It is mentioned in RV I.126.7 as a sheep of the Gandharis. The verse contains the words of a young girl said to the hundred-years-old seer Kakshivat, the author of the hymn, who obtained the girl together with horses and cows as a present from an Asura king after having carried out a big sacrifice for him. A maiden together with women and cattle is generally given as a present to the sacrificing priest in Vedic times. The words of the verse are:

Come near and embrace me closely!

Do not believe that I have few (hair);

I am full of hair like a sheep of the Gandharis.

Though a virgin the girl invites the seer like a prostitute. Her bad quality, her hair, becomes her adornment. She is a bride by nature. The bride is still adorned like a goddess in India. The adornment of the goddess Istar belonged to her divine Me, her magic powers. In the Old Testament, the sacred prostitute was called zenot, the adorned. If the girl had only few or no pubic hair, the seer would not have been entitled to have sexual intercourse with her, as Geldner states in a note. Full of hair, Romasha, is also her name. The Gandharis are probably identical to the Gandharas, after whom the Graeco-Buddhist style of art is named. The name of the king Romapada (hair-footed) is related to romasha. In the foregoing verse the seer compares the girl with the female of an ichneumon. The ichneumon or mongoose is a holy animal, because it kills venomous snakes.

They cannot defend themselves with their poison against it on account of a certain drug it produces. The mongoose is also appreciated because of its hide like other animals of this family. On account of the smell of the drug it produces it is a fit partner for the sacred marriage and for procuring fertility in the eyes of the Vedic seer. Since he is a seer, the girl does not hesitate to yield to him inspite of his hundred years. The markhor is an element in the motif of several Indus seals. Among them is the famous seal 2430, where it takes part in a sacrifice (cf. § I.8). Its hair was used for the sieve, in which the soma was purified. Hence it is related to the sacred marriage, too, which was not only celebrated to obtain fertility, but also for the purification from sins, which is a precondition to regain immortality. With regard to this verse the cup-sign can be read as hair of the pudenda.

The two curves would signify embrace me closely. It is also possible, however, to read the inscription in regard to the soma. Then we can affiliate it to RV IX.74.9: Mixed with water, purified soma, your sap flows over the wool of the sheep (in the vat). The meaning is almost as erotic as in the other verse. Only the personal relation is missing here. Moreover, the two signs can be read as girdle contained the name of the author of the hymn I.126.

The Great Seer Agastya

The motif of a seal or tablet can be helpful to a great extent in the understanding of the inscription. To demonstrate this we shall study the four-sided tablet 2719 (M-1431). The image of the fourth side is almost totally worn, but it can be deduced from the illustration in Kalyanaran, that it consists of three parts.

On account of its short tail the animal at the left must be a markhor. It stands on a railing or in a boat. In the middle a kneeling man is sacrificing a vessel to a deity standing in an arch of pipal leaves as on seal 2430 (cf. § I.8). At the right a composite elephant is depicted as on the middle side of tablet 2734 (M-1430) that we shall study later on. On the third side the simplified soma pressing is illustrated as it is described in RV I.28.1,2:

Where the stone is erected on the broad fundament there you may swallow with greed the soma pressed in the mortar, Indra!

Where the two boards (on which the press is put) resemble the thighs (of the woman), there you may swallow with greed the soma pressed in the mortar, Indra!

The woman at the left uses her thighs instead of the two wooden boards, on which the soma-press is put normally. It can be seen on the tablet that the upper pressing stone has the form of a pistil and that the lower is round and deepened in the middle like a mortar. After the soma has been pressed by the kneeling woman, the sap is poured from the mortar in a vessel by the woman standing in the middle. Both women could be priests, too. The vessel is covered by a sieve, as it is indicated by several points on its rim that have been omitted in the drawing. With regard to the Vedic verse the figure behind the vessel is the god Indra to whom the soma is dedicated. He runs to the vessel with speed to swallow it with greed.

The hymn I.28 was composed by the boy saint Shunahshepa, but it is not very likely that he is illustrated on the tablet, because on side three there are two persons engaged in pressing the soma. This makes it likely that the motif refers to the famous seer Agastya and his young wife Lopamudra who could also be depicted on the first side as the tiger and the person in the tree. The squatting position of the person in the tree that is also found with the woman with the pestle on side three is an image of seduction. According to RV I.179 Agastya's problem was to get progeny in spite of his old age. The file of animals on side two with a crocodile and fowls on the top can be a hint to a sacred marriage and to initiation going along with it. Lopamudra can also be represented by the two gazelles or goats eating from the tree at the left of side 3. The tree can be a symbol of Agastya, whose name means be (asti) immovable (aga) (like) a tree or hill. As the tree Agastya is the enjoyed, when he gets progeny he is the enjoyer.

Agastya and Lopamudra can also be illustrated on the fourth side of the tablet, the markhor in the boat or railing can symbolize the soma, the composite animal at the left may represent the goddess of language, Vac, who is personified in Lopamudra. The motif in the middle can be explained as Agastya praying for remission of his sin. The three motifs of this side can be read as: By venerating the goddess of Language she will reveal her two aspects to you.

The two aspects are also contained in the motif of the tiger and the deity in the tree on side one. Through the inscription on the first side of the tablet that can be restored as we are directed to RV I.179.6:

> *Agastyah khanamanah khanitraih prajam apatyam balam icchamanah ubhau varnav rshir ugrah puposha satya deveshva asisho jagama Agastya ploughed with (wooden) pegs, desiring children, descendants and power; both colours the mighty seer let bloom, with the gods his desires became true.*

The man-sign in curved lines can be identified with Agastya making furrows, the leaf-sign can stand for the soma and the peg, the first cup-sign consisting of two hands folded together can be read as to desire, the second cup-sign can denote the truth. This renders: The desires of the furrow-making seer Agastya became true (by the gods).

By drinking soma not only his desires became true, Agastya gets also remission for the sin of having broken his vow of abstinence:

> *To the Soma drunken with the heart I call without anything in between: The sin which we have done he may forgive, for the mortal has many desires.*

The name of Agastya does not only appear on this tablet. This is not to be wondered at, since he is one of the most famous seers in the Veda as well as in later time. Thus the inscription of a pipal leaf and a cup-sign on tablet 2734 that designates the divine nature of the Soma can be referred to RV I.179.6 and the motifs of the tablet can be related to the mythology of Agastya.

Since Agastya is venerated like a wishing tree, many people go to it as illustrated on the first side by the three human figures in front of it. Agastya can also be identified with the priest, by whom the bull is sacrificed. The gazelle or goat eating from the tree on side 3 can be regarded as Lopamudra and Agastya again. The motif at the right is a bull with three heads. On its back a man stands on his head. This is perhaps the earliest illustration of this yoga posture, that symbolizes the mastership over the power of gravity that is also obtained by urdhvaretas, the drawing upward or inward of the semen (cf. § 8). The three heads of the bull can be identified with the three worlds.

The two foot-prints on side two standing in opposition to each other can be explained as a symbol of Agastya and Lopamudra in cohabitation. The composite animal on the second side is again an image of Lopamudra. According to later Indian mythology, Agastya created her by taking a part from each animal. On a miniature painting from Rajasthan of the 17th century the Gayatri, a synonym of the goddess of wisdom, is depicted in the form of a composite animal.

The Bull and the Scorpion as Attributes of the Goddess of Wisdom

A number of seals and tablets have a motif or several motifs that can be read as an inscription as in the case of tablet 2719d. Sometimes it renders the name of Meluhha, as in case as of a round seal found in Dilmun and of a cylinder seal with Indian motifs found in Ur.

The motif of the Dilmun-seal shows a bull and a cow in cohabitation, the cow being on top contrarily to the natural position. The three symbols above it can be explained as a scorpion, a garment and a fish that may be female. This is contained in RV X.85.34: Like poison is the shirt of the bride. If the scorpion is read as mer (Deimel 11) and the second sign as luh, to purify, we obtain the reading Merluyya. This is nearer to the Indian pronunciation of mrla-vac than Meluhha.

In the upper part of a seal from Ur a goddess with her legs spread apart is giving birth to a tree as on tablet 3304. The Vedic name for the mother-goddess is Uttanapad (cf. § I.3). She is identical with Vac, the goddess of language. She beats the bull in front of her with a stick, one of her toes is placed upon the scorpion's tail, whilst the vaginal fluid trickles down on its head. The scorpion is called vrshcika in the Veda, which is equal to 'small bull'. The partners of the goddess in the sacred marriage are the big bull and the small bull which stand for her two aspects, the life-giving and the death-giving.

The palm-tree in front of the bull is an attribute of Ea, the Akkadian god of wisdom. If the scorpion is read as mrdhra, the goddess as Vac, the bull as vrshan, which is homophonous with vrsha, region, we obtain the name Mrdhra-vac-vrsha or Me(r)luhha(r) in Akkadian. The bull seems to be safe and well-fed through the bundle of grass in front of him, though he is attacked by the scorpion and beaten by the goddess. But to beat means also to kill or to sacrifice that goes along with marriage (cf. chapter I.7). The goddess kills her lover as it is known from the Akkadian goddess Istar.

The Standard as an Image of the Soma-press

On the Indus seals the tree in front of the bull is replaced by a standard in front of a unicorn. Its function is unknown so far. Its prototype is found together with a bull on a sherd from Mehi in Baluchistan, where it is combined with a tree:

> *A small ivory sculpture that has recently been excavated in Harappa, shows that the contrivance is an image of the soma-press that is described in Rigveda I.28.1,2 (cf. § 5). The conic upper piece is the pistil, its rectangular part is the handle that was moved with both hands. The hemispherical lower piece is the mortar. The mortar was placed on two wooden boards that had the form of segment of a circle. They resemble the root of a tree on the Mehi sherd. The small side of the segment was yoked to the lower piece of the press that has an excavation at the bottom for this purpose. There is no pipe in the lower stone. The marks on it are only for decoration. The soma was poured with the hand from the mortar through a sieve into a vessel as it is shown on tablet 2719 (cf. § 5). The bull that is fastened to the contrivance on the Mehi sherd is a simile of the soma-juice in the*

Veda, but the pistil could also be drawn by an ox like a whim. Such a whim is referred to in RV X.135.3. On the Indus seals the bull is replaced by the unicorn. The 'hair' on its lower part can be explained as the ends of the twigs, fruits or the bark that were pressed. The tree standing behind the standard is a pipal or ashvattha (ficus religiosa). It has been venerated in India until today as the cosmic tree, though it suffocates other trees. Its fruits have berry-form and are sweet like dates. They would render the sweet variant of the soma juice called madhu (honey).

The soma-pressing can be compared with the rubbing of the fire by the two fire-sticks. Therefore the standard can also be explained as a fire-altar as it is depicted on Kushan coins. The Gandharvas, who are the guardians of the soma in the Veda, are also credited with the knowledge of making fire. They give a fire-vessel to king Pururavas, who brought the fire to the earth. The bull on the Mehi sherd can also represent the king or Agni, the fire-god himself.

The triangle between the horns of the animal is a symbol of the sun, the horns represent the moon. The wavy lines on the back of the bulls and between the leaves of the fig-tree that are similar to the two snakes on the Ur-seal are a symbol of the tongue and of the goddess of Language that is also represented by the pipal tree. The comb-signs refer to the same goddess, but in this connection they can also represent the fix-stars that are female in the Veda. The triangle sign on the back of the first bull can be explained as a virile member. The five goats under each bull, two of which are also found under the seat of the yogi on seal 2420 (cf. § 8), are sacrificial animals like the bull. Inside the stomachs of the bulls leaves have been depicted that they have eaten before. The rumination of this animal is a symbol of resurrection like the soma-pressing.

A similar bull is depicted on vessel from Nindowari. Here we find about 30 comb-signs around the animal. This number is approximately identical to the star-houses the moon visits on his way along the ecliptic. In addition there are five wheel-signs which can be identified with the five planets. There is only one wavy line which is almost identical to the cup-sign. It indicates that the origin of this sign was a the snake which is an image of the goddess of language, as already mentioned, and of the cosmic snake, the Kundalini.

There is an additional 'wheel' between the horns of the animal as on the Mehi sherd. In this context the bull can be identified with the heavenly bull also mentioned in the Gilgames epic. When all planets and sun and moon are appearing on the sky at the same time a new era is inaugurated according to the teaching of the Akkadian astronomers. The tree the bull is fastened to is probably a mimosa. There are twigs of the pipal tree and of an acacia in front and behind it. Both trees can be identified with the cosmic tree or the axis mundi. These trees are also illustrated on a sherd from Nausharo c. 2600, too (cf. A. Parpola, Deciphering the Indus Script).

A standard is also found on many Failaka seals. Here the 'net' is at the bottom, however: In the Sumerian script the net-sign is used as a determinative for plants (Deimel sign 593), particularly for a medicinal plant (Akkadian shammu). Since the standard has the form of the crescent of the moon on the Failaka seals we can translate the whole symbol as 'moon-plant'. This is identical to the soma plant, for Soma is a name of the moon also.

The 'hair' issuing from the lower part of the standard can be interpreted as the rays of the moon in this connection. On several Failaka seals the net-sign appears together with a plant that has pinnate leaves, on others with a temple-door confirming the sacred purpose of the plant. The motif of a tree in a railing, sometimes together with a swastika, is found on several North Indian coins from the time of 300 to 100 ante. Like the standard it can be explained as a symbol of the cosmic tree. This is a further reason that the standard has roots on the Mehi sherd.

A stylized pipal tree with the heads of two unicorns attached to its trunk is depicted on seal 1387. Their necks meet in a round plate filled with drops and 'lamellas' beneath it that illustrate their blood. The tree can be the cosmic tree, the two unicorns would then represent the cosmic male and female.

This is corroborated by the leaves of the tree, five of them pointing upwards, four downwards. In a similar way the inner triangles of the Shri-Yantra are arranged. The five signs of the inscription can be read according to X.85.13:

The wedding car of the sun-daughter went ahead which Savitar (the father) sent off; in the lunar mansion Agha the bulls are killed (sacrificed), in the lunar mansion Phalguni she (the bride) is brought home.

The initial compound is equal to the wedding car of the sun-daughter, the second and the third sign render first or oldest seer, which is an epithet of the sun-god Savitar, the lance-sign corresponds to sent off. The field-sign, that is also found on seal 2279 with the motif of a bull-sacrifice, stands for the place of sacrifice, where the bulls were killed and the bride was given to the husband.

A great feast is held together with marriage all over the world. In ancient India a lot of bulls had to be killed to provide the food for the retinue and relatives of the bridegroom and the bride. The name of the lunar mansion Agha, when the bulls were killed, can be derived from the weak stem gha of the root han, to kill. Agha means not killed, however, because the bulls that were sacrificed, were not killed in our sense of the word, but sent to heaven. They became immortal. In later time the mansion was called Magha, enjoyment, obtained at the feast. The bloody forms of the sun-daughter are mentioned in X.85.35.

Two Seals with Cosmogonic Inscriptions

Cosmogonic conceptions play an important part in the Veda and on this ground a lot of inscriptions can be read, in particular those of the often discussed seal 2420 (M-304) with the motif of a horned figure in a yoga or dancing position surrounded by four animals and the equally famous seal 2430 (M-1186) with the motif of a deity in a pipal tree accompanied by seven pigtailed persons and venerated by a kneeling adorer having a head on a dais at his right and a markhor at his left side:

The inscriptions of the two seals are nearly identical. On seal 2430 the field-sign that we have met on seal 1387 appears again, here it is written separately under the deity in the tree.

The similarity of the two inscriptions can best be recognized when they are written under each other: The first man-sign is missing in 2430. If the additional stroke signifies the virile member, it can be read as Daksha, literally potency. Daksha is the cosmic father. His daughter who is also his mother is called Aditi and Uttanapad, who spreads her legs for conceiving and giving birth, in the cosmogonic hymn X.72 (cf. chapter I.3). Verse 4 and 5 of this hymn read:

> *This world was born by her, who spreads apart the legs, from the world were born the (four) regions; from Aditi Daksha was born, from Daksha Aditi in return.*
>
> *For Aditi was born as your daughter, Daksha! after her the beneficial gods were born, the friends of the drink of immortality.*

The sequence of the first two signs on seal 2420 has been changed in the Vedic hymn. The two triangle-signs represent the mother-goddess. The first sign refers to her as the daughter, the second as the mother. The cup-sign with two additional strokes represents Daksha again. The strokes stand for the seed. The last three signs of both inscriptions correspond to the last half of X.72.5. The beneficial gods are equal to the fish-sign, bhadra, beneficial means shining literally. The cup-sign stands for the drink of immortality here, the man-sign for the friend. On seal 2430 the first sign can be read as Aditi in her aspect of the mother again, the second in her aspect of the daughter.

The gods are equal to the fish-sign, the cup-sign to the drink of immortality, the man-sign renders friend here. The complete verse can be affiliated to the inscription of seal 2430. The first sign can be read as Aditi again, the second as to be born as the daughter, the fish-sign with additional stroke renders the beneficial gods, the cup-sign and the man-sign the friends of the drink of immortality. The field-sign has the same meaning, since it represents the standard or whim, in which the soma was pressed.

Daksha can also be identified with the central figure on seal 2420. The four animals surrounding him can be explained as the four castes whose emanation is mentioned in X.90.12. The elephant corresponds to the brahmins, the tiger to the kings, the rhino to the vaishyas, the farmers and merchants, and the water-buffalo to the shudras, whose main feature is inertia. That the elephant looks in the opposite direction can be explained with the dignity of the brahmins.

The deity has male and female attributes, which corresponds to the description of the cosmic man as being born reciprocally from man and woman. It can also be called lord of the beasts, but in another sense as Marshall did. The animals are inherent the cosmic man, therefore he can become their creator. This is expressed by the compound sign on the elephant seal 2058 that we have discussed in chapter I.3.

The Indian name for the lord of the beasts is pashupati. Pashu are the domesticated animals generally, but according to RV X.90.8 the animals of the air, of the forest and of the village are made of the Purusha. This means that the lord of the beasts is an aspect of the cosmic man. There are no birds on the seal, but we find two goats under the dais instead whose wild specimen lives in the high air of the mountain. The same kind of animal is found under the bull on the Mehi sherd. The goats are a sacrificial animal like the bull. According to Indian philosophy creation is based on sacrifice (cf. Bhagavadgita 3.9-15).

The seven persons in the lower register of seal 2430 are referred to in X.82.2 as the seven seers. It is said there that the creator of the world is still beyond them. According to the following verse the seers of ancient times have sacrificed to him like those of the present time. The head beside the main priest in the middle of the seal is mentioned in the cosmogonic hymn X.125 addressed to the goddess of Language, who declares in X.125.7: I give birth to the father in the head of this (world).

The head is equal to a certain constellation, where all planets stand in one line. Besides, it is a simile of the virile member of the cosmic father. The sacrifice of the head is equal to the sacrifice of the male potency. This was replaced by urdhvaretas, leading the semen upwards, in the later tradition. This process together with pranayama, the controlling of the breath, and certain positions of the body like standing on the head is said to be the fundament of yoga in the Tantric Samhitas. It leads to a temporary austerity called tapas, heat, in the Veda. The sexual activities can be resumed if necessary as the story of Agastya reveals, only the dissipation of the semen, especially in day time is prevented (cf. Prasna Upanishad I.13). As a liquid, soma is the substitute of the semen. It is represented by the markhor on the seal.

I do not believe that a nomadic people as the Aryans describe themselves in some hymns of the Veda would have been able to develop such lofty philosophic ideas. They must have been composed in an earlier time, when the Aryans were still barbarians as they thought in a later time their enemies, the Dasyus, to be.

The Parable of the Elephant and the Blind

The parable of the elephant and the blind has been told by a Buddhist monk to overcome the obstacles impeding the further spreading of the Buddhist teaching (dhamma). Buddhism has left its impact on Indian history, but it was also influenced by the preceding oral tradition of the Veda and the Upanishads. The Buddha was no friend of mythical thought in general and of the Veda in particular, but this does not mean that he and the Buddhist teachers who followed his dhamma rejected the Vedic tradition altogether. Instead, they tried to bring it in a historical frame and to incorporate it in this way in their own teaching.

The parable of the elephant and the blind is an example for this dealing with an older tradition. It was applied by other creeds and religions, too, notably by Christianity. The parable is based on the ancient myth that a blind man can regain his eyesight by touching a sacred person or object. This myth has also found its way in the Christian New Testament. In the Buddhist version, however, the blind men do not regain sight, on the contrary, they quarrel with each other about the nature of the elephant they touch. The reason of their quarrelling is that they do not follow the dhamma and this is a sort of blindness. The parable that is narrated in Udana 6.4, a rather late Buddhist text, reads as follows:

When the Buddha stayed in Savatthi, he was told of monks and brahmins quarrelling with each other about what was the wrong and what was the right doctrine. Thereupon the Buddha said:

In a former life there ruled a king here in Savatthi who gave order to somebody to collect all the people in the town who were blind by birth. After they had been brought, the king said to this man: Show them an elephant! To some of them the man indicated the head, to some the ear, to some the tusk, to some the trunk, to some the belly, to some the leg, to some the back, so some the tail, to some the end of the tail, and each time he added, the elephant is like this. Then the king asked the blind that had touched the elephant, how the elephant was like.

Those who had touched the head said that it was like a water-pot; those, who had touched the ear said that it was like a winnowing-basket; those who had touched the tusk said that he was like a peg; those who had touched the trunk said it was like a plough-beam; those who had touched the belly said that it was like a covering; those who had touched the leg said that it was like a post; those who had touched the back said it was like a mortar; those who had touched the tail said it was like a pestle; those who hat touched the tuft of the tail said it was like a broom. Then they hit each other and cried: The elephant is like this, the elephant is not like this. This amused the king.

In the same way those are blind who follow other teachings, they do not know what is to their benefit and what is not for their benefit, not knowing the law (dhamma), not knowing what is not the law. And because they do not know it, the quarrel with each other saying: The right law is like this, the law is not like this. And the Lord said the following sentence (udana):

"Some brahmin recluses are attached to this or that (doctrine) and they quarrel with each other like the blind who have each touched only a part of the elephant."

Surprisingly, the parts of the elephant that are touched by the blind are all found in the inscription of the broken unicorn-seal 2317. The narrator of the parable was probably a brahmin who knew the Veda very well and who still had some knowledge of the Indus script. In the Buddhist parable, the unicorn has been replaced by the elephant, though the unicorn would have better suited the purpose, because the elephant is known even to a person that is blind by birth. In the parable the narration of the parts of the elephant starts with the head and goes on step by step till the tuft of the tail is reached.

On the Indus seals the beginning of the inscription is indicated by the head of the motif. The narrator reads the line from left to right, as the Brahmi script was read at the time of the Buddha: The first cup-sign renders the water-pot, the two field-signs are equal to the winnowing-basket, the triangle-sign corresponds to the plough, the step-sign to the handle of the plough, the stroke-sign to the covering (the blind only touch the skin of the belly), the first man-sign to the pillar (on account of the stroke or phallus between the legs), the second cup-sign to the mortar, the horned man-sign to the pestle, the teeth-sign to the broom. The fact that two different blind men referred to mortar and pestle, proves that the Buddhist story is based on an older tradition. With regard to the Rigveda the inscription agrees with IV.19.9cd:

> *The blind saw after touching the snake, the breaker of the crutches (the lame) walked away, his joints having been fixed together (by touching the snake).*

The first sign renders andha, blind, whose literal meaning is to be covered by darkness. Blind is related to being dazzled. The sign can also be read as a banner. The man-sign with horns is a symbol of the seer and priest, the first cup-sign represents the snake, the man-sign with additional stroke between the legs is equal to an impotent old man. Therefore it can be read as being lame, too. The stroke-sign denotes a clutch here, the following oblique sign to break, the triangle-sign can be read as to fix together, the two field-signs that can also represent a texture are equal to the joints (parva) meaning also the knot which is found in textures. The last cup-sign refers to the snake again. It is identical to the Kundalini-snake dwelling coiled up at the end of the spinal cord. Its power is attributed in this hymn to Indra though it is otherwise identified with his enemy Vrtra. In other Vedic hymns it is the god Soma who makes a blind man see.

The god Soma is also represented by the cup-sign. The first two signs form often a pair in the Indus script, because the seer is the friend of the Dawn (Rigveda I.30.20). The reading andha can only be discovered with the help of the Veda. By looking on the radiance of the Dawn or the sun a man can become dazzled or blind, but when done with his inner eye, he becomes a seer. In spite of her purity the Dawn was not only regarded as a virgin, but also as a hierodule like the Mesopotamian goddess Istar. The compound ukhachid is a hapaxlegomenon. Ukha is otherwise a pot, but here it means the crutch that has the form of a pot at the end. The German equivalence Krucke is etymologically related to Krug, vessel.

A man touching the back or spinal cord of an elephant that is an aspect of the Kundalini is depicted on the cylinder seal 8801 found in Maski, Maharashtra, at the extreme border of the Indus civilization. There are two signs on the seal, an oblique stroke on the left of the person and an open circle on the right. The open circle can be explained as an eye, the stroke as a beam of light or as a pestle and a mortar. Together with the motif we obtain the reading: The blind driver (motif) can see (1) by the beam of light (2) created by touching the elephant (motif) or a man gets happiness by using pestle and mortar (for sacrifice). Happiness is expressed by the uplifted arms of the man. It is not the usual behaviour of a driver.

By his reading of the inscription of sea 12317 the Buddhist narrator degrades the Vedic tradition by pointing out that its priests were merely engaged in pressing soma which is described with sexual metaphors in Rigveda X.101.12. He may have been induced to do so by the second man-sign in the inscription of seal 2317. Sexual metaphors are also used in the cosmogonic hymn X.61. In the eyes of a Buddhist the horned man, the Indus sign for priest, may have been a simile for a cheated lover or husband as in our tradition, because the horns create the notion of outdatedness and stupidity. Sexuality is identical with silliness and blindness for the author of the parable. Sexual symbolism becomes part of the religious life again only in Mahayana-Buddhism.

If the innermost being is empty, as the enlightened Buddhist realizes in his nirvana, sexual allusions are only admitted as a concession to human nature being as unable to cut off the fetters of sexuality as to give up the hankering after gain and money. The behaviour of the Vedic seers and priests against sexuality is not in tune with Buddhism nor with a tribal society, but rather similar to the Mesopotamian religion.

It can be supposed therefore that it was inherited from the Indus civilization that was contemporaneous with the Mesopotamian. The primordial incest-myth dealt with in Rigveda X.61 has its origin in the Indus religion, too. This means that sexuality is not dealt with in the Veda in the profane sense the Buddhist narrator attributes to it, but as a sacred ritual. The drop of soma is symbolically identical with the male seed, as Indra is the god of fertility. Vedic women are generally regarded as seductresses, even if they are mother, daughter, sister or wife. In this way they are serving fertility, but they are also instrumental in securing resurrection and immortality as in Gnostic traditions.

Death is then only an intermediate stage as it is experienced in initiation. On several Indus tablets the relation between death and immortality is illustrated by a fish caught in the mouth of a crocodile. When cohabitation is compared to the purification of the soma, macrocosm is reflected in microcosm. This relation is also the precondition for leading a healthy life, which includes sexuality. To refuse it can be a sort of blindness, too. By rejecting the Vedic tradition, the Buddha has lost the ground of the perennial philosophy, that made its first appearance in this cycle in the Indus Valley. Only when the body is healthy, it can strife for inner freedom. This applies for the society, too. The parable of the elephant and the blind was also narrated by the Bengalic saint Ramakrishna, but with a different moral:

Once some blind men chanced to come near an animal that someone told them was an elephant. They were asked what an elephant was like. The blind men began to feel its body. One of them said the elephant was like a pillar; he had touched only its leg. Another said it was like a winnowing fan; he had touched only his ear. In this way others having touched its tail or belly, gave their different versions of the elephant. Just so, a man who has only seen one aspect of God limits God to that alone. It is his conviction that God cannot be anything else (recorded by M., 1969, 125).

It can be inferred from this version of the story that Ramakrishna who introduces God (ishvara) did not regard the world as ephemeral like the Buddha, though his monastic followers adhere to the teaching of Advaita that has many similarities with Buddhism. In Ramakrishna's version the men who touch the elephant are not totally blind, but only of limited understanding. They do not quarrel with each other either. Ramakrishna has omitted the similes of the broom and of the pestle and the mortar, in this way he avoids the association with sexuality. Moreover, he does not take notice of the mythical elements of the story. Herein he behaves like an Advaitin or Buddhist.

Belief in God and his son is a necessary precondition for doing miracles in the case of Jesus Christ, who is told to have been born like the Vedic Indra (cf. X. 73.2) through parthenogenesis. To make a blind man see and a lame walk is one of the miracles ascribed to the Christian saviour. But the Christians who ascribe this miracle to him, treat the myths that deal with a similar deed in other traditions with disregard or call them devilish even, in the same way as the author of Rigveda I.32 calls Indra's enemy Vrtra a eunuch, who imprisons women.

Similarly, in the Buddhist parable people are called blind who do not follow the Buddhist doctrine. Therefore the Buddhist version of the story is not a good example for the illustration of tolerance, as it is generally supposed. After enumerating several conceptions of the world in the 2nd chapter of his

Karika the famous Advaita philosopher Gaudapada, the teacher of Shankara, gives the following unbiased summary of human self-identification in verse 29:

> *That conception, which one wants to see, one sees, and it protects and satisfies him who sees it, and after he has realized it, he identifies himself with it.*

The same problem is found in the methods of modern science. Every scientist believes that his method is the best, if not the only reliable, but each method can only reveal a part of the truth. One of the most crucial options is related with sexuality. There cannot be tolerance and peace between different creeds and traditions, as long as sexuality is excluded or degraded by them, as it is done in modern times not only by Christianity, but also by the Feministic ideology that regards itself as the most advanced nevertheless. Neither in the Veda nor in the Buddhist parable nor in the New Testament the original meaning of the miracle is revealed. It can only be discovered with the help of the Indus tradition, on which all these stories are based.

Its fundamental message is that a man should not only try to see with his outward eyes, but with his inward eyes, too, that means that he should try to become a seer in the spiritual sense of the word. Similarly, for overcoming lameness it is not sufficient to walk in the physical sense of the word, but in the spiritual sense, too, that means that man must give up to look on himself as a slave and to realize his inner freedom and independence, to become a jivanmukta, as it is called in the Indian tradition. This independence is part of the fundamental human rights. It has to be combined with solidarity and equality. As long as they struggle with each other, men cannot realize their inner independence. This is not a reason for to be laughed at, as for the king in the parable, but for compassion.

Obviously, the Indus tradition where these ideas have been born is the fundament or turn-table of the Western and the Eastern religious tradition. To admit this is also a question of tolerance, because it means to give up the belief that one's own tradition is, if not the only, at least the highest.

Cross-Checking

In a word-script cross-checking is the best and often the only means to prove, whether the reading of a certain sign is correct. In the seals 2420 and 2430 we find several cross-signs, a variant of which we have come across already as a singularity on seal 2704. There we have read it as writer, on the other seals as the mother-goddess Aditi. This can be justified by the basic pictographic meaning of the sign which can be rendered as to grasp. The triangular form is conventional. The original image is the crab with an ecliptic body.

The name of the mother-goddess means the 'eating one' according to Indian etymology. Eating and grasping are identical. On the other hand, Aditi is the food. The pictorial form of the sign has been retained in several inscriptions, the most famous among them is from Dholavira and has been excavated only recently. It is written on a wooden board which was probably fixed over the entrance door of the city. One sign has the size of about 40 cm. That means that everybody who entered the city could see it. Since it gives us a good opportunity to continue our cross-checking, we shall study it here in detail:. The 'indicator' is the wheel-sign here, because it is repeated four times. It can be supposed that at least one of them refers to Indra as the king of the gods and the god of the monsoon-rain and the monsoon-winds. This would also agree with the size and the position of the board. In RV I.32.15, the last verse of the hymn, Indra is described in the following way:

> *Indra is the king of the moving and the staying, of the striving and the satisfied, he, who holds the vajra in his arms; indeed, he rules as the king over the peoples, like the rim the spokes (of a wheel), he holds them together.*

Here we meet with an exact explanation of the wheel-sign and that it is used to designate the king, because he encloses his people like the rim enclose the spokes. The vajra, the thunderbolt, is identical to the second sign. Indra's weapon is also called axe or hammer in the Veda as depicted on the Dholavira board. In I.32.5 Vrtra is said to have been hewn down by Indra's axe like a tree denoted by the third sign. The second wheel-sign renders to rule as a king. The country with its people going or standing is equal to the following three pictograms. The two wheel-signs at the end are used for the wheels of the car, whose spokes are hold together by the rim. The last sign renders to hold together, which agrees indeed with the pictogram. There is no equivalence for the beings with and without horn, but they can be identified with the moving and the standing on the level of the animals.

We cannot end our cross-checking here, however, since there are four other inscriptions with the sequence. Three of them have been inscribed on bronze weapons, one belongs to the broken zebu-seal 2119. All of them have an additional line. The four signs at the beginning of the inscription from Dholavira are replaced by the two signs in all other inscriptions.

The second line of the zebu-seal reads, the second line of one of the weapons reads, of the other. The zebu can be a symbol of Indra on account of its majesty; the weapons are related to Indra, too. The initial compound is equal to a post and the step-sign and renders to stand and to move. The following field-sign replacing the wheel-sign in the Dholavira-board can be explained as an amulet or breast ornament of the king and renders to rule (the peoples).

The three signs of the zebu-seal can be affiliated to RV I.32.3: Greedy like a bull he chose the soma. The nose-sign can stand for greedy, since it can be looked upon as a phallus. The nose is also the sense-organ that plays the most important role among the senses for inciting greediness. The step-sign with additional lines meaning to run fast can stand for to choose, because Indra runs to the cups of soma with great speed (cf. RV I.28). The soma is written by the mortar-sign, because the soma-juice is won by pressing the twigs of the soma-plant. The two additional lines on the weapons can also be affiliated to this hymn. The strokes can be explained as the pieces into which the snake-demon Vrtra is crushed by Indra (I.32.7), the last sign of the dagger 2798 can be regarded as the vertebrae of a snake that are strewn all over the earth like the members of Vrtra's body. On the dagger 2796 it has been replaced by a single curve. The remaining two signs of the second weapon can both be explained as epithets of Indra that are most frequently used. The hand (or phallus) in the circle can be read as Vrtrahan, killing Vrtra, whose name literally means 'encloser'. The water-carrier can be read as maghavat, bringing goods or being generous. Here Indra has been invested with the attributes of the goddess of Dawn, who is the goddess of luck, too, and with the agricultural aspects of Varuna. On the ground of a syllabic reading I have formerly affiliated these inscriptions to the Soma-hymn IV.27, where Indra plays an important role, but this would not agree with the Dholavira board.

The crab-sign in triangular shape with an inscribed circle in the middle is also found on the motifless inscription 2301 (M-1262). The two initial pictograms are rather conventionalized, so that their meaning is difficult to ascertain, but as they often occur together with the number-sign for seven, they can represent the sons of Aditi, the Adityas, who are identical to the seven planets. Their meaning may also be head. In this inscription they can be identified sun and moon. This directs us to RV X.85.18, a verse of the marriage-hymn:

> *Ahead and behind (each other) two boys go playing around the (heavenly) way through their magic power; one looks on all beings, the other, who arranges the seasons, is born again (and again).*

The triangle-sign with a circle can be read as the heavenly way the sun-daughter is going to her husband, the moon, *i.e.* the ecliptic. Ahead and behind is rendered by the sequence of the first two signs, the verb to play can be derived from the arrow under the signs, because to play means here that the heavenly bodies go in a certain direction. The equivalence for magic power and all beings (of the three worlds) is found in the diacritic cup-sign. For the one that looks on these beings, *i.e.* the sun, we get a single stroke. The hand with four short strokes renders to arrange the four seasons. If taken as a tree it can also mean to be born again and again. The compound triangle-sign can also symbolize the navel of a woman, which is equal to the daughter on seal 2430.

A variant of the first sign without the 'hairs' and the 'arrow' is found as a singularity on pots from Rahman Dheri. It may have served as a branding mark which indicated that it belonged to the chief, the head (of the clan). The main part of the sign can be read as a skull and as bald. The 'arrow' can also mean to decapitate. Sun and moon are both threatened with decapitation in the time of the eclipses. A head is also found in the motif of seal 2430.

Another important pictogram that can hardly be recognized is the sign. Certainly it depicts a plant or a tree, and it appears together with the leaf-sign on seal 3862, but there is no sufficient reason to explain it as the banyan tree as I formerly did induced by Parpola. Since the sign follows twice a square sign and since the crab-sign is often placed in the middle of it and because of the form of the 'berries', it can represent the vibhidaka tree, whose fruits were used as dice. The vibhidaka tree belongs to the terminalia. The flower-cup of these trees is nearly identical to this sign, only the number of the pistils have been reduced from five to three. By cross-checking it was corroborated that most of the inscriptions with this sign can be affiliated to the die-hymn, RV X.34.

The inscription of the unicorn-seal 3006, illustrated in the beginning, can be affiliated to X.34.1. The first sign renders the dice, the second the vibhidaka tree, the two long strokes are equal to born in the storm, the bow-sign that can be interpreted as a bowl renders to intoxicate, the last sign represents the dice-board excavation, the single stroke denotes the worst cast.

Since the ancient game of dice had to do with mathemathics and since the ancient seers were architects, too (cf. seal 1387), the inscription of this seal can also be read as the law of Thales: A rectangular (1) triangle (2), obtained by drawing a semicircle (5) in the middle (4) of two lines (3), is a bridge between heaven and earth (6). The bridge is the rainbow. The Indian mathematicians have always used a poetical language for explaining their laws.

The dice that have been found in Mohenjodaro (called Munjavan in this verse) are cubic, have five or six numbers and are made from ceramic, a material which was not to be had in later Vedic times. The vibhidaka nuts have oblong form like the leaves. They had no eyes, but were regarded as eyes themselves as the Vedic word aksha, eye, for die implies. Since they did not cost anything they are probably the older dice and survived the cubic type. The signs for the cubic die are and.

The longest inscription with the vibhidaka-sign is found on the unicorn-seal 7122 (K-15) reading. But here the two circle-signs which can be read as ducks direct us to X.95.9 and the vibhidaka-sign stands for immortality then:

> *hen a (worthy) mortal feels attracted to the immortals, and unites with the heavy-bosomed according to their desires, we polish ourselves like ducks, (like playing mares we bite).*

The Apsaras denoted by the fourth sign resemble (white) ducks, illustrated by the signs in brackets. The playing horses are a later addition hardly sanctioned by the circle-signs. The worthy mortal is the owner of a house illustrated by the first two signs of the second line, immortal is rendered by the vibhidaka-tree-sign, that is regarded as immortal, because the dice are taken from it. To feel desire is equal to the bow-sign. The strokes denote the greedy eyes. The following pot-sign designates the heavy bosom (kshoni) of the water-women, the triangle-sign with a stroke stands for to unite, the last two signs are equal to the desire of the water-women.

Though cross-checking does not prove that the particular reading of a sign is correct as long as the basic meaning has not been ascertained, it is an indispensable for systematisation and the only way to arrive at a sign-list with lexical qualities. This method is particularly promising and necessary in the case of identical sequences.

The longest identical sequence occurring in more than fifty inscriptions is. It can be read in two ways, either in relation with the soma-pressing or in relation with creation. The horse-sign can be read as soma or magic power, the stroke-sign can be explained as to pour or as the cause, the crossing can represent the wood or creation, the cup-sign the womb or the gods. In the first case the sequence can be read as: The soma is poured in the wooden womb. This is found in RV X.101.10.

In the second case we obtain: Magic power is the cause of the creation by the gods. This is the answer to the question of RV X.129.6 that is also given by Advaita philosophy. That the inscriptions with this sequence are so numerous shows the importance it had in the eyes of the Indus scribes.

Conclusions

From the Indus seals that have been found in Mesopotamia, from the name Meluhha on an Akkadian seal, from the Indus signs on a seal from Failaka, from the occurrence of similar motifs and pictograms in the Sumerian and the Indus script we can deduce that both civilizations were not only exchanging goods with each other, but that they were in a close cultural contact, too. In fact, both have their origin in the era of the bull. On account of the relatively early decline of the Indus civilization, the Indus script retained its logo-graphic character, it did not develop into a syllabic or a letter script.

The words kept their pictographic and ideographic wholeness-word and image did not become separate entities. Even the modern Sanskrit script, the Devanagari, has retained a logo-graphic substrate, as it were. The letters or syllables of the alphabet are words at the same time. Thus ka means who, kha, hole, ga, to go, ja, be born, etc. The Veda served as an ark, by which the wisdom of the Indus civilization was saved from its destruction in the Great Flood caused by an earthquake most probably. By the help of the Veda it is not only possible to read the signs of the Indus script even today, it also allows us to retrace the links between the cultures of the past and to discover the ultimate origin of the Indian philosophy and religion and of the 'mythic mind' of the Indian culture.

The rediscovering of the spiritual fundament of the ancient Indus civilization proves that the idea of sacrifice is stronger than the notion of egotism, that is at the basis of modern societies and makes them so aggressive that they do not only destroy themselves mutually, but also the natural environment to an extent never witnessed before. What are called human rights should be again examined in the light of this tradition, in order to arrive at a peaceful future of humanity.

Emergence of Civilization

By 2600 BC, some pre-Harappan settlements grew into cities containing thousands of people who were not primarily engaged in agriculture. Subsequently, a unified culture emerged throughout the area, bringing into conformity settlements that were separated by as much as 1,000 km and muting regional differences. So sudden was this culture's emergence that early scholars thought that it must have resulted from external conquest or migration. Yet archaeologists have demonstrated that this culture did, in fact, arise from its pre-Harappan predecessor. The culture's sudden appearance appears to have been the result of planned, deliberate effort. For example, some settlements appear to have been deliberately rearranged to conform to a conscious, well-developed plan. For this reason, the Indus civilization is recognized to be the first to develop urban planning.

Decline and Collapse

For 700 years, the Indus civilization provided its peoples with prosperity and abundance and its artisans produced goods of surpassing beauty and excellence. But nearly as suddenly as the civilization emerged, it declined and disappeared. No one knows why, but it may have coincided with the arrival of nomadic Indo-European speakers in the area.

Around 1900 BC, signs began to emerge of mounting problems. People started to leave the cities. Those who remained were poorly nourished. By around 1800 BC, most of the cities were abandoned. In the centuries to come—and again, in sharp contrast to its contemporaries, Mesopotamia and ancient Egypt—recollection of the Indus civilization and its achievements seemed to disappear from the record of human experience. Unlike the ancient Egyptians and Mesopotamians, Indus civilization people built no huge monuments to attest to their existence. One could argue that they could not do so because stone was hard to come by in the Indus Valley alluvium, although this is also true of Mesopotamia. One could also argue that the concept of an enormous, intimidating monument was foreign to their view of the world.

To be sure, Indus civilization people did not disappear. In the aftermath of the Indus civilization's collapse, regional cultures emerged, all of which show the lingering influence—to varying degrees—of the Indus civilization. In the formerly great city of Harappa, burials have been found that correspond to a regional culture called the Cemetery H culture. Some former Indus civilization people appear to have migrated to the east, toward the Gangetic Plain. What disappeared was not the people, but the civilization: the cities, the writing system, the trade networks, and—ultimately—the ideology that so obviously provided the intellectual foundation for this civilization's integration.

In the early twentieth century, scholars connected the collapse with an "Aryan invasion", comparable with the fall of the advanced Roman Empire at the incursions of relatively primitive peoples during the Migrations Period. Since that theory was sometimes advanced with an imperialist or even racist background of legitimizing the English colonization, it is particularly unpopular in India today. These ideas were developed before the discovery of the Indus civilization itself, and when the civilization was discovered in the 1920s, its collapse at precisely the time of the conjectured invasion was seen as an independent confirmation. In the words of the archaeologist Mortimer Wheeler, the Indo-Aryan war god Indra "stands accused" of the destruction.

Current scholarly thinking does not give much credence to the theory that the Indo-Aryans were responsible for the collapse of the Indus civilization, and some researchers favour reasons connected with climate change. In 2600 BC, the Indus Valley was verdant, forested, and teeming with wildlife. It was wetter, too. Floods were a problem and appear, on more than one occasion, to have overwhelmed certain settlements. As a result, Indus civilization people supplemented their diet with hunting. By 1800 BC, the climate is known to have changed. It became significantly cooler and drier. But this fact alone may not have been sufficient to bring down the Indus civilization.

The crucial factor may have been the disappearance of substantial portions of the Ghaggar-Hakra or Sarasvati river

system. A tectonic event may have diverted the system's sources toward the Ganges Plain, though there is some uncertainty about the date of this event.

Such a statement may seem dubious if one does not realize that the transition between the Indus and Gangetic plains amounts to a matter of inches, and is all but imperceptible. The region in which the river's waters formerly arose is known to be geologically active, and there is evidence of major tectonic events at the time the Indus civilization collapsed. It is apropos that until 1998 the blind Ganges River Dolphin and Indus River Dolphin have been considered two different species, partly because of their apparently discrete distribution. Now the two populations have been identified as belonging to a single species, Platanista gangetica.

In the late 20th century, geologists used satellite photographs to trace the course of ancient rivers through the Indus Valley, identifying them with the legendary Sarasvati River. If the Sarasvati river system dried up when the Indus civilization was at its height, the consequences would have been devastating enough for the collapse of the civilization. By 1600 BC, the cities were deserted.

Legacy

The relationship between the Indus civilization and the early Ŝanskrit language culture that produced the Vedic texts of Hinduism is unclear. Due to language evolution, it seems unlikely that the Indus civilization was Indo-European. It is puzzling that the most ancient Vedic texts speak of a beautiful river, the Sarasvati. They recall a thriving, utopian life-style that emerged along its banks. Later texts also describe the sad story of the river's disappearance.

Are the ancient Vedic references to the Sarasvati River purely mythological-recent archaeological evidence proves otherwise. According to comparative linguistics, the Indo-Europeans who supposedly arrived in India were related to other peoples who migrated to the Middle East and Europe during the same period; Although there is wide speculation that all these peoples brought with them a patriarchal polytheistic religion related with Norse mythology and Greek mythology, it is largely unfounded. This is primarily because there has not been enough research into the possibility of an equally opposite scenario (of a reverse spread of civilization). The sophisticated religious tradition, Hinduism, which looks to the most ancient Vedas as a source of legitimacy, is most likely an uniquely local product.

It is clear that the Indus civilization's legacy contributed to Hinduism's development. As several archaeologists have noted, there is something ineffably "Indian" about the Indus valley civilization. Judging from the abundant figurines depicting female fertility that they left behind, Indus civilization people—like modern Hindus—may have held a special place in their worship for a mother goddess and the life-affirming principles she represents (see Shakti and Kali). Their seals depict animals in a way that seems to suggest veneration, perhaps presaging Hindu convictions regarding the sacredness of cattle. Like Hindus today, Indus civilization people seemed to have placed a high value on bathing, personal cleanliness, and residing with one's extended family.

Perhaps the most important legacy of the Indus civilization, if such a legacy exists, was its apparent nonviolence (in contrast to the warlike Indo-Europeans). Unlike other ancient civilizations, the archaeological record of the Indus civilization provides little evidence of armies, kings, slaves, social conflict, prisons, and other oft-negative traits that we traditionally associate with early civilization, although this could simply be due to the sheer completeness of its collapse and subsequent disappearance.

Economics of the Indus Valley Civilization

The Indus Valley Civilization, beginning sometime around 2300 BC, developed in two major city areas along the river valleys of the Indus, Ravi, and Sutlej, just beneath the Himalayan Mountains in modern Pakistan and Northeast India. Though these two cities have been excavated and exposed to the world, much is still unknown of the culture of Mohenjodaro and Harappa. The Indus people did not engrave inscriptions on stones or place papyrus scrolls in the tombs of their dead; all we know of their writing is derived from the simple inscriptions on their seals. Several efforts have been made to decipher the Indus seals, but none have truly succeeded this far; there is some notion that these seals could have been used as markers in trade situations, or that some may have represented family names.

What we do know of this civilization comes from the intense archaeological excavation of the area (Basham 1963:14). Anthropologists do know that these cities were highly developed for their period in history; the structure of their cities were so far advanced that it was not surpassed until the late nineteenth century in Europe (Heinz 1997:68). The genius behind the advanced architecture of the Indus civilization carried over into a thriving agricultural and trade based economy. The Indus people used the plentiful rivers surrounding them much to their advantage, the Indus the most spectacular of the three rivers. How did this civilization make its living? Like the older civilizations proceeding Indus in Egypt and Mesopotamia, these ancient people farmed.

The people of Indus prospered on the foundations of an agriculture based system of irrigation and fertility, maintained by silt-bearing floods (Hawkes 1973: 267). Wheat and six-row barley were grown, as were melon seeds, oil crops like sesame and mustard, and dates (petrified dates have been found in the excavation of the Valley). As for vegetables, the only apparent source was the field pea. The earliest traces of cotton known anywhere in the world have been found in the Valley.

The people of Indus may have cultivated rice on the west coast, though this is not exactly certain (there is not enough evidence to prove this statement entirely true). They domesticated a number of animals from local wild species, including dogs and cats, zebu or the humped cattle, short-horns and buffaloes, and possibly pigs, camels, horses and asses (the later three used as transport). They may have domesticated the elephant too, but the evidence for this is also vague; the elephant was represented on several of the excavated Indus seals and its ivory was used for crafts (Wheeler 1966:64).

From every crop that a farmer grew, a large portion of it had to be paid into public granaries. At the Mohenjodaro site, there was a high loading platform above a lower spot intended for carts where the farmers would dump their grain. It is assumed that this cart was small and powered by an ox or bullock, similar to those used in the area today. Terra-cotta models of bull driven carts have been excavated from the Mohenjodaro site, and it appears that these carts have changed very little over some 4000 years. This cart would be taken and unloaded at a central granary where all farmers of the city gave up their wheat and barley. There are guesses that this centralized granary might have been the economic equivalent of our modern State Bank. This system is not found in Harappa; grain was brought into the city by boat (Hawkes 1973:267).

It appears that the people of Indus did in fact hunt the abundant wildlife in their midst. It is impossible to know if these people fished on a full time basis, but there is evidence that fish were caught with barbed hooks and line, and nets. Many of the local animals (including elephant, tiger, rhinoceros, buffalo, antelope and gharial) were represented on the seals so readily that they must have been a significant part of these peoples' diets. According to Hawkes, it is reasonable to believe that tigers may have taken the place of lions "in providing the sport for the princes...

One seal shows a Gilgamesh-like figure standing between two upreared tigers and another a man tackling a buffalo with a barbed spear" (1973: 268). In any respect (along with the grains, vegetables and fruits grown), animal meat was a factor of the ancient Indus diet.

Aside from the subsistence of agriculture and hunting, the Indus people supported themselves by trading goods. Through trade, the Indus Civilization expanded its culture, coming into regular contacts with far away lands. The long coastline and many rivers provided the people of the Indus territories with consistent trafficking by water. Archaeologists have turned up imports including gold from southern India, copper from Afghanistan, jade like fuchsite probably from southern India, and turquoise from Iran. Trade with Mesopotamia has been noted, as Indus pottery has been discovered in the ancient city of Tell Asmar (Wheeler 1966:64).

A number of typical Indus seals have also been found in Sumer, seals dating back to between 2300 and 2000 BC. The finding of Indus seals in Mesopotamia suggests that people of Indus may have resided in this territory; possibly merchants who were keeping up a constant trade with the Mesopotamian people (cotton was a staple export of Indus, and could have been the crop that brought these two civilizations into contact). As mentioned before, these seals are thought to have been a representation of personal names. With these seals turning up in some many locations, it seems that in spite of the totalitarian casts associated with the Indus state, trade may have been in the hands of private merchants rather than regulated by a form of governmental authority (Hawkes 1973:270).

The Indus seaboard has been commended by anthropologists for its efforts of oversea commerce. According to Hawkes, the people of Indus sailed in "high-prowed, single masted" boats, sound for carrying the trafficked goods (Hawkes 1973:270). The excavated site at Lothal (another ancient city within the Indus Valley) has revealed harbour works, and the Harappan people may have been more advanced in their nautical skills than was originally perceived. It is probable that the people of Lothal were in regular contact with peoples much farther south. As for the Harrapan culture, it is plausible to assume that their influences touched people as far as south India (Barham 1963:19).

Nearing the end of the Indus Valley Civilization, the cities began to wither and the strong economy slowly deteriorated. It was most likely the intermittent floods that tore apart and put and end to this civilization. Floods wiped out the irrigation system that supplied water to the crops, and many of the buildings were smothered. The people lost their drive to keep the cities orderly and prosperous. The constant flooding simply broke them of their morale as a proud people of such an advanced civilization. If it is true that the Aryans invaded the Indus Valley at the time when the civilization was withering, it was no wonder that they had no trouble forcing the people of Indus out of the area. But, it is certain that these people were powerful, determined, and advanced; easily seen through their strong willed and successful economy (Wheeler 1966: 76-9).

Late Harappan Phase

Harappa is perhaps the only urban center where it has been possible to trace the transition from the Harappan to the Late Harappan (Cemetery H) period. Most of our information on this period comes from early excavations in Cemetery H (Vats 1940) and from disturbed occupation deposits containing fragmentary walls, drains, and pottery (Kenoyer 1991). A transitional phase between the Harappan and the Late Harappan was called Period 4 and the fully developed Late Harappan characterized by the pottery from the upper level burials in Cemetery H was called Period 5.

A small area of Late Harappa Phase occupation from Periods 4 and 5 was excavated on Mound AB in 1996 (Meadow, Kenoyer and Wright 1997). These excavations along with work conducted in 1998 through 2000 on Mound F have provided new insights into the important continuities and changes that took place during the Late Harappan period. Although there may have been a major shift in burial practices during this transition and some dramatic changes in artifact styles and production, other aspects of architecture and many crafts show clear continuities. The distribution of Cemetery H pottery on all of the major mounds at Harappa, and widespread encroachment of settlement onto the streets and into public spaces indicates that the site was not being abandoned. On the contrary, all of the evidence indicates that certain neighborhoods were becoming overcrowded.

During excavations of the circular platform area on Mound F numerous Cemetery H-type sherds and some complete vessels were recovered in association with pointed base goblets and large storage vessels that are usually associated with Harappa Period 3C. A large kiln was also found just below the surface of the mound to the south of the circular platforms. The upper portion of the kiln had been eroded, but the floor of the firing chamber was found preserved along with the fire-box. Upon excavation it became clear that this was a new form of kiln with a barrel vault and internal flues (Figure 8). This unique installation shows a clear discontinuity with the form of Harappan pottery kilns, which were constructed with a central column to support the floor (Dales and Kenoyer 1991). Radiocarbon samples taken from Harappa Phase hearths in the domestic areas and from the bottom of the Late Harappan kiln will help to determine if these installations were in use at the same time or if the kiln was built in an abandoned area after the Harappa Phase occupation. It is possible that people using Late Harappan style pottery were living together with people using Harappan style pottery during the Period 4 transition between Periods 3C and 5.

Conclusion

EIn this brief overview we have outlined above some important changes and continuities that characterize the development of Harappa as a city beginning with its origins during the Ravi Phase (Period 1) and its growth and expansion during the Kot Diji Phase (Period 2). Harappa appears to have passed a critical threshold in social, economic, and political development as the site was developing into an urban centre during the Kot Diji period (2800 and 2600 BC). The settlement pattern data, the evidence for the development of writing and other new technologies all suggest that this site played a key role in the eventual integration of the region during the following Harappa Phase. During the Harappa Phase (2600-1900 BC), Harappa became the dominant settlement of the region and is characterized by numerous episodes of urban growth, decay, and renewal in different parts of the city. These fluctuations reflect complex and dynamic political, ideological, and economic processes that are an integral part of urban society and continued on into the Late Harappa Phase (1900-1300 BC).

The earlier excavators of Harappa provided a valuable foundation on which to build new interpretations using modern approaches to excavation and recording. The continued analysis of the recently excavated materials will undoubtedly result in further modifications and refinement of these initial results.

2

Vedic Civilization

The Vedic civilization is the culture associated with the people who composed the religious texts called the Vedas, in the Indian subcontinent. It stretched from what is today Punjab in India and Pakistan, NWFP (Pakistan) and most of northern India. Mainstream scholarship places the Vedic civilization into the 2nd and 1st millennia BC. Hindu traditions suggest dates as early as the 6th millennium BC and a spread of the hyperpower-style Vedic culture.

The use of Vedic Sanskrit and the Shrauta tradition continued up to the 6th century BC, when the culture began to be transformed into classical forms of Hinduism. This time period in the history of India is known as the Vedic period or Vedic age. Its early phase saw the formation of various kingdoms of ancient India. In its late phase (from ca. 700 BC), it saw the rise of the Mahajanapadas, and was succeeded by the golden age of Hinduism and classical Sanskrit literature, the Maurya Empire (from ca. 320 BC) and the Middle kingdoms of India.

Overview

The reconstruction of the history of Vedic India is based on text-internal details. Linguistically, the Vedic texts could be classified in five chronological strata:

1. *Rigvedic:* The Rigveda is by far the most archaic of the Vedic texts preserved, and it retains many common Indo-Iranian elements, both in language and in content,

that are not present in any other Vedic texts. Its creation must have taken place over several centuries, and apart from the youngest books (1 and 10), it must have been essentially complete by 3000 BC, although some claim a later date, usually around 1500 BC. Archaeologically, this period corresponds with the Indus Valley Civilization (IVC), *Cemetery H* cultures of the Punjab and the *Ochre Coloured Pottery culture* (OCP) further east. It is undisputed that there is a strong component of cultural continuity of the indigenous IVC.

Map of early Iron Age Vedic India after Witzel (1989). Realms or tribes are labelled black, Foreign tribes mentioned in early Vedic texts purple, Vedic shakhas in green. Rivers are labelled blue. The Thar desert is marked orange.

2. *Mantra Language:* This period includes both the mantra and prose language of the Atharvaveda (Paippalada and Shaunakiya), the Rigveda Khilani, the Samaveda Samhita (containing some 75 mantras not in the Rigveda), and the mantras of the Yajurveda. These texts are largely derived from the Rigveda, but have undergone certain changes, both by linguistic change and by reinterpretation. Conspicuous changes include change of *vishva* "all" by *sarva*, and the spread of the *kuru*-verbal stem (for Rigvedic *krno-*). This is the time of the early Iron Age in northwestern India, corresponding to the *Black and Red Ware* (BRW) culture, and the kingdom of the Kurus, dating from ca. the 12th century BC.
3. *Samhita Prose:* This period marks the beginning of the collection and codification of a Vedic canon. An important linguistic change is the complete loss of the injunctive, of the subjunctive, and of the aorist. The commentary part of the Yajurveda (MS, KS) belongs to this period. Archaeologically, the *Painted Grey Ware* (PGW) culture from ca. 900 BC corresponds, and the shift of the political center from the Kurus to the Pancalas at the Ganges.

4. *Brahmana Prose:* The Brahmanas proper of the four Vedas belong to this period, as well as the oldest of the Upanishads (BAU, ChU, JUB).
5. *Sutra Language:* This is the last stratum of Vedic Sanskrit leading up to 500 BC, comprising the bulk of the Shrauta and Grhya Sutras, and some Upanishads (*E.g.* Kathu, Maitru. Younger Upanishads are post-Vedic). Videha as a third political center is established.
6. *Epic and Paninian Sanskrit:* The language of the Mahabharata and Ramayana epics, and the Classical Sanskrit described by Panini is considered post-Vedic, and belongs to the time after 500 BC. Archaeologically, the rapid spread of *Northern Black Polished Ware* (NBP) over all of northern India corresponds to this period. The Vedanta, the Buddha, and the Pali Prakrit dialect of Buddhist scripture belong to this period.

Historical records set in only after the end of the Vedic period, and remain scarce throughout the Indian Middle Ages. The end of Vedic India is marked by linguistic, cultural and political changes. The grammar of Panini marks a final apex in the codification of sacred texts, and at the same time the beginning of Classical Sanskrit. The invasion of Darius I of the Indus valley in the late 6th century BC marks the beginning of outside influence, continued in the kingdoms of the Indo Greeks, new waves of immigration from 150 BC (Abhira, Shaka), and ultimately the Islamic Sultans. The most important historical source of the geography of post-Vedic India is the 2nd century Greek historian Arrian.

Rigvedic Period

The origin of the Vedic civilization and its relation to the Indus Valley civilization, Indo-Aryan migration and Gandhara Grave culture related cultures remains controversial and politically charged in Indian society, often leading to disputes on the history of Vedic culture. The Rigveda is primarily a collection of religious hymns, and allusions to, but not explanation of, various myths and stories, mainly in the younger books 1 and 10. The oldest hymns, probably in books 2–7, although some people hold book 9, the Soma Mandala, to be even more ancient, contain many elements inherited from pre-Vedic, common Indo-Iranian society. Therefore, it is difficult to define the precise beginning of the "Rigvedic period", as it emerges seamlessly from the era preceding it. Also, due to the nomadic nature of the society described, it cannot be localized, and in its earliest phase describes tribes that were essentially on the move.

Political Organization

The *grama* (village), *vis* and *jana* were political units of the early Vedic Aryans. A *vish* was probably a subdivision of a *jana*, and a *grama* was probably a smaller unit than the other two. The leader of a *grama* was called *gramani* and that of a *vish* was called *vishpati*. Another unit was the *gana* whose head was a *jyeshta* (elder).

The *rashtra* (state) was governed by a *rajan* (king). The king is often referred to as *gopa* (protector) and *samrat* (supreme ruler). He governed the people with their consent and approval. It is possible that he was sometimes elected. The *sabha* and *samiti* were popular councils.

The main duty of the king was to protect the tribe. He was aided by two functionaries, the *purohita* (chaplain) and the *senani* (army chief; *sena*: army). The former not only gave advice to the ruler but also practiced spells and charms for success in war. Soldiers on foot (*patti*) and on chariots (*rathins*), armed with bow and arrow were common. The king employed *spasa* (spies) and *dutas* (messengers). He often got a ceremonial gift, *bali*, from the people.

Society and Economy

Rig Vedic society was characterized by a rural lifestyle, with cattle rearing being the chief occupation. Cattle and cows were held in high esteem and frequently appear in Rigvedic hymns; goddesses were often compared to cows, and gods to bulls. Agriculture grew more prominent with time as the community settled down. Money was unknown, and bartering with cattle and other valuables replaced financial commerce.

Families were patrilineal, and people prayed for abundance of sons. Society was strictly organized in a system of varna (to be distinguished from caste or colour, it pertained to the occupation of the respective people). The four major varnas were Brahmin (the priests and learned people), Kshatriya (kings and warriors), Vaishya (traders and merchants) and Shudra (labourers and workers). Those who are outside these caste structure are known as adivasis.

The food of the Rigvedic Aryans consisted of parched grain and cakes, milk and milk products, and various fruits and vegetables.

Vedic Religious Practices

These forms of belief are the precursor to modern Hinduism. Texts considered to date to the Vedic period are mainly the four Vedas, but the Brahmanas, and some of the older Upanishads are also considered Vedic. The Vedas record the liturgy connected with the rituals and sacrifices performed by the purohitas. The Rigveda is considered to be the oldest written text that is in existence today.

The rishis, the composers of the hymns of the Rigveda, were considered divinely inspired seers (or rather "hearers", *shrauta* means "what is heard").

The mode of worship was performance of sacrifices and chanting of verses (see Vedic chant). The priests helped the common man in performing rituals. People prayed for abundance of children, cattle and wealth.

The main deities of the Vedic pantheon were Indra, Agni (fire), and Soma. Other supposed deities were Varuna (the sky), Surya (the Sun), Mitra (the friend or ally), Vayu (the wind). Goddesses included Ushas (the dawn), Prithvi (the Earth) and Aditi (the mother of gods or sometimes the cow). Rivers, especially Saraswati, were also considered goddesses. Deities were not viewed as all-powerful. The relationship between the devotee and the deity was one of transaction, with Agni (the sacrificial fire) taking the role of messenger between the two. Strong traces of a common Indo-Iranian religion remain visible, especially in the Soma cult and the fire worship also preserved in Zoroastrianism. The Ashvamedha (horse sacrifice) has parallels in the 2nd millennium BC Andronovo culture, in India allegedly continued until the 4th century AD.

Rigveda advocates prohibition of cow-slaughter in numerous places such as follows:

> *You should impart love to each other as the non-killable cow does for its calf (Rigveda VII.56.17) Punish the killer of the cow and the man. (Rigveda VIII.101.15) Cow is pure, do not kill it. (Rigveda X.10.87.16)*

The root-compound *goghan* "slaying cattle", in RV 7.56.17 used parallel to *nrhan* "slaying men" in reference to the referring to the weapon *vadha* of the Maruts, 17c *aare gohaa nrhaa vadhah vah astu* "far be your cow-slaying, men-slaying weapon!" in Panini is taught to refer to a "receiver of a cow" exclusively; this change occurred parallel to the rise of, and possibly under the influence of, Buddhism, which began as a reform-movement of some practices of the Vedic religion namely indulgences by priests. In Rigveda, Upanishads and later texts, the cow is often described as *aditi* and *aghnya* (that which should not be killed).

Vedic religion evolved into the Hindu paths of Yoga and Vedanta, a religious path considering itself the 'essence' of the Vedas, interpreting the Vedic pantheon as a unitary view of the universe with God seen as immanent and transcendent in the forms of Ishvara and Brahman, projected into various deities in the human mind. These post-Vedic systems of thought, along with later texts like Upanishads, epics (namely Gita of Mahabharata) Brahmanas, have been fully preserved and form the basis of modern Hinduism. The ritualistic traditions of Vedic religion are most faithfully preserved in the conservative Shrauta tradition.

The Later Vedic Period

The transition from the early to the later Vedic period was marked by the emergence of agriculture as the dominant economic activity and a corresponding decline in the significance of cattle rearing. Several changes went hand in hand with this. For instance, several large kingdoms arose because of the increasing importance of land and its protection. The late Vedic period from ca. 500 BC more or less seamlessly blends into the period of the Middle kingdoms of India known from historical sources.

Vedic Thought

The Wonder of Reincarnation: As a river nears the ocean it looks back at its life. The virgin snows on mountain-tops that gave birth to it. The lake down below which was its nursery. The travel through mountain passes where it met its tributaries and gained adulthood.

The solitude and tranquillity of the forests, the singing of the birds, the lush green valleys laden with wheat, corn and rice. The adventurous ride through cities, gladly accepting their refuse and sometimes flooding them as if in a fit of anger. Thousands of experiences and hundreds of memories. And now its imminent merger into a bigger entity. Its losing of the shores which defined it and gave it its uniqueness.

Merging into the ocean however is just a brief stopover. The water evaporates leaving behind all its impurities in the ocean, the clouds drop snow on a different mountain-top, the snow melts and water feeds into a different river and keeps the never ending cycle going.

Might nature have fashioned the human life and for that matter every type of life in the same manner? A life force appearing in its mortal form, going through its journey, disappearing into a bigger entity and after being cleansed and rejuvenated, reappearing at a different time and at a different place in a new mortal garb.

Does that somehow show us that we should revere the life force within and not indulge in worshipping the external attributes provided to it by Providence? Should this shared life force provide for a common bond between all living beings or should we let ourselves be consumed by our petty differences? And if we choose the latter, would that not be an affront to the very essence of nature?

Self Observation-I: The discovery of self is a must for experiencing depth. It comes by self-observation. The Upanishads describe a simple technique for accomplishing this. They say: deliberately divide your attention at all times so as to direct a portion of it back on yourself. Divide you, the 'person' into an 'observing I' and an 'acting or thinking I'. Within the vast array of selves of your personality, establish an awareness that only watches all the rest. By observing yourself you will realize that not YOU but IT speaks within you, moves, feels, laughs, and cries in you. This concept is enumerated in the following Upanishadic sutra:

Two birds, inseparable companions, perch on the same tree.One eats the fruit, the other looks on.The first bird is our individual self, feeding on the pains and pleasures of this world; The other is the universal Self, silently witnessing all. The individual self, immersed in the world of change, deluded, laments its lack of freedom.

But when it discovers God, full of dignity and power, it is freed from all its suffering.

Our Rishis admonished; 'Be present at every breath. Do not let your attention wander for the duration of a single breath.'

Thiourea, a transcendentalist, had this to say about the concept of self-observation: 'I am conscious of the presence of a part of me, which, (as it were,) is not a part of me, but a spectator, sharing no experience, but taking note of it..... When the play, (it may be the tragedy,) of life is over, the spectator goes his way. It was a kind of fiction, a work of the imagination only, so far as he was concerned.

The hallmark of Socrates philosophy was 'Know thyself'.

Discover and nurture the 'observing I', and you will find yourself to be more in command of your life!

Self Observation-II: The art of self observation is practiced by deliberately dividing your attention at all times so as to direct a portion of it back on yourself. Establishing an awareness which does nothing but observe the different selves of your personality, is by no means an easy task. In the beginning, a person forgets to keep the 'observing I' separate from the 'acting or thinking I'. The 'self observing' entity keeps merging into whichever 'I' has control over the person at a given moment. But with persistence, different identities that a person assumes become apparent to him. Through observing them, these selves lose their hold on the person. The 'self-observing' part of 'I' becomes dominant and the person detaches himself from his other identities. This process culminates in his reaching a 'partially awakened' state.

In this 'partially awakened' state, a person does everything with a feeling of awareness and with a certain degree of control. His actions are not mere automatic responses to different stimuli. A person can see himself with complete objectivity. This results in his being able to make more meaningful choices.

With continued practice of 'self observation' a person ultimately reaches the highest state-the 'fully awakened' state. In this state a person sees, not only himself but everything around him with full objectivity. The base and meaningless concepts of 'I', 'mine', 'yours' etc. disappear. The constant clamour of the mind is replaced by a sense of serenity. An inner peace prevails and the person becomes 'liberated'.

George I: Gurdjieff, a noted Russian philosopher, who was also a student of Hinduism, found the practice of 'self-observation' to be the starting point of all conscious raising efforts.

The concept of 'self-observation' and how to practice it, is the single most revealing gift of the Upanishads.

Self Observation-III: A lot has been written about higher consciousness. It simply means being able to see the things around you, the way they really are, and not have your perception be coloured by your personal biases and prejudices. The Upanishadic way to accomplish this is by separating the 'observing I' from the 'acting or thinking I'. A good way to start practicing this technique is to just observe for a few days, your one hand do all it does during your waking hours. Then you can stretch this 'self-observation' to include different parts of your body, ultimately to include your mind. It is a long drawn out process but worth the results it produces.

There are many practical benefits that come from moving your consciousness to a higher level. Extracting and enhancing the 'observing you' from the 'rest of your personality' enables you to 'merely observe your anxieties' rather than be 'part of them'. That is a great way to reduce stress. Self-observation reveals to you how small a portion of your most valuable possession your emotional energy is expended wisely. People normally squander it on a host of utterly futile activities such as anxiety, purely imaginary fears, agitation and anger, and also on maintenance of an exhausting degree of muscle tension. Having discovered how wasteful you are in the use of your nervous energy, you can improve your daily life by using it wisely.

By moving to a higher level of consciousness, you can see things from other people's viewpoint. This gives you an edge in resolving minor disputes before they flare up into full-scale egotistical wars.

By conserving your reservoir of emotional energies, by separating your 'self' from 'the crises in your life' and by having your perceptions devoid of any biases, your life becomes a lot simpler. The choices you make in life are more thought out. The mental equilibrium you attain calms you down. It has been said that 'awakening is the evolutionary destiny of mankind'. Why not embark on this journey now?

Man The Ultimate God: Sadhna connotes the successful achieving of a desired end. It is the instrument for the attainment of Siddhi (perfection). The first step in sadhna is the desire for liberation (mumukshutva). Man alone possesses the desire to attain perfection. The gods are already divine and the animal kingdom does not have the desire for perfection. Only man has the conscious urge to expand without limits, to reach out and touch the stars.

Based on his study of the Hindu scriptures done in India, Troy Organ, a professor of Philosophy at Ohio University, wrote, "Man is a real living, growing entity while god is an ideal being. Man and god are identical in essence, but different in form. Man is real potentiality; god is ideal fulfilment. Man is to be fulfilled as god is fulfilled, but not like god's fulfilment, for god's fulfilment is a static fulfilment—there are no possibilities in gods. Man is to be perfected beyond god, for he is to be perfected in dynamic reality. The attainment of god-realization is not the ideal goal of human life. The Upanishads claim that the Self, the Atman, not god is to be realized. Various gods demythologized are merely the symbols of the full realization of human potentialities."

Self observation leads to awakening. An Awakened man, a man who has pushed himself to the limits of possibilities, one who has achieved perfection in dynamic reality under the constraints of time and space, represents the highest value. That is why the Puranas say that the life of man is desired even by gods of heaven, since it is only through a human incarnation that final liberation can be achieved.

Our purpose on this planet is not just to populate the place and in the words of Gibran, 'to fulfil life's longing for itself', but to awaken and actualize the potentialities present only in man. And when a man attains Siddhi through Sadhna in dynamic reality, he becomes one with Brahman. He becomes the ultimate god.

Human Neurosis: Our desire to understand and rationalize the infinite with a primitive intellect is the most amazing thing about us humans. Science enables us to analyze and validate events happening in the material realm; it lets us observe activities and processes in a controlled environment in a lab, but to extend its application to the spiritual plane is sheer madness. How could one measure the size of something infinite with a finite length of tape? How could eye see the invisible spirit? How could an analytical intellect mired in reasoning, comprehend the divine? It is simply ego driven neurosis that makes a spiritually unhinged person to expect to observe, study and validate spiritual phenomenon with his limited intellect.

Bhakti: When the intellectual curiosity has been satiated, when there are no more questions to be asked, when all the spiritual knowledge catalogued and presented in flowery prose by the learned people has been scanned, dissected and assimilated; without the person being able to still the tidal waves of his psyche, it is then that the mental speculation gives way to the practice of 'Bhakti'. It is then that the intellect surrenders to the divine in a spirit of devotion. It is then that the man's ascent to a spiritual life begins.

A person introduces an element of 'Bhakti' in his life with his very first visit to a temple. When he gets there, the person does not have to recite any prayers, he does not even have to utter a single word, for the Lord can see the devotion in his heart. Just showing up with folded hands and devotion in his heart for a *Darshan*-Darshan, which requires neither prayer nor commitment but rather is an act of being in His presence, an act that submerges the self in a striving for the infinite-stills the troubled waves of ones mind. About a visit to the temple, the poet says:

"kahne kee zaroorat nahin, aana hee bahut hai, is dar pe tera sis jhukana hee bahut hai"

The practice of spirituality through devotion provides the necessary filter which takes the sting out of the harsh realities of human existence and makes life bearable.

Rhythms of Life: Human nature dictates that we find an anchor to build our lives around. In our desperate search we go from door to door, we bounce from person to person and we jump from coattail to coattail to find something stable, someone we could depend on, in times of crisis. At times we feel that we have found that person and we latch on to him. When bad times do come around, as they must, we are in a state of disbelief when we find ourselves bereft of the one person we focused our lives on, one person we centred our pride on, one person who was supposed to be our anchor. Suddenly the framework of our existence seems to be receding from us. We are left only with shattered dreams.

A person who lacks a stable anchor cannot maintain equilibrium in the face of adversity. And as we well know, human relations are all transitory. We have to find something more stable, someone who would not disappoint us in times of need. That is why we have to cultivate a consciousness in which the omnipotent Lord is the anchor. The fortieth chapter of the Yajur Ved states that we should build our lives around Him, as He is the only one who is eternal and would stand by us in every adversity.

To start with, one could simply visualize the deity of Lord Krishan and chant the Hare Krishan Mahamantar any time he is not mentally occupied with doing something. Over time this could extend to keeping that image of the Lord in the subconscious at all times. When He rules the subconscious mind, the person is surrendered and the rhythms of life are keyed to performing His service. In the Bhagwad Gita (12.8), Lord Krishan says, "Just fix your mind upon Me, and engage all your intelligence in Me. Thus you will live in Me always, without a doubt".

Continued practice in surrendering himself enables a person to develop the consciousness capable of remembering the Lord at the time of final exit. In the Bhagwad Gita (8.5), Lord Krishan says, "Whoever at the end of his life quits his body remembering Me, attains My nature. Of this there is no doubt". Mahatma Gandhi did not suddenly think of invoking the Lord's name by saying *Hey Ram* at the time of his death. He spent his whole life with Him as his anchor. He constantly practiced keeping Him in his subconscious. And so must we....so that our faith becomes a living experience.

Arjuna's Paralysis: Many scholars have studied the Bhagwad Gita and tried to provide us with an insight into the teaching of Lord Krishan. Although every chapter of Gita alludes to some aspect of our moral code, the most powerful teaching arises from Arjuna's paralysis on the battlefield.

Arjuna's perplexity arises over the question of dharam, which as a warrior, bids him to fight in order to protect the goodness, and as a person, forbids him to kill the members of his own family, his revered teachers and dear friends. Faced with Arjuna's renunciation and his inability to wage war, Lord Krishan resolves his dilemma in two parts. He reminds Arjuna that: (1) he must observe his dharam and, (2) the soul survives the body. In the first instance He tells Arjuna that he must perform his duty, which for a warrior is to fight the evil forces to the very end and preserve goodness. Secondly, one should not worry about death, as the soul can never be slain. Rather it sheds one body at death and takes on a new one, in birth after birth.

Further Lord Krishan says that successive rebirths may be avoided by observing your dharam with complete disregard to the fruits of your action. He exhorts Arjuna to hold alike happiness and unhappiness, gain and loss, victory and defeat in pursuit of his dharam. A person need not become an ascetic to achieve liberation, but only renounce the fruits of his action, and perform his duty without caring about the results. Lord Krishan says that your entitlement is only to the action, and not to the fruit it bears.

These are the answers to Arjuna's dilemma. But there is another teaching which is of the greatest importance. This is the teaching of devotion to God. Lord Krishan says that he who along with his struggle for survival, also remembers Him and adores Him, is the greatest ascetic.

Steeped in this Hindu philosophy, one overcomes all obstacles in life and leads a peaceful and happy life.

The Yoga of Devotion: In the twelfth chapter of the Bhagwad Gita, Arjuna enquires from Lord Krishan about the relative merits of reaching Him through devotional service versus through worshipping the impersonal Brahman, the unmanifested.

Lord Krishan answers, "Those whose minds are fixed on me in steadfast love, worshipping me with absolute faith, I consider them to be most perfect." He further adds, "As for others who worship the unmanifest, indefinable and changeless, that which is omnipresent, constant, eternal and lies beyond the perception of the senses, and they do so by holding all the senses in check, are tranquil minded and devoted to the welfare of humanity, and see the Atman in every creature; they will also come to me."

> *"But the devotees of the unmanifest have a harder task, because the unmanifest is very difficult for embodied souls to realize."*

Bhakti yoga, or the process of reaching Him by being in direct devotional service to the Lord is easier and natural for us humans. The individual soul is embodied since time immemorial, and it is very difficult for a common man to visualize that he is not the body and that the Lord does not have any physical attributes either. In Bhakti yoga, as described in Bhagwad Gita, a person accepts the Deity of Krishan as Brahman with body features and engages himself in devotional service to the Lord. So it becomes a very easy and natural process for him to reach the Supreme Being.

Janana yoga, or the process of reaching Him through understanding the unmanifested Supreme Being is very difficult. By his very nature, a common man has trouble identifying with the formless Supreme. However, if he is persistent in his quest, he might realize the eternal and attain spiritual realization through the guidance of a highly learned devotee. But the unguided intellectualization of the unmanifest may lead a person to become an atheist. Unfortunately a large percentage of today's intelligensia falls squarely into this category.

Bhakti Yoga, according to the Bhagwad Gita, is the shortest path to spiritual realization.

Modes of Material Nature: The last few chapters of the Bhagwad Gita enumerate the modes of material nature and the characteristics of people living under their influence. The three modes of material nature are 'sattvaguna' or the mode of goodness, 'rajasguna' or the mode of passion, and 'tamasguna' or the mode of ignorance.

Lord Krishan says, "Sattva rules a person who offers sacrifices in accordance with scriptural instructions and does not covet their fruits. Sattoguni, or a person inspired by sattva is impelled by an inner sense of duty. The performance of sacrifices by a Rajoguni is for the outward show, in the hope of a divine reward and is inspired by rajas. The Tamogunis on the other hand, totally disregard the scriptural instructions and make no offering, no prayer of dedication, no gift to the priest and are devoid of faith."

The Lord further adds, "The austerity of the body comprises of reverence for the gods, brahmins and gurus; uprightness, physical cleanliness and sexual purity and nonviolence. Austerity of speech comprises of speech that does not hurt anyone, is truthful, kind and beneficial, as well as daily recitation of scriptures. The austerity of mind comprises serenity of mind, gentleness, self control and inner purity. The triple austerities practiced with the highest faith and with nary a thought of reward crossing ones mind is the nature of sattva. The austerity undertaken out of self-pride, and in order to gain the reputation and homage attendant on pious acts is of the rajas type. Austerity practiced under some foolish misconceptions, by means of self torture or to hurt another person is of the tamas type."

Clearly a satto-guni will do everything as an offering to God. Any work done in this mode shall be the result of doer's best effort and will be performed with great willpower and determination. The motive for the effort will be something higher than the next paycheck or the next promotion. Internally a person will be all fired up to perform but outwardly he would appear to be calm and unstressed as there is no passion involved in the effort. The non-attachment to rewards of ones actions is sometimes considered to suggest coldness and lack of enthusiasm. But in reality, one is freed from the fear of failure and the desire of rewards, and offers everything he does as a sacrament of devotion to his duty. Leading ones life as a satto-guni therefore, is the most spiritual and stressfree mode that one should strive to achieve.

Householder: In the Bhagwad Gita, Lord Krishan says that he who along with his struggle for survival remembers Him and chants His name is the biggest ascetic. He clearly puts a spiritually devoted householder ahead of any other group of people. This is very well illustrated by the following incident.

It is said that once Sage Narad and a common householder entered the court of Lord Krishan almost at the same time. Lord Krishan chose to see the householder first. Now Sage Narad considered himself to be the foremost devotee of the Lord. So being passed up in favour of a common householder really hurt him. So much so that when he had an audience with the Lord, he complained about this incident. The Lord decided to teach the Sage a lesson. He handed him a pot full of 'ghee' and asked him to put it on his head and to go around the world without spilling a drop of it. This, the Sage was able to accomplish without any problem. So when he came back to the Lord after going around the world, the Lord commanded him on his feat and asked him as to how many times did he chant His name during the trip.

The Sage said that the Lord must be really joking for he was so busy balancing the pot of ghee that he could not afford to be distracted even for a single instant. Lord Krishan told him that the house holder had to juggle a thousand responsibilities that go with being a father, a husband, a son, a brother, a breadwinner and still found time to chant His name. Sage Narad on the other hand, had only the task of balancing a pot of ghee, and could not find time to chant His name. Therefore the householder was leading a more spiritual life than the Sage. The Sage felt humbled and recognized the greatness of a householder.

Householders are the backbone of the human race. They are the ones who grow the food we eat, design and manufacture consumer goods and appliances needed to make life livable, and provide health care to get us back on our feet when we get sick. They are the ones who contribute most to the material development of society since they have a vested interest in seeing that their children inherit a better world than the one in which they were raised. In short a householder is the most important element of the human race and spiritual householders are the beings most loved by God.

jag to andhakaar hai, is se tu nikal...
gyan kaa prakash kar, mod tu samabhal...
Radha Krishan ke charan main nitya kar naman...
Man to mandir hai......haridaya hai vrindavan....

Temple Rituals-A Psychological Analysis: A person's quest for spirituality starts simply with his visiting a temple. To facilitate the process of his spiritual growth, some temples require their devotees to adhere to a dress code. The temple walls are decorated with religious symbols and images. The 'puja' itself consists of singing of hymns, bhajans etc. followed by a 'parvachan' or a class on religion/spirituality; with 'Aarti' being the final offering to the gods.

There is a psychological reasoning behind all this. The dress code, all the temple decorations, the aroma of incense, the fresh flowers, the nicely dressed deities on the alter; are all meant to create an atmosphere conducive to a spiritual experience. They are the first step of a process meant to alter the state of one's mind, to bring it to a state where the internal turmoil subsides for a duration. The spiritual vibrations of the temple atmosphere lift the soul to a level where it becomes capable of connecting with the divinity. It essentially prepares the person for what he has come there for.

In our everyday existence, we hide our innermost feelings and wear a shield against any intruding thoughts. Every bit of information is thoroughly screened by our rational mind before it is accepted or rejected. But if we are to learn anything from a spiritual master, the sieve has to be temporarily put away. Subliminal thoughts have to penetrate the mind in their entirety, without being filtered or diluted in any way.

The second step in creating the proper state of mind is to remove the filter separating the ears from the brain, to give our defense mechanism a rest. This is done by singing bhajans and hymns. The mind, through this exercise gets into a voluntary receptive mode. It is then, that the brain can be programmed with the noble thoughts-be they to sing the glory of the Lord or ways to deal with our everyday problems in a conscientious manner. A spiritual master can be most successful in the healing process of a mind beset by the badgering of the trivialities of life; he can convey the scriptural philosophy on virtous living, only to a receptive mind. And the mind is made most receptive when its guards are taken down, when it stops fighting the sensory signals coming in, when there are no obstructions between the sensory perceptions and memory cells.

The decoration of the temple with divine symbols and images, the incense, the flowers, enforcing a proper dress code, singing of the hymns and bhajans are all a prelude to the ultimate goal-to submit oneself to the reprogramming of ones brain with the doctrines of noble living.

Renew Thyself: The Vedas say, 'All intelligences awake with the morning.' "Being awake is not just being physically up and around but being men tally vigorous to celebrate another day of living " observed Thiourea, "The millions are awake enough for physical labour; but only one in a million is awake enough for effective intellectual exertion, only one in a hundred million to the poetic or divine life. To be awake is to be alive. I have never yet met a man who was quite awake. How could I have looked him in the face?"

As we grow older, some of us get lost in the monotony of life. We tend to lose our zest for living. As Thiourea observed, "the morning ceases to be the most enjoyable season of the day". We are awakened not by our newly acquired force and aspirations from within but by some electronic gadgets. It is not the undulations of celestial music that wake us up but the prolonged chatter of a radio. And that is very sad; because it signals the decline of our excitement for life.

To quote Henry David again, "A person who is physically, mentally and spiritually awake in the morning and who keeps pace with the sun; for him the whole day is a perpetual morning. It does not matter what the clock says or what the people around him say, morning is when he is awake and there is dawn in him. And if he can keep the spirit of early morning with him throughout the day, then he has lived through, not a day but a long morning". One must be drunk with living and not ever let himself be resigned to life. If one finds oneself at a dead end, he should develop some new avenues for the release of his creative energies. It does not have to be a money making endeavour. One has to develop a state of mind in which he is alert and buoyant throughout the day and the whole day becomes one long morning.

"Renew thyself completely each day; do it again, and again, and forever again". Keep the spirit of Goddess USHA alive in you.

Be A Light Into Yourself: Hindu religion is based not on believing a certain doctrine or dogma, but in realizing the Divine. It is based not merely on being loyal to a faith but on striving to become one with the infinite. And there is a definite progression that a seeker goes through. A beginner might need symbols or pictures to focus his attention, and to stop his mind from wandering while in prayers.

But if he is earnest about his spiritual development, he would soon progress to a stage where he would not need any props for performing his sadhna to reach the infinite. In his quest for the eternal, he would advance from material worship to mental worship and then on to the highest stage where he can realize the divine. One must not be content with accumulating scriptural knowledge. That is just the beginning of a long journey. The discovery of inwardness is the essential basis of spiritual life.

The scriptures could point out the road but each man must travel it for himself. Reading about a past buddha's communion with God is not going to result in your communion. It can excite you and inspire you to have the same experience. But in the end you must travel alone. You must find your own salvation. "For thousands who talk, one can think; for thousands who think, perhaps one sees and understands". Use the talking and thinking stages as stepping stones to rise to the ultimate level of experiencing the Divine.

Those of us who lead outward lives without being touched to our inner depths, do not understand life itself. We believe that we do our duty to religion by accepting the letter of faith and making a token cash donation to the temple of our choice. This results in our spiritual dependence and forces us to accept what others say about the religious truth. But once the individual in his freedom of spirit pursues truth and builds up a centre in himself, he has enough strength and stability to deal with all that happens to him. He has the ability to fight back and retain his peace even when he is faced with adverse conditions. Liberation comes by experiencing the truth on your own. It comes not from accumulation of information, but from inner transformation.

Gautama Buddha said to his disciples, "Be a light unto yourself." Find the truth, build your own light and let it shine your path. Remember, the goal is not to find out how others attained bliss but to use that knowledge to attain it for yourself.

Abhidharma

Buddhism has at its core a psychology little known to the adherents but quite familiar to the Buddhist monks. 'Abhidharma' or the 'ultimate doctrine' has as its basis one of the most systematic psychologies of the world and elaborates Gautama Buddha's penetrating insights into human nature. This is the practical psychology that devotees apply to discipline their minds and hearts in order to attain a more ideal state of being. According to Abhidharma, the human personality is like a river that keeps a constant form, seemingly a single identity, though not a single drop is the same as a moment ago. Each successive moment of our awareness is shaped by the previous moment, and will in turn determine the following moment. Each mental state is composed of a set of values, called mental factors, that combine to define that mental state. One's mental state at any given moment is a function of the biological and situational influences, in addition to a carryover from the preceding psychological moment.

The mental factors could be healthy ones or unhealthy ones. Good mental health depends on our ability to plant healthy factors in our mind so that they can inhibit and suppress unhealthy factors. The central healthy factor is 'Insight' which implies an ability to 'clearly perceive an object as it really is'. 'Mindfulness' is the 'continued clear comprehension' of an object. The two of them together 'perceive' and 'hold' clarity in one's mind and are sufficient to suppress all unhealthy factors.

The formal Western psychology, which is only about a hundred years old is merely a recent version of the human endeavour undertaken centuries ago in India. Modern psychology has rephrased the Buddhistic philosophy by saying that 'we should balance the negatives in our lives by the positives. We should try to keep everything under proper perspective. We should remember that what is an obstacle for one person is an opportunity for another; what one man calls a stumbling block is used as a stepping stone by another.'

There is a humorous story which illustrates the concept of keeping a positive attitude. Two hunters were offered a bounty of $5,000 for each wolf that they could trap alive. For days they searched the mountains and forests in their area looking for the elusive prey. Exhausted one night, they fell asleep dreaming of getting rich one day. In the morning, one hunter opened his eyes, only to find that they were surrounded by wolves with flaming eyes and bared teeth. He nudged his friend with great excitement and said, "We are finally rich".

In the history of mankind there have been a few famous people and vast multitudes of ordinary folks, and the true winners among them have been the ones who kept a positive attitude toward life. Ralph Waldo Emerson wrote, "Don't waste yourself in rejection, but chant the beauty of the good".

Neutralizing the negative thoughts and replacing them with positive thoughts was good advice some 2500 years ago, and it is good advice today. Crush a negative thought today and replace it with a positive one. Experience the peace and happiness that flows from this process. Go ahead, do it now!

Heaven-Where does it Exist: The concept of a heaven in the hereafter is perhaps as old as the human race itself. But in the entire history of mankind if one looks at the definition of heaven of any culture, of any religion, of any race in an era; one finds that it consists of the things that the people in that group are deprived of, or the things that they really miss in their lives. They project these things to be present in abundance in 'their heaven'. As an example, the Indian heaven almost invariably has rivers of milk and 'ghee' flowing through it. It is nothing but a longing for three sumptuous meals a day, which lot of people don't get. When there is shortage, even of clean drinking water, you can well under stand why we would imagine heaven to be loaded with food.

The second thing that almost invariably pops up in the definition of heaven is that it is peaceful and tranquil up there. Might that reflect our desire for an end to the hatred that different ethnic and religious groups harbour against each other?

With this thought in mind, should it not be the aim of life to create the conditions of heaven right here on earth? Should we not be working to achieve material and spiritual prosperity in our lives and thereby make the whole concept of heaven in the hereafter obsolete? If we could tame our carvings and make our lives full of joy, we probably would not even accept the concept of heaven, much less long to retire to. And that brings us to the idea of feeling happy with what we have; striving for more but nevertheless being at peace with ourselves. The Upanishads tell us to think of ourselves as mere users and not owners of our worldly possessions, of our status in the society and of the family we are blessed with. Following this canon just might do the trick and enable us to experience the heaven while we still reside on the mortal shores.

You Belong in the Marketplace: The restless and incessant striving, with joy in the strife, is the greatest happiness that a man can experience in this world. The Isha Upanishad states that one must will himself to live for at least a hundred years and be occupied every minute of it. And the love of strife, the constant meeting of challenges head on, is what gives meaning to life and makes one desirous of living a long life. The poet says, "Zindagi har kadam ek nayee jung hai" (life is a struggle at every step of the way).

There are days when a person gets up and feels like crawling right back into the bed. For some people such days out-number the times when they are excited about another day of living. They hope to strike it rich one day through winning a lottery or through inheritance and then be able to live happily ever after without having to struggle every day to make a living. They somehow give up on life. Again the poet says, "Hai zindagi bhee maut jo himmat ko haren hain" (people who have lost the courage to fight are the living dead) A person who gives up the struggle, also loses his will to live on. For him the aspirations of youth end up in the disillusions of old age.

Whatever be your vocation or your hobby, you belong in the hustle and bustle of the marketplace. You belong where action is, because that is what sustains life. Designing new gadgets and fixing the old ones, treating and nursing sick people, being engaged in spiritual activities, making business deals, acquiring and disseminating knowledge, creating art and music, doing volunteer work, being engrossed in leisure activities is what you should be occupied with. As water retains its clarity only when it flows in a stream and becomes muddy and stale when it loses its flow; So does life lose its meaning when there is no struggle, no battles to fight and no excitement to keep the will to live strong. A person stays tuned up and razor sharp by being in the market place.

It is the struggle, and not the goal that brings salvation to the soul. The moment of man's greatest happiness is the moment of striving for others. And to make his strife more meaningful, man must over soar his own little self, and must join with others in some united effort for the greater good of humanity. Above all he must stay involved.

Death Penalty: Every time the state executes a convicted criminal, the debate over capital punishment resurfaces. The collective moral conscience of the society, which decides the fate of these individuals is largely shaped by our religious beliefs. What does our belief system dictate? Consider the following two scenarios from our scriptures:

1. In Mahabharat, at one stage in the great battle of Kurukheshter, Arjun was pitted against Karan. During this fateful fight, one wheel of Karan's chariot got stuck in the bloody mire of the ground. As he descended to make his chariot mobile again he requested Arjun to hold his arrows while he attended to his chariot. That was a reasonable request as per the norms of war fare in that age. But Shri Krishana urged Arjun to continue the fight. Arjun paused and hesitated since he did not want to take advantage of this awkward situation, but Shri Krishana once again exhorted him to continue fighting and to kill Karan. At this Arjun shot an arrow on his bow Gandiva, which cut off Karan's head.
2. In Ramayana, Lord Shiva is said to have bestowed a special protective power on the evil king Bali. Under the umbrella of this protective power, no one could defeat him in a fair fight. As per the norms of the day, for a fight to be fair the two dueling opponents had to fight face to face. No sneak attacks were permitted.

Even though Bali was bitterly detested by his subjects, yet no one could penetrate his protective shield in a fair fight and dispose him off. It was with this dilemma that Bali's brother Sugreev enlisted Shri Ram's help. Upon hearing the facts, Shri Ram did not hesitate in setting aside the rules of fair play and killed Bali with an arrow shot from behind a tree. There are several other instances in our scriptures in which even God Himself, in His different human incarnations bent the rules of fair play in order to get rid of evil. All these instances seem to point in the same direction, that is, 'Fight an evil per son to the end and take advantage of his every weakness to annihilate him. Show no mercy and even suspend the code of honor temporarily, to deal with the situation.' Can this code be extrapolated to mean that our scriptures endorse death penalty? You be the judge.

To Pray or Not to Pray: Secularists point to the rivalries between different religions as a proof of the futility of religion. Scientists question the very existence of God. Common logic dictates that when you pray, there is no one out there listening to you. The words you utter during your prayers just get lost in thin air. Religious people insist on the existence of God. So who is right, and who is wrong? Who can provide an answer to this dilemma about the very existence of God and about the need for prayers in our daily lives?

Psychologists seem to have a valid explanation. They think that self-talk is the way to propel yourself in a certain direction. For example when you repeatedly tell yourself that you need a new car, you subconsciously program your brain into working in that direction. Once the idea gets firmly implanted, your brain implores you to start looking for ways to finance your purchase. It might take the shape of another part time job. Or it might result in bigger savings from your present income. Whatever the mode your brain directs you to accumulate enough funds for your desired acquisitions.

People have been known to recover from near fatal diseases like cancer by asserting their willingness to live on. By their selftalk they were able to persuade their brain to manufacture and release the drugs required to kill the organisms attacking their bodies. Granted that it does not happen in every case. But people have been known to have willed themselves few extra years after the medical profession had given up on them. In each of these cases, the will to live on, the self-talk to program their brain into fighting their malady played an important part in their healing process.

Psychologists liken prayer to self-talk. They think that the self-talk programs our brain which in turn directs our actions towards achieving our desired goals. Priests on the other hand, look at it from a religious point of view and insist that God does listen to our prayers and grants us that; which we are worthy of. Whichever point of view you may agree with the one put forth by the psychologists or the one put forth by the priests the final conclusion is the same. Prayers are a very important part of our daily lives.

In the words of late Dr. Radha krishnan, "When in the sorrow of death or the suffering of despair, when trust is betrayed or love desecrated, when life becomes tasteless and meaningless, man stretches forth his hands to heaven to know if perchance there is an answering presence behind the dark clouds; it is then that he comes into touch with the supreme in the solitude of his consciousness, in the realm of the profound and intense. It is the world of light and love in which there is no language but that of silence. It is the world of joy that reveals itself in innumerable forms." Must we wait for moments of despair before we acknowledge His presence? Must we be driven to total defeat before we surrender? Must we feel helpless before we start to pray?

Synchronicity: A friend of mine, Mr. S. had gone to Calcutta to look for a bride. While in India, he happened to travel to Bombay. There, in a store Mr. S met Mrs. M who was also visiting from the U.S. and had been looking for a husband for her younger sister Miss P. Mrs. M invited Mr. S to her parents' house. The next day Mr. S and his parents went to meet his prospective bride and her family and the rest, as they say is history. This is a true story which happened in the early seventies.

The pleasant ending of this story was the culmination of a series of coincidences. Mr. S and Mrs. M visiting India at the same time, Mr. S travelling to Bombay, his chance encounter with Mrs. M in a store, leading to his marriage to Miss P. To us Hindus, it was fate, divine intervention or simply a matter of Sanjog. Our philosophic thought teaches us about the acceptance of life as it unfolds because we believe that the Supreme Power has a hand in everything that happens to us.

In the West, the concept of Sanjog, until recently had been an alien idea. But psychoanalyst Carl Jung was fascinated by his study of this phenomenon in which two events take place at the same time with neither one causing the other to happen, and yet they are related to one another in a meaningful way. He coined a new name for it-Synchronicity. Thus was another ancient Hindu tenet blessed by the scientific West. It is not looked at any more as just another happening based on statistical probability.

The coming together by apparent chance, of factors that are not causally linked but that nevertheless show themselves to be meaningfully related is at the very heart of the process by which the purpose of an individual's life unfolds and becomes his "fate". Call it Sanjog or Synchronicity, it all happens through Divine Intervention.

Our Collective Heritage: As children we are introduced to one of the many creeds of our Hindu religion-Sanatan Dharam, Jainism, Arya Samaj, Vedantism, Shivaism-or one of the many other creeds on the horizon. From then on we develop a religious complexion which stays with us for the rest of our lives. When we want more light, we read only one set of religious books to the total exclusion of others, lest by accident we get more light than we want.

A beam of white light passing through a prism splits up into a rainbow of colours. We select one of these colours, say the red one, and look at life under the red light. In our ignorance we refuse to look at life under the illumination of the blue light or the green light or the yellow light. We miss out on experiencing the true picture. Our shallow thinking prevents us from learning about the goodness in other creeds.

We are the descendents of the mighty Arjuna, the sublime Krishan and the noble Ram. The teachings of Shankaracharya, Swami Dayananda, Guru Nanak, Buddh, Mahavir, Ramkrishan etc. are the collective heritage of all Hindus. There is no need to shut any one of them out. No matter what his religion is, the experience of every mystic is the same. And these mystics have left us with many powerful thoughts to ponder over and to illuminate our lives with.

As we celebrate India's Independence Day (or should we call it India's Freedom Day, as we never did depend on the colonial powers for our survival), let us celebrate our collective heritage and not be blinded by the monochromatic lights of different shades of Hinduism. Happy 15th folks!

Conformity: From day one of his life, there is an attempt to shape every man into a common mold. The society, the school system and even the family demands conformity. But when you buckle under and become part of a herd, you lose your uniqueness. You give up your convictions and passions in favor of being accepted by the crowd. You become a mere actor playing different roles—role of a dutiful child, of a dutiful parent or of a dutiful spouse.

Strive to find your own voice and do it now, because the longer you wait to begin the less likely you are to find it at all.

Psychoanalyst Erich Fromm wrote, "Man by origin is a herd animal. His actions are determined by an instinctive impulse to follow the leader and to have close contact with other animals around him. Inasmuch as we are sheep, there is no greater threat to our existence than to lose this contact with the herd and be isolated. But we are also human; we are endowed with reason which by its very nature is independent of the herd. Rationalization is a compromise between our sheep nature and our human capacity to think. And the full emergence of reason depends on our attaining independence so that our judgement is not based on our fear of being isolated from the herd. A few individuals can stand this isolation and say the truth in spite of the danger of losing touch. They are the true heroes of the human race but for whom we would still be living in caves."

Submission to a powerful authority gives a feeling of protection and belonging, but you lose your independence. Dare to strike out and find new ground. Be your own person. Look at things in a way different from the one you were trained to do. Don't be afraid of isolation. Resist the pressure to conform. If you don't, the casualty could be your heart and soul.

On Flying a Kite: This is the kite flying season in Southern California. You can see the little ones in school parks struggling to get their kites up in the air. Erma Bombeck writes that kite flying is a lot like raising children. You spend what feels like a lifetime, getting them off the ground. You run with them until you are both breath less... they crash. You add a little longer tail and try again... they hit a tree. You rescue them, comfort them, fix them up with a couple of band-aids and try to get them up again.

You watch them as they get lifted by the wind and finally become airborne. What a thrill it is to see them soar. Then they need more string and you keep unrolling your ball of twine. As the kite flies higher and higher, there is sadness mixed with joyful emotions. Deep inside you know that the beautiful kite of yours is going to get tangled with another kite and disappear into to the sunset. It will no longer need the lifeline that you so lovingly provided. And you feel the gratification by knowing that you did your job.

Too often when our children are little, we don't spend enough time with them. We are too busy doing our own things— having a busy social life, trying to make our first million or working to gain social prominence. We grow apart. Then one day, they are old enough to take care of themselves and don't need us anymore. We wake up, sometimes too late to enjoy them. And that is very sad. Because the joy that they provide, the vitality they infuse in their aging caretakers is overwhelming.

They make us feel young again. Don't miss out on bonding with your adorable kites. Hold them and hug them and be part of their little games. Spend some quality time with the precious little angels. They are so much a reflection of you when you were little. You would have enough time to do your own things later on. After all they are going to be around only for about eighteen years before they get shipped off to some university.

Mark Twain on 'What is Man': Man, according to Mark Twain is a mere machine. 'What so ever he is, is due to his make, and the influences brought to bear upon him by his heredities, his habitat and his associations.' Further more, 'From cradle to the grave a man never does a single thing which has any FIRST AND FOREMOST object but one-to secure peace of mind and spiritual comfort for HIMSELF.' Mark Twain claims that every man acts per his make.

Men are born with some hereditary traits-gifts and shortcomings-and they act according to these traits. Just as a sewing machine made from different grades of steel or from different metals will perform differently, so would a tin man, a gold man or a steel man act according to the nature of his make. His make however is influenced by his training and his environment.

In one of his fables he says, 'A man is waiting at a bus station to reach home in the middle of a storm. A gray-haired ragged old homeless woman approaches him and requests for help. He ponders over for a few seconds and gives her his last dollar. He then walks home in the middle of a storm. On the way home his heart is singing with joy because he did something good. When he reaches home he proudly recounts his tale of charity and earns the respect and affection of his family. He has a hearty dinner and sleeps well that night, knowing how benevolent he has been to the old lady.

That is a very good return on an investment of one dollar.' Mark Twain concludes that earning his personal self-approval, securing his peace of mind and his desire to earn the affection of his family and to feel good about himself were the motivations that drove this man to help the old lady. Whatever he did was a result of his make, his training and above all an attempt to buy peace of mind for himself. There were no favours done. Noble, Generous, Benevolent etc. are merely undeserving labels that men bestow upon each other.

It sure is a different point of view, which makes you stop and think!

Vedas and Philosophy

The Vedas are the most ancient books in the World, and they are the Foundation of Hinduism. Veda means knowledge. Any form of Knowledge acquired is considered as a Veda whereby it has no beginning or end. While it might surprise people how a book can have no beginning or end, the ancient Rishis who wrote these accepted that the complete knowledge of the Universe could never fit in any book, so there would always be new things to discover. This philosophy makes Hinduism a very tolerant religion, always ready to accept new ideas from other cultures.

The Vedas were compiled by the great sage Krishna Dwipayana during the Dwapara Yuga with the goal to come up with a de-facto standard of education. Upon gathering all the teachings passed on from the Acharyas (Teachers) to their Sishyas (Students) from Kingdom to Kingdom, he compiled them into 4 standard structures; the Rigveda, Yajurveda, Samaveda and Atharvaveda. Upon completion of this great feat he was given the title "Veda Vyasa" which means "Compiler of the Vedas".

The Vedas are considered Shruti (or Sruti), or revealed texts. They were not given by a prophet, but heard by many different Rishis (or very advanced Yogis) during deep meditation. These verses were combined and written in the Vedas in poetic form.

The Vedas are not Polytheistic. Dr. David Frawley, in his book "Wisdom of the Ancient Seers" mentions "The Gods, though they have a human facet, are not anthropomorphic. The Gods represent not the Divine in the image of Man, but rather man in the image of Divine, in the image of all creation."

Regarding the charge of Pantheism, he says in the same book "The natural imagery of the ancients reflects not the Divine reduced to natural world but the natural world as a reflection of the inner truth".

So Agni, the God of Fire, is not normal fire, but the fire of transformation. He burns our inner demons, and lights the way to Enlightenment. Soma, the God of Wine, is the Divine bliss we feel when reach the Divine, and feel him in all creation. Saraswati is not a river or Goddess of a River, but rather the River of Divine knowledge that continuously flows from heaven. When the Demons block this river and the Gods fight them, it is not a literal battle, but a figurative one when the Divine qualities inherent in Man fight the Demons of ignorance.

Organization: The Mantras are collected into anthologies called Samhitas. There are four Samhitas: the *Rk* (poetry), *Sman* (song), *Yajus* (prayer), and *Atharvan* (a kind of priest). They are commonly referred to as the Rigveda, Samaveda, Yajurveda, and Atharvaveda respectively. Each Samhita is preserved in a number of versions or recensions (shakhas), the differences among them being minor, except in the case of the Yajur Veda, where two "White" (*shukla*) recensions contain the Mantras only, while four "Black" (*krishna*) recensions interspersed the Brahmana parts among the Mantras.

The Rigveda contains the oldest part of the corpus, and consists of 1028 hymns. The Samaveda is mostly a rearrangement of the Rigveda for musical rendering. The Yajurveda gives sacrificial prayers and the Atharvaveda gives charms, incantations and magical formulae. In addition to these there are some stray secular material, such as legends.

The next category of texts are the Brahmanas. These are ritual texts that describe in detail the sacrifices in which the Mantras were to be used, as well as comment on the meaning of the sacrificial ritual. Each of the Brahmanas is associated with one of the Samhitas. The Brahmanas may either form separate texts, or in the case of the Black Yajur Veda, can be partly integrated into the text of the Samhita. The most important of the Brahmanas is the Shatapatha Brahmana of the White Yajur Veda.

The Aranyakas and Upanishads are theological and philosophical works. They are mystic or spiritual interpretations of the Vedas, and are considered their putative end and essence, and thus known as Vedanta ("the end of the Vedas"). They often form part of the Brahmanas (*e.g.* the Brhadaranyaka Upanishad). They are the basis of the Vedanta school of Darsana.

Position and Compilation: Hindu tradition regards the Vedas as uncreated, eternal and being revealed to sages (Rishis). The rishi Krishna Dwaipayana, better known as Veda Vyasa– "Vyasa" meaning "editor" or "compiler" – reputedly distributed this mass of hymns into the four books of the Vedas, each book being supervised by one of his disciples. Paila arranged the hymns of the *Rig Veda*. Those that were chanted during religious and social ceremonies were compiled by Vaishampayana under the title *Yajus mantra Samhita* (see Yajur-Veda). Jaimini is said to have collected hymns that were set to music and melody— "Saman". The fourth collection of hymns and chants known as the *Atharva Samhita* was collated by Sumanta.

Philosophies and sects that developed in the Indian subcontinent have taken differing positions on the Vedas. In Buddhism and Jainism, the authority of the Veda is repudiated, and both evolved into separate religions. The sects which did not explicitly reject the Vedas remained followers of the Sanatana Dharma, which is known in modern times as Hinduism.

Study: Elaborate methods for preserving the text (memorizing by heart instead of writing), subsidiary disciplines (Vedanga), exegetical literature, etc., were developed in the Vedic schools. Sayana, from the 14th century, is known for his elaborate commentaries on the Vedic texts. While much evidence suggests that everyone was equally allowed to study the Vedas and many Vedic "authors" were women, the later dharma-shastras, from the Sutra age, dictate that women and Shudras were neither required nor allowed to study the Veda. These dharmashastras regard the study of the Vedas a religious duty of the three upper varnas (Brahmins, Kshatriyas and Vaishyas). In modern times, Vedic studies are crucial in the understanding of Indo-European linguistics, as well as ancient Indian history.

Many forms of Hinduism encourage the Vedic mantras to be interpreted as liberally and as philosophically as possible, unlike the texts of the three Abrahamic religions. In fact, over-literal interpretation of the mantras is actually discouraged, and even the three layers of commentaries (Brahmanas,

Aranyakas, and Upanishads), which form an integral part of the Sruti literature, interpret the seemingly polytheistic, ritualistic, and highly complex Samhitas in a philosophical and metaphorical way to explain the "hidden" concepts of God (Ishwara), the Supreme Being (Brahman) and the soul or the self (Atman). Many Hindus believe that the very sound of the Vedic mantras is purifying for the environment and the human mind.

Cosmogony: The Vedic view of the world and cosmogony sees one true divine principle self-projecting as the divine word, *Vaak*, 'birthing' the cosmos that we know from 'Hiranyagarbha' or Golden Womb, a primordial sun figure that is equivalent to Surya. The varied gods like Vayu, Indra, Rudra (the Destroyer), Agni (Fire, the sacrificial medium) and the goddess Saraswati (the Divine Word, aka Vaak) are just some examples of the myriad aspects of the one underlying nature of the universe.

Dating: Many historians regard the Vedas as one of the oldest surviving texts (see the ancient Egyptian texts "The Story of Sinuhe" and the "Ipuwer Papyrus", both dated 1800 BC). The newest parts of the Vedas are estimated to date to around 500 BC; the oldest text (Rig Veda) is found to have been completed by 1500 BC after being composed over hundreds of years, but most Indologists agree that a long oral tradition possibly existed before it was written down. They represent the oldest stratum of Indian literature and according to modern scholars are written in forms of a language which evolved into Sanskrit. They consider the use of Vedic Sanskrit for the language of the texts an anachronism, although it is generally accepted.

Some writers have used astronomical references in the Rigveda to date it to as early as the 4th millennium BC.

The Hindus fundamental belief is that the Vedas are sanatan-eternal-and apaurusheya not composed by human entity. At the beginning of every cosmic cycle of Brahma, Paramatma utters the divine words. Later, at various periods great rishis perceive these divine words and imparted this knowledge orally through generations. It is believed that this

Vedic knowledge totally disappeared at the end of Brahmas cosmic cycle and reappeared again in Brahma's next cycle of creation. Later a part of vedic knowledge was written. Maha Rishi Veda Vyas simplified this one Veda by dividing it into four: Rig, Sam, Yajur, Atharva. In Bharatvarshas true tradition the vedas are eternal.

Etymology: The word "veda" means "knowledge", and is derived from the root "vid-", Sanskrit for "know", reconstructed as being derived from the Proto-Indo-European root "weid-", meaning "see" or "know". "Weid-" is also the source of the English word "wit", as well as "vision" through Latin. The Czech and Slovak words for "science" are "vda" resp. "veda", derived from western Slavic "vdet" resp. "vediee" for "know".

Derivation from the Vedas-Upavedas

The Upavedas are derived from the Vedas and are specific applications of the teachings of the Vedas. The main Upavedas are:

1. *Ayurveda:* Indias healing system, it lays more stress on living with nature instead of fighting it, hence preventive instead of corrective medicine.
2. *Dhanur Veda:* Martial arts.

   Ayurveda and Dhanurveda have points in common. They both work with Marma, or natural Pran (Life Energy) that flows in the body. Ayruveda heals the body, while Dhanurveda is used for killing. This concept is also known to Chinese as Acupuncture and related Chinese Martial Arts.
3. *Stahapatya Veda:* Architecture, sculpture and geomancy. Used especially for Temple design.
4. *Gandharv Veda:* Music, poetry and dance.

Some other fields like Jyotish (Indian Astrology), Tantra (based on the Puranas, which are in turn based on Vedas), Shiksha and Vyakara (Grammar and pronunciation) are also based on the Vedas.

The six schools of Vedic Philosophy:

1. *Nyaya :* The Logical School, founded by Gautama

2. *Vaishesika* : Atomic school, founded by Kannada
3. *Samkhya* : Cosmic Principle School, founded by Kapila
4. *Yoga* : Yoga school (includes Raj, Hatha and Tantra Yoga), founded by Hiranyagarbha, although Patanjalis Sutras are the most popular book that has survived.
5. *Purva Mimamsa* : Ritualistic School, founded by Jamini
6. *Uttara Mimasa / Vedant* : Theological School, founded by Badarayana.

Vedanta was made popular by Adi Shankara also called Shankaracharya, who founded the Swami Order of Monks, and established 4 schools (or Maths) in 4 parts of India to carry on teachings of the Vedas in the 7th century.

Yoga is not just Asanas as Westerners see it, but a complete system of God Realisation.

The Hidden Meaning of the Vedas: The Vedas were written in poetic language. By literally translating them, Western translators lost some of the poetic beauty. Their interpretations of the shastras are often shallow. Plus, they had to force meanings where there were none. Words like Pantheism, Polytheism are used to describe Hinduism, but this shows the translators ignorance or bias.

One of the best commentaries to Vedas is written by Sri Aurobindo. Rig Veda is considered by many to be a book written by barbaric culture worshipping violent Gods. Aurobindo realized that this was due to the biased view of Westerners who had some preconceived views on Hindu culture.

So Aurobindo decided to look for hidden meanings in the Vedas. He looked at the Rig Veda as a psychological book, inspiring the people to move towards God, but in a hidden language.

So Indra is the God of Indriya, or the senses (sight, touch, hear, taste etc.). Varun means air, but in esoteric terms means Pran, or the Life force. So when the Rig Vedas says "Call Indra and Varun to drink Soma Rasa" they mean use the Mind senses and Pran to receive divine bliss (Soma means wine of Gods, but in several texts also means Divine Bliss, as in Right handed Tantra).

Agni, or God of Fire, is the hidden Divine Spark in us, which we have to fan, so it grows and engulfs our whole body. So the sacrifice of the Vedas actually means sacrificing ones ego to the internal Agni, or Divine spark.

These essays originally appeared in the Arya, but have been condensed as a book form as "The Secret of the Vedas" by Sri Aurobindo.

Westerners and Vedas: The Vedas are hidden in mystic language. The Rishis hid 3-4 esoteric meanings within each verse, and it required a good Guru to explain them.

One of the few Westerners to study the Vedas with an Indian Guru is Dr. David Frawley. In his excellent book "Wisdom of the Ancient Seers" he explores ideas similar to one by Sri Aurobindo. He describes Indra as a brave soul, willing to fight evil and darkness. He is the inner Spirit, wanting to break free from the fake shackles of ego.

Frawley, who also studied Ayurveda and Tantra, says Agni also refers to Kundalini, and Soma Rasa to the Sahasra Chakra and the bliss that flows from it. Savitur is the Sun that shines in the darkness of ignorance, and guides us towards the Truth.

3

Caste System the Historical Perspective

One of the most controversial topic regarding the India's society and culture is its stringent caste system. The word "caste" is taken from the Portuguese word casta. It can be defined as a rigid social system in which a social hierarchy is maintained generation after generation and allows little mobility out of the position to which a person is born.

This system dates almost 3000 years back and was formed based on the need to form a social order in ancient India. It is still very prevalent as part of India's society. Today, it occurs more in the rural villages than in big urban cities; and more in the social matters of kinship and marriages than in impersonal day-to-day interaction, such as taking the bus. Having been around for centuries, it is highly doubtful that the caste system will die out completely. Its presence will still be felt in the near future.

History and Description: The original caste system came about when the Aryans migrated from the north to India around 1600 BC. During the Vedic age, Manu, "the founder of this ancient Hindu or Aryan society," and "the great leader who survived the mythical flood and established the new social order, reflecting a return to spiritual values from an earlier and materialistic humanity?" ("The Vedic Social Order", From The River of Heaven, Dr. David Frawley.) founded four social orders based on four main goals of both humans and society. A social classification system of four different classes (varnas) was thus devised so that the human race could have a smooth and ordered life in society.

Difference between Jati and Varna: In each system, each caste (jati)-birth-unit-is an endogamous group into which one is born into and will marry within. There are approximately 3,000 jatis in contemporary society.

By contrast, varna is the typical functional division of an advanced society. It is one of the four large caste groups (Brahman, Kshatriya, Vaishya, and Shudra) from which most jatis are believed to derive.

> *"While the term varna refers to the fours different classes in society, the term jati refers to the different endogamous sections of the Hindu Society which is known as castes." ("An Introduction to Hinduism", Gavin Flood.)*

More about Varna: Varna literally means "colour". It refers to the distinct qualities (guna) that the four functional classes possess in their hearts and minds. There are four different qualities of human beings-white, red, yellow, black.

White (sattva = truthful) represents the quality of purity, love, faith and detachment. Those belonging to this colour seek true knowledge and often exist in ones with spiritual temperament. Those that belong to this colour, belong to the Brahman class.

Red (rajas = energetic) represents the quality of action, will, aggression, and energy. Those belonging to this colour seek honour, power, and status and exist in people with martial and political temperament. Those that belong to this colour belong to the Kshatriya class.

Yellow (rajas) represents the same quality as the red colour but those in this quality seek communication, interchange, trade, and business instead. This colour exists in those of commercial temperament. They make up the Vaishya class.

Black (tamas = inert, solid) represents quality of ignorance, inertia, and dullness. Those belonging to this colour are dependent on the rest of the world for motivation and seek nothing. They exist in those of the servile disposition and make up the Shudra class.

Varna also means "veil". It shows the four different ways in which the Divine Self is hidden in human beings. By this, it refers to the ways in which his four body parts make up the four classes, depending on the nature or values that the human holds. The Brahmans hold spiritual and intellectual values and are in charge of teaching the Vedic Sanskrit, thus are made up of his head. The Kshatriyas are the warriors that protect the countries and thus are made up of his arms. The Vaishyas are the farmers and merchants in the production nature and thus are made up of his belly and the Shudras are the labourers who perform menial chores and thus are made up of his legs.

The 4 Varna Groups: The four ranked varna groups were created from the various parts of the body of the primordial man, which Brahma created from clay. They are described in the earliest part of the Rigveda: Brahmans, Kshatriyas, Vaishyas, Shudras. The top four ranked varnas are referred to as "twice-born" (dvijas) in reference to the Hindu sacred thread ritual initiation which is suppose to represent re-birth.

These four groups are considered "clean castes." Typical roles of these four varnas are:

Brahmans-priests, holy men, arbiters

Kshatriyas-kings, warriors, soldiers that protect and guard the country

Vaishyas-businessmen, traders, commercial class

Shudras-farmers, producers, peasants

The Untouchables: Below the four varna castes lays a fifth group-The Untouchables. This group is not mentioned in the Vedas records until the Bhagawad Gita and is supposed to be considered outside of the human society and of no caste. Unlike the upper four, it is not considered a "twice-born," having not gone through the Hindu sacred thread ritual initiation. The fifth varna is deemed "unclean" and polluting. Their role in life and society is to perform menial, degrading jobs.

The Untouchables are known by a variety of names. They call themselves "Dalits", priding themselves for the struggles they have fought against society. Mahatma Gandhi calls them "Harijans"-Children of God-when he adopted, against the caste rules, an Untouchable child. Finally, the Untouchables are also known as the "Scheduled Castes" after the 1935 constitution was erected to protect them in society both economically and socially:

"In India there are approximately 240 million Dalits. This means that nearly 25% of the population is Dalit. It also means that in a country, where everybody is supposed to have equal rights and opportunities, 1 out of 5 persons is condemned to be untouchable."

Despite the professed equal rights and duties in the Indian society, the Untouchables are still bounded in ways that keeps them in their place. They do not receive any education that can help them climb up in society and they live in poverty with scarce means of amenities, food, health care, and all other key survival needs in life.

Dharma and Reincarnation: Different castes have different designated codes of proper conduct (dharma), according to their ranks on the hierarchy that they are obligated to perform to contribute to their society. For example, Brahman's proper behaviour will be to be nonviolent, religious and have a vegetarian diet; Kshatriyas are expected to be aggressive warriors who fight and defend and consume meat and alcohol.

The original caste system supported the moving of individuals from one caste to another based on one's actions and performances (karma) in society. The mass population believe that the suffering in their present life is a result of the bad deeds they committed in their past life. The karma that they accumulate is the deciding factor as to which position in the caste hierarchy they will belong to in their next lives. They believe that the faithful execution of the duties obligated in their position in life, thus good karma performed, will be a promise to raise them up through the different classes in reincarnation until they reach the top of the ranks and take the next proceeding step to liberation (moksha). The rigid caste system is justified by this belief and it is thus possible to see why the masses stay muted and accept their suffering in life.

Purity vs. Pollution: Other than the roles in life (dharma), what makes the castes different from one another?

Inequalities amongst castes are a part of the ordained natural order and it is explained or justified in terms of purity and pollution. High-caste status is associated with purity and low-castes status, with pollution. Those born into high-ranking class would have inborn purity, like the Brahmans and similarly, the low caste Dalits are born into pollution. The Dalits can easily pollute a Brahman just by physical contact and the latter will have to perform ritual cleanliness like bathing in flowing water and changing clothes.

This explains for the distance the upper and lower castes maintain in terms of intercaste relationships. One of the theories of purity is that when a person is alive, both his body and soul are connected spiritually as one. When any part of the body leaves the whole entity, its connection to spirituality is broken and it is considered impure. Polluting. So anything emitted from the body is considered polluting. For example, corpses, manure, dirt, bodily fluids, etc. Similarly, anyone who deals or is in contact with such impure matters is considered tainted and polluting too.

Low-castes that hold perform menial jobs that deal with burying corpses, killing or skinning animals, cleaning toilets and clearing rubbish and body excretion, are considered tainted and polluting. They are kept away from any sacred learning and ritual and away from the mainstream society. The Untouchables have to live outside the villages and have their own wells so as not to pollute the rest of the people.

Since occupational specialization is believed to be in accord with the ordained order of the universe, and since purity or pollution is traditionally hereditary, low castes who hold demeaning jobs have their lives remain polluted forever. For example, a Sweeper will be a Sweeper for his entire life and his children will have to inherit the same job and be polluted as well. Similarly, the upper-class groups like the Brahmins will always retain their inherent purity from their parents, as long as they carry out the daily cleanliness rituals and do not violate any purity codes.

Intercaste Relations

Purity Pollution: Intercaste relations are also affected by the purity and pollution dogma. High-caste groups shun and keep their distance from the lower castes. Dalits are suppose to be so polluting that even the cast of their shadows would stain the higher-castes. In some cases, they even have to wear bells to warn others of their presence.

Distance is maintained in all situations, even in the case of preparation of food. A Brahmin who accepts water or a meal from the hands of a Sweeper or any Dalit will immediately be polluted and could face social rejection from his fellow caste members. Certain exceptions hold. For example, only members of the Waterbearer caste who are employed to supply water from wells to homes can offer water by hand to all castes without polluting them. Only completely raw uncooked food like rice grains, uncooked vegetables, mangoes, or bananas can be accepted by anyone from anybody.

Another instance of inter-caste relation that is forbidden is inter-caste marriage. Given that even the issue of dining has so many regulations, marriage and consummation issues are under even heavier scrutiny. Marriages are traditionally arranged and within one's own caste. The background of each bride and groom are thoroughly studied to make sure they fit. Caste is the key qualification sought, and like how it affects basic socialization of society, is a filter system when seeking potential life partners. Pollution and Purity have very strict rules and regulations to abide by. Every action in every single day (a drink of water, a meal, talking, touching, bathing) has immediate consequences to it. And one would have to take the necessary purifying rituals to correct the violation. These daily rules and regulations serve as a constant reminder of the multi-ranked caste society and shows how important and essential the hierarchy is to the lives of Indians.

Atrocities: Intercaste Relations can be seen as either economically cooperative or exploitative. In the prior perspective, the lower castes that perform jobs as farmers, carpenters, shoemakers, potters are hired by upper castes who owns lands and business to afford to pay them. In the latter perspective, since the higher-ranking castes are the ones with both social and economic power, they can economically exploit or plainly discriminates the low classes. Such cases range from minor levels of degrade and abuse to shocking states where the low castes are even killed by these high-ranked castes. Evidence of such atrocities appears in several controversial news reports in different parts of India.

> *"In 1990, blatant subjugation of low-caste labourers in the northern state of Bihar and eastern Uttar Pradesh was the subject of many news reports. In this region, scores of Dalits who have attempted to unite to protest low wages have been the victims of some 500 villagers."*

> *"In 1991 the news magazine India Today reported that in an ostensibly prosperous village about 160 kilometres southeast of Delhi, when it became known that a rural Dalit labourer dared to have a love affair with the daughter of a high-caste landlord, the lovers and their Dalit go-between were tortured, publicly hanged and burnt by agents of the girl's family in the presence of some 500 villagers."*

Caste Structure

In Goa, the Bamonn or the Brahmins belonged to the originally priestly class taking upon other occupations like agriculture, trade and commerce (merchants), gold smithy etc. The Chaddho or the Kshatriyas were the noblemen, warriors and related soldiery taking up commercial avocations also. The Vaishya-Vanis were engaged in trade and among them were the 'shetts' or goldsmiths pursuing the craft of gold and gold ornaments. The Sudir or the Sudras were the workers and agricultural labourers engaged in the servicing professions. The Gavddi or Kunnbi were the landless labourers, earlier dislodged by the above high castes and living in their own wards in the village. There were the Gauddo or Gaudde, probably the Vaishya counterparts in Goa of the neighbouring Karnataka's Gowda, as there is 'Gaud' found in the Canacona taluka of Goa on Karnataka's border.

The caste structure in Goa was somewhat like pre-eminence in the social hierarchy based on the nobility of blood, very much resembling the idea of family nobility in the rest of India. All the castes or rather sub-castes or jatis like Saraswats, Karades, Chitpavans, Padhyes etc. among the various segments of the population of Goa, particularly the goldsmiths and some merchants probably, as seen from the surnames of members of communes purportedly all-Brahmin, were lumped into the Christian caste of Bamonn or Brahmin.

The various groups among the Kshatriyas or locally known as Chaddho were mainly the noble and warrior class. Some of them engaged in the trading profession, known as Chatim, which was an occupational appellation common to Brahmins also. The caste appellation of Chaddho gradually fell into disuse. Later among the Hindus of this caste in Goa who did not embrace Christianity began preferring the appellation of Maratha. The Marathas and Vanis were incorporated into the Christian caste of Chaddho.

Those of the Vaishya-Vani caste men who could not get themselves merged as Christian Bamonn or Chaddho, appear as Gauddo in place in Bardez Taluka of Goa, among Christians and those among the Hindu remnants of this caste in the present Canacona taluka etc. Gauddo caste among Christians is treated as one of the three high castes. It is believed that large number of Vaishya-Vanis emigrated to the adjoining district of Sindhudurg in Maharashtra. Their descendants trace their origin to Goa and the flight of their ancestors at the time of the conversion fever. The Christian counterpart of the Hindu Vani is the Gauddo Christian caste. The goldsmiths call themselves 'Daivednya Brahmins' and are known in Goa as 'Shetti', they were put into the Christian caste of Sudir or Sudras, which is a lower caste. They did not get into the caste deemed superior because they were known as 'Panchal' or the artisan group of castes.

The aboriginal stock in Goa is known as the 'Gavddi', is a higher caste. The Christian convert of the Gavdi aboriginal was termed as Kunbi. The Kunbis are found in large number in the Salcete taluka than in any other taluka of Goa.

At the time of the conversions carried out by the Portuguese missionaries, there were untouchables like the 'Mahara' and Chambars, who were converted to Christianity. They are found in Chandor village. Chambars have later merged with the Sudras among Christians. Bamonn and Chaddho are the two advanced castes among the Hindus in Goa. They continued to attach their caste to the Christian names and surnames even after conversion. The first mass baptisms or conversions to Christianity were effected in the two prominent villages in the vicinity of the then city of Goa, Divar Island and Carambolim villages, the first of the Bamonn and the second of the Chaddho.

The majority of the total number of village communes converted to Christianity belonged to the two high castes. The priests in the Goan community should be recruited from the Bamonn and Chaddho. At some places the Christian name, is mentioned along with the old Hindu name while at others the Christian name is mentioned with the person's father name in the Hindu original or in case of the father being a Hindu. The surnames of Poi, Kamat or Vamotim, Desai Kudav, Naik, Prabhu or Porbu etc. are common to both the high castes of Bamonn and Chaddho. Christian Bahmonns and Chaddhos are the two leading rival classes among the Goan's.

The continued maintenance of the caste system among the Christians in Goa is attributed to the mass conversions of entire villages, as a result of which the religious complexion of the whole village was given a new coat of Christianity without affecting its age-old social structure which was rooted in caste foundations. The old usages and customs and age-old traditions, including superstitions of a varied order, especially the caste-system were transferred. The Portuguese, fearing the relapses of their coverts to Hinduism, destroyed all available material reminiscent of the old religion including literary works which are stated by historians to have been in Konkani, mainly religious or socio-religious in nature.

History of Caste System

Origin: Some researchers believe that the caste system began with the Indo-Aryan migration to India. The early Indo-Aryans organized among themselves in groups that later led to the caste system. A 2001 study, led by Michael Bamshad of the University of Utah, revealed that Indians belonging to higher castes are genetically closer to Europeans than are individuals from lower castes, whose genetic profiles are closer to those of Asians. The researchers believe their results support the theory that Europeans who migrated into India may have merged with or imposed their social structure on the native northern Indians and placed themselves into the highest castes.

However, the theory of Indo-Aryan migration itself is a highly disputed topic. The critics claim that it was formulated to undermine the historical significance of India, and was exploited by the British to show that they had the right to invade India, as the Indians supposedly themselves were invaders. A 2006 genetic study by India's National Institute of Biologicals supported the idea that Indians have acquired few genes from Europeans, thus disputing the Aryan Invasion Theory. Megasthenes, the Greek ambassador to Chandragupta Maurya's court in India classified people of India into seven classes: philosophers, peasants, herdsmen, craftsmen and traders, soldiers, government officials and councillors.

Hindu Scriptures: Although the Hindu scriptures contain some passages that can be interpreted to sanction the caste system, they also contain indications that the caste system is not an essential part of the Hindu religion, and both sides in the debate are able to find sections in scriptures that support their views.

The most ancient scriptures-the Shruti texts, or Vedas, place very little importance on the caste system, mentioning caste only rarely and in a cursory manner. A hymn from the Rig Veda seems to indicate that one's caste is not necessarily determined by that of one's family:

> *I am a bard, my father is a physician, my mother's job is to grind the corn. Rig Veda 9.112.3*

In the Vedic period, there also seems to no discrimination against the Shudras (which later became an ensemble of the so-called low-castes) on the issue of hearing the sacred words of the Vedas and fully participating in all religious rights, something which became totally banned in the later times.

Later scriptures such as Bhagawad Gita and Manusmriti state that the four varnas are created by God. However, at the same time, the Gita says that one's varna is to be understood from one's personal qualities and one's karma (work), not one's birth. Some scholars believe that, in its initial period, the caste system was flexible and it was merit and job based. One could migrate from one caste to other caste by changing one's profession. This view is supported by records of sages who became Brahmans. For example, the sage Vishvamitra belonged to a Kshatriya caste, and only later became recognized as a great Brahmin sage, indicating that his caste was not determined by birth. Similarly, Valmiki, once a low-caste robber, became a great sage. Veda Vyasa, another sage, was the son of a fisherwoman. Vashishtha was a shudra and he became sage later.

Manusmriti, dated between 200 BC and 100 AD, contains some laws that codified the caste system. Varna is mentioned as caste equivalent in Manusmriti. However, the Puranas use the term in the context of skin colour too. Manusmriti and some other shastras mention four varnas: The Brahmins (teachers, scholars and priests), the Kshatriyas (kings and warriors), the Vaishyas (traders, landowners and some artisan groups), and Shudras (agriculturists, service providers, and some artisan groups). Another group of untouchables excluded from the main society was called Parjanya or Antyaja. A varna can be viewed as a group of castes or a social division that consists of various sub-castes called jatis.

Passages in Manusmriti and other scriptures suggest that the Indian caste system was originally non-hereditary:

As the son of Shudra can attain the rank of a Brahman, the son of Brahman can attain rank of a Shudra. Even so with him who is born of a Vaishya or a Kshatriya Manu Smriti X:65

The various smritis, like the Yagnavalkyasmriti and the Manusmriti strongly disapprove of marrying outside one's caste. The smritis also argue that new, despicable castes are formed out of such cases. According to these smritis, the chamars were born out of the union of a vaideha and a nishada, the chandals were born out of the sexual relations between a Brahmin and a Shudra.

Historical Advantages of the Caste System: Historically, the caste system offered several advantages to the population of the Indian subcontinent:

1. Preservation of order in society through the use of institutional stratification of social groups.
2. Integration of foreigners and invading forces into Indian culture by assigning a caste to them (a process that historian Jawaharlal Nehru referred to as "Indianization"): India has faced repeated invasions from outside the region, dating back to the Macedoniaan invasion by Alexander the Great. Most invaders were swiftly assimilated into ancient Indian society by assigning them specific castes. Examples include the Kambojas, believed to be of Indo-Scythian descent, who were retroactively assigned a social position in the Manusmriti.
3. The Varna system, with its normative interpretation as a division of labour, had and continues to have a heavy bias towards spiritual evolution. The deep religious proclivities and the urge for spiritual uplift had induced the people to search for simpler and effective ways to achieve the spiritual goal which led to innovations like the Bhakti movement which had a powerful impact on the socio-cultural-spiritual life of the people even at mass level without distinctions of caste or class or other social differences. It is these deeply run cultural roots which caused an abiding following for Hinduism even in the face of unrelenting assaults by other religions and had in fact continued to influence the lives of people even after their conversion to other faiths. Thus,

the caste system can be said to have preserved ancient cultural values in Indian society.

4. The caste system played an influential role in shaping economic activities. The caste system functioned much like medieval European guilds, ensuring the division of labour, providing for the training of apprentices and, in some cases, allowing manufacturers to achieve narrow specialisation. For instance, in certain regions, producing each variety of cloth was the speciality of a particular sub-caste.
5. Philosophers argue that the majority of people would be comfortable in stratified endogamous groups and have been in ancient times. Membership in a particular caste, with its associated narrative, history and genealogy would instill in its members a sense of group accomplishment and cultural pride. Such sentiments are routinely expressed by the Marathas, for instance.

Emergence of Rigid Caste Structures: In its later stages, the caste system is said to have become rigid, and caste began to be inherited rather than acquired by merit. In the past, members of different castes would not partake in various activities, such as dining and religious gatherings, together. In addition, the performance of religious rites and rituals were restricted to Brahmins, who were the designated priesthood. In recent years, more egalitarian reforms have enabled lower castes and even outcastes such as the Dalits to become religious clerics.

The "Pandaram" priests are an example of an order of Dalit priests, based in Nepal and South India. The Pandaram maintain the same tradition as the Brahmin priests, including the use of the Sanskrit language (traditionally reserved for the Brahmins) for the rituals. While they are not generally as well trained as the Brahmin priests, they are highly respected within their community and are addressed with reverence.

According to the Manusmriti, every caste belongs to one of the four varnas (Brahmin, Kshatriya, Vaishya, and Shudra). However, there have been many disputes about the varna of many castes, such as castes being considered Kshatriya by some scholars, while described as Shudra by others. While texts such as the Manusmriti attempted to rationalize ambiguous castes by placing them in varna-sankaras (*i.e.* mixed varna), the fact remains that Indian society was, and is, composed of numerous geographically diversified but endogamous groups. With many occupational groups practicing endogamy within a particular region, as well as numerous sub-divisions within the four main castes, a more complex system of sub-castes and jatis is evident. The jatis have broken up into clans like Agarwal, Iyer, etc.

Mobility Across the Castes: The view of the caste system as "static and unchanging" has been disputed by many scholars. For instance, sociolgists such as Bernard Buber and Marriott McKim describe how the perception of the caste system as a static and textual stratification has given way to the perception of the caste system as a more processual, emprical and contextual stratification. Other sociologists such as Y.B Damle have applied theoretical models to explain mobility and flexibility in the caste system in India.. According to these scholars, groups of lower-caste individuals could seek to elevate the status of their caste by attempting to emulate the practices of higher castes.

Flexibility in caste laws permitted very low-caste religious clerics such as Valmiki (of the Naga tribal caste) to compose the Ramayana, which became a central work of Hindu scripture.

According to some economists, mobility across broad caste lines may have been "minimal", though sub-castes (jatis) may change their social status over the generations by fission, re-location, and adoption of new rituals..

Sociologist M. N. Srinivas has also debated the question of rigidity in Caste. In an ethnographic study of the Coorgs of Karnataka, he observed considerable flexibility and mobility in their caste hierarchies. He asserts that the caste system is far from a rigid system in which the position of each component caste is fixed for all time. Movement has always been possible, and especially in the middle regions of the hierarchy. It was always possible for groups born into a lower caste to "rise to a higher position by adopting vegetarianism and teetotalism" *i.e.* adopt the customs of the higher castes. While theoretically "forbidden", the process was not uncommon in practice. The concept of sanskritization, or the adoption of upper-caste norms by the lower castes, addressed the actual complexity and fluidity of caste relations.

Historical examples of mobility in the Indian Caste System among Hindus have been researched. The "Noniya" Caste of salt makers have claimed to the higher status of the "Chauhan Rajput". They have risen well above the untouchable line and their leaders have, in the past, mobilized upwards along the caste hierarchy. There is also precedent of certain Shudra families within the temples of the Shrivaishava sect in South India elevating their caste.

British Rule: The caste system was first exposed to the modern Western world during the Portuguese occupation and rule of sections of India. The word 'caste' in this context is derived from the Portuguese, 'casta'. Later, other European empires, including the British, occupied parts of the subcontinent. British anthropologist Herbert Risley's The Tribes and Castes of Bengal, published in 1892, was one of the first works on the caste system in India written by a Western scholar.

Some scholars state that the caste system was broken up greatly during British Raj in India. However, some other historians suggest that the impact of British reforms has been greatly exaggerated.

Initially, the British strengthened the caste system. They gave the Brahmins back special privileges the Muslim rulers had taken away. During the initial days of British East India Company's rules, caste privileges and customs were encouraged in the Bengal Army. But, British law courts disagreed with the discrimination against the lower castes. Many believe that the lack of British respect for sepoys' caste traditions was one of the reasons behind the Indian Rebellion of 1857.

During British rule, the reservation of seats for the "Depressed Classes" was incorporated into the Government of India Act 1935, which went into force in 1937. The Act brought the term "Scheduled castes" into use, which was later clarified in The Government of India (Scheduled Castes) Order, 1936 which contained a list of scheduled castes.

British Census Officers determined caste hierarchy based on the principle, *e.g.* someone who accepts food and water from another person but the other person does not reciprocate the same way, then the other person is superior to the former.

It was contested at many places (a notable example is that the Koris of UP who said they won't accept water from Brahmins, and so should be placed higher than them). Because it was met with rampant controversies, arbitration was very common during those days. The most notable arbitration stories are:

1. Caste status of Bhumihar
2. Caste status of Kayastha
3. Caste status of Kurmi
4. Caste status of Yadav

It raised more questions than it answered and subsequent census records varied radically, making it free for all, after some time.

Major Caste Groups: According to the 1891 census data, the major caste groups in India were following (listed in the order of population):

Caste-group	*Example*	*Population %*
Cultivators	Kurmi, Mali, Lodha	20%
Village Menials	Chamar, Dosadh, Dom	13%
Military	Jat, Rajput, Maratha	12%
Artisans	Lohar, Sunar, Julaha	12%
Pastoral	Ahir, Gadaria, Dhangar	7%
Forest tribes	Santhal, Gond, Bhil	7%
Professionals	Nambudri, Bhat, Kayasth	6%
Services	Nai, Dhobi, Kandoi	6%
Traders	Agrawal, Khatri, Balija, Barnwal	5%
Labourers	Musahar, Bagdi, Bawari	3%

Contd...

Caste-group	***Example***	***Population %***
Fishers	Kahar, Mallah	3%
Other professionals	Vaidya, Mirasi, Bhand	2%
Vagrants	Waddar, Nat, Beldar	1%

Reform Movements: Traditionally, Dalits (Untouchable Castes) were not allowed to let their shadows fall upon a non-Dalit caste member (particularly a Brahmin, for fear of ritually contaminating them), and they were required to sweep the ground where they walk to remove the 'contamination' of their footfalls. Dalits were forbidden to worship in temples or draw water from the same wells as caste Hindus, and they usually lived in segregated neighbourhoods outside the main village. However, there have been cases of upper caste Hindus warming to the Dalits and Hindu priests, demoted to outcaste ranks, who continued practising the religion.

An example of the latter was Dnyaneshwar, who was excommunicated into Dalit status from society in the 13th century, but continued to compose the Dnyaneshwari, a Dharmic commentary on the Bhagawad Gita. Other excommunicated Brahmins, such as Eknath, fought for the rights of untouchables during the Bhakti period. Historical examples of Dalit priests include Chokhamela in the 14th Century, who was India's first recorded Dalit poet, Raidas, born into Dalit cobblers, and others. The 15th century saint Ramananda also accepted all castes, including untouchables, into his fold. Most of these saints subscribed to the Bhakti movements in Hinduism during the medieval period that rejected casteism. Nandanar, a low-caste Hindu cleric, also rejected casteism and accepted Dalits.

Many movements in Hinduism have welcomed Dalits into their fold, the earliest being the Bhakti movements of the medieval period. Early Dalit politics involved many Hindu reform movements which arose primarily as a reaction to the advent of Christian Missionaries in India and their attempts to mass-convert Dalits to Christianity under the allure of escaping the caste system (however, the Caste system among Indian Christians remained in full force even after conversions).

In the 19th Century, the Brahmo Samaj under Raja Ram Mohan Roy, actively campaigned against untouchability. The Arya Samaj founded by Swami Dayananda also renounced discrimination against Dalits. Sri Ramakrishna Paramahamsa founded the Ramakrishna Mission that participated in the emancipation of Dalits. Upper caste Hindus, such as Mannathu Padmanabhan also participated in movements to abolish Untouchability against Dalits, opening his family temple for Dalits to worship.

While there always have been places for Dalits to worship, the first "upper-caste" temple to openly welcome Dalits into their fold was the Laxminarayan Temple in Wardha in the year 1928 (the move was spearheaded by reformer Jamnalal Bajaj). Also, the Satnami movement was founded by Guru Ghasidas a Dalit himself. Other reformers, such as Mahatma Jyotirao Phule also worked for the emancipation of Dalits. Another example of Dalit emancipation was the Temple Entry Proclamation issued by the last Maharaja of Travancore in the Indian state of Kerala in the year 1936. The Maharaja proclaimed that "outcastes should not be denied the consolations and the solace of the Hindu faith". Even today, the Sri Padmanabhaswamy temple that first welcomed Dalits in the state of Kerala is revered by the Dalit Hindu community.

The 1930s saw key struggles between Mahatma Gandhi and B.R. Ambedkar, most notably over whether Dalits would have separate electorates or joint electorates with reserved seats. The Indian National Congress was the only national organisation with a large Dalit following, but Gandhi failed to gain their commitment. Ambedkar, a Dalit himself, developed a deeper analysis of Untouchability, but lacked a workable political strategy: his conversion to Buddhism in 1956, along with millions of followers, highlighted the failure of his political endeavours. India's first Prime Minister, Jawaharlal Nehru, based on his own relationship with Dalit reformer Ambedkar, also spread information about the dire need to eradicate untouchability for the benefit of the Dalit community.

In more contemporary times, India has had an elected Dalit president, K. R. Narayanan, who has stated that he was well-treated in his community of largely upper-caste Hindus (24 July 2002). Another popular Harijan includes Babaji Palwankar Baloo, who joined the Hindu Mahasabha and was both a politician and a cricketer. He was an independence fighter. In addition, other Hindu groups have reached out to the Dalit community in an effort to reconcile with them, with productive results. On August 2006, Dalit activist Namdeo Dhasal engaged in dialogue with the Rashtriya Swayamsevak Sangh in an attempt to "bury the hatchet".

Also, the "Pandaram" are an order of Dalit Hindu priests (a task traditionally reserved for the Brahmins) based largely in Nepal and parts of South India. These Pandaram priests maintain the same tradition as the Brahmin priests, including using Sanskrit for the rituals (a language traditionally reserved for the Brahmins). They perform religious ceremonies from weddings to death rituals. They are not generally as well trained as the Brahmin priests, but are highly respected within their community and are addressed reverentially. Also, Hindu temples are increasingly more receptive to Dalit priests, such as Suryavanshi Das, the Dalit priest of a notable temple in Bihar.

Discrimination against Hindu Dalits is on a slow but steady decline. Many Hindu Dalits have achieved affluence in society, although vast millions still remain poor. Recent episodes of Caste-related violence in India have adversely affected the Dalit community. In urban India, discrimination against Dalits in the public sphere is largely disappeared, but rural Dalits are struggling to elevate themselves. Government organizations and NGO's work to emancipate them from discrimination, and many Hindu organizations have spoken in their favour.

Religious Form of Caste System

In Hinduism there exists four castes arranged in a hierarchy. Anyone who does not belong to one of these castes is an outcast. The religious word for caste is 'Varna'. Each Varna has certain duties and rights. Each Varna members have to work in certain occupation which only that Varna members are allowed. Each

Varna has certain type of diet. The highest Varna is of the Brahman. Members of this class are priests and the educated people of the society. The Varna after them in hierarchy is Kshatriya.

The members of this class are the rulers and aristocrats of the society. After them are the Vaishya. Members of this class are the landlords and businessmen of the society. After them in hierarchy are the Sudra. Members of this class are the peasants and working class of the society who work in non-polluting jobs. The caste hierarchy ends here. Below these castes are the outcasts who are untouchable to the four castes. These Untouchables worked in degrading jobs like cleaning, sewage etc.

The first three castes had social and economical rights which the Sudra and the untouchables did not have. The first three castes are also seen as 'twice born'. The intention in these two births is to the natural birth and to the ceremonial entrance to the society at a much later age. Each Varna and also the untouchables are divided into many communities. These communities are called Jat or Jati (The caste is also used instead of Jat). For example the Brahmans have Jats called Gaur, Kokanastha, Sarasvat, Iyer and others.

The outcasts have Jats like Mahar, Dhed, Mala, Madiga and others. The Sudra is the largest Varna and it has the largest number of communities. Each Jat is limited to professions worthy of their Varna. Each Jat is limited to the Varna diet. Each Jat members are allowed to marry only with their Jat members. People are born into their Jat and it cannot be changed.

This is the how the caste system is supposed to be in its religious form. But in reality it is much more complicated and different from its religious form.

Beginning of the Caste System

There are different theories about the establishment of the caste system. There are religious-mystical theories. There are biological theories. And there are socio-historical theories. The religious theories explain how the four Varnas were founded, but they do not explain how the Jats in each Varna or the untouchables were founded. According the Rig Veda, the ancient Hindu book, the primal man-Purush-destroyed himself to create a human society.

The different Varnas were created from different parts of his body. The Brahmans were created from his head; the Kshatriyas from his hands; the Vaishyas from his thighs and the Sudras from his feet. The Varna hierarchy is determined by the descending order of the different organs from which the Varnas were created. Other religious theory claims that the Varnas were created from the body organs of Brahma, who is the creator of the world.

The biological theory claims that all existing things, animated and inanimated, inherent three qualities in different apportionment. Sattva qualities include wisdom, intelligence, honesty, goodness and other positive qualities. Rajas include qualities like passion, pride, valour and other passionate qualities. Tamas qualities include dullness, stupidity, lack of creativity and other negative qualities. People with different doses of these inherent qualities adopted different types of occupation. According to this theory the Brahmans inherent Sattva qualities. Kshatriyas and Vaishyas inherent Rajas qualities. And the Sudras inherent Tamas qualities.

Like human beings, food also inherents different dosage of these qualities and it affects its eater's intelligence. The Brahmans and the Vaishyas have Sattvic diet which includes fruits, milk, honey, roots and vegetables. Most of the meats are considered to have Tamasic qualities. Many Sudra communities eat different kinds of meat (but not beef) and other Tamasic food.

But the Kshatriyas who had Rajasic diet eat some kinds of meat like deer meat which is considered to have Rajasic qualities. Many Marathas who claim to be Kshatriyas eat mutton. The drawback of this theory is that in different parts of India the same food was sometimes qualified to have different dosage of inherent qualities. For example there were Brahmans who eat meat which is considered Tamasic food.

The social historical theory explains the creation of the Varnas, Jats and of the untouchables. According to this theory, the caste system began with the arrival of the Aryans in India. The Aryans arrived in India around 1500 BC. The fair skinned Aryans arrived in India from south Europe and north Asia. Before the Aryans there were other communities in India of other origins. Among them Negrito, Mongoloid, Austroloid and Dravidian. The Negrito have physical features similar to people of Africa.

The Mongoloid have Chinese features. The Austroloids have features similar the aboriginals of Australia. The Dravidians originate from the Mediterranean and they were the largest community in India. When the Aryans arrived in India their main contact was with the Dravidians and the Austroloids. The Aryans disregarded the local cultures. They began conquering and taking control over regions in north India and at the same time pushed the local people southwards or towards the jungles and mountains in north India.

The Aryans organized among themselves in three groups. The first group was of the warriors and they were called Rajayana, later they changed their name Rajayana to Kshatriya. The second group was of the priests and they were called Brahmans. These two groups struggled politically for leadership among the Aryans. In this struggle the Brahmans got to be the leaders of the Aryan society. The third group was of the farmers and craftsmen and they were called Vaishya. The Aryans who conquered and took control over parts of north India subdued the locals and made them their servants. In this process the Vaishyas who were the farmers and the craftsmen became the landlords and the businessmen of the society and the locals became the peasants and the craftsmen of the society.

In order to secure their status the Aryans resolved some social and religious rules which, allowed only them to be the priests, warriors and the businessmen of the society. For example take Maharashtra. Maharashtra is in west India. This region is known by this name for hundreds of years. Many think that the meaning of the name Maharashtra is in its name, Great Land. But there are some who claim that the name, Maharashtra, is derived from the Jat called Mahar who are considered to be the original people of this region. In the caste hierarchy the dark skinned Mahars were outcasts. The skin colour was an important factor in the caste system. The meaning of the word "Varna" is not class or status but skin colour.

Between the outcasts and the three Aryan Varnas there is the Sudra Varna who are the simple workers of the society. The Sudras consisted of two communities. One community was of the locals who were subdued by the Aryans and the other were the descendants of Aryans with locals. In Hindu religious stories there are many wars between the good Aryans and the dark skinned demons and devils. The different Gods also have dark skinned slaves. There are stories of demon women trying to seduce good Aryan men in deceptive ways. There were also marriages between Aryan heroes and demon women. Many believe that these incidences really occurred in which, the gods and the positive heroes were people of Aryan origin. And the demons, the devils and the dark skinned slaves were in fact the original residence of India whom the Aryans coined as monsters, devil, demons and slaves.

As in most of the societies of the world, so in India, the son inherited his father's profession. And so in India there developed families, who professed the same family profession for generation in which, the son continued his father's profession. Later on as these families became larger, they were seen as communities or as they are called in Indian languages, Jat. Different families who professed the same profession developed social relations between them and organized as a common community, meaning Jat.

Later on the Aryans who created the caste system, added to their system non-Aryans. Different Jats who professed different professions were integrated in different Varnas according to their profession. Other foreign invaders of ancient India-Greeks, Huns, Scythains and others-who conquered parts of India and created kingdoms were integrated in the Kshatriya Varna (warrior castes). But probably the Aryan policy was not to integrate original Indian communities within them and therefore many aristocratic and warrior communities that were in India before the Aryans did not get the Kshatriya status.

Most of the communities that were in India before the arrival of the Aryans were integrated in the Sudra Varna or were made outcast depending on the professions of these communities. Communities who professed non-polluting jobs were integrated in Sudra Varna. And communities who professed polluting professions were made outcasts. The Brahmans are very strict about cleanliness. In the past people believed that diseases can also spread also through air and not only through physical touch. Perhaps because of this reason the untouchables were not only disallowed to touch the high caste communities but they also had to stand at a certain distance from the high castes.

Caste and Stages of Life in Hinduism

The pattern of social classes in Hinduism is called the "caste system." The chart shows the major divisions and contents of the system. Basic caste is called *varna*, or "colour." Sub-caste, or *jati*, "birth, life, rank," is a traditional subdivision of *varna*.

The *Bhagawad Gita* says this about the varnas:

The works of Brahmins, Kshatriyas, Vaishyas, and Shudras are different, in harmony with the three powers of their born nature. The works of a Brahmin are peace; self-harmony, austerity, and purity; loving-forgiveness and righteousness; vision and wisdom and faith.

These are the works of a Kshatriya: a heroic mind, inner fire, constancy, resourcefulness, courage in battle, generosity and noble leadership. Trade, agriculture and the rearing of cattle is the work of a Vaishya. And the work of the Shudra is service.

There are literally thousands of sub-castes in India, often with particular geographical ranges, occupational specializations, and an administrative or corporate structure. When Mahatma Gandhi wanted to go to England to study law, he had to ask his sub-caste, the Modh Bania, for permission to leave India. ("Bania", means "merchant," and "Gandhi" means "greengrocer"—from *gandha*, "smell, fragrance," in Sanskrit—and that should be enough for a good guess that Gandhi was a Vaishya.) Sometimes it is denied that the varnas are "castes" because, while "true" castes, the jatis, are based on birth, the varnas are based on the theory of the gunas (the "three powers" mentioned in the Gita). This is no more than a rationalization: the varnas came first, and they *are* based on birth.

The gunas came later, and provide a poor explanation anyway, since the guna *tamas* is associated with both twice born and once born, caste and outcaste, overlapping the most important religious and social divisions in the system. Nevertheless, the varnas are now divisions at a theoretical level, while the jatis are the way in which caste is embodied for most practical purposes. Jatis themselves can be ranked in relation to each other, and occasionally a question may even be raised about the proper varna to which a particular jati belongs. As jati members change occupations and they rise in prestige, a jati may rarely even be elevated in the varna to which it is regarded as belonging.

Associated with each varna there is a traditional colour. These sound suspiciously like skin colours; and, indeed, there is an expectation in India that higher caste people will have lighter skin—although there are plenty of exceptions (especially in the South of India). This all probably goes back to the original invasion of the Arya, who came from Central Asia and so were undoubtedly light skinned. The people already in India were quite dark, even as today many people in India seem positively black. Apart from skin colour, Indians otherwise have "Caucasian" features—narrow noses, thin lips, etc.—and recent genetic mapping studies seem to show that Indians are more closely related to the people of the Middle East and Europe than to anyone else.

Because Untouchables are not a varna, they do not have a traditional colour. I have supplied blue, since this is otherwise not found, and it is traditionally used for the skin colour of Vishnu and his incarnations. Chief among those is *Krishna* whose *name* actually means "black" or "dark," but he is always shown blue rather than with some natural skin colour. The first three varnas are called the *twice born*.

This has *nothing* to do with reincarnation. Being "twice born" means that you *come of age* religiously, making you a member of the Vedic religion, eligible to learn Sanskrit, study the Vedas, and perform Vedic rituals. The "second birth" is thus like Confirmation or a Bar Mitzvah. According to the *Laws of Manu* (whose requirements may not always be observed in modern life), boys are "born again" at specific ages: 8 for Brahmins; 11 for Kshatriyas; and 12 for Vaishyas. A thread is bestowed at the coming of age to be worn around the waist as the symbol of being twice born.

The equivalent of coming of age for girls is marriage. The bestowal of the thread is part of the wedding ceremony. That part of the wedding ritual is even preserved in Jainism. Ancient Iran also had a coming of age ceremony that involved a thread. That and other evidence leads to the speculation that the *three* classes of the twice born are from the original Indo-European social system—the theory of George Dumezil. Even the distant Celts believed in three social classes.

The three classes of Plato's *Republic* thus may not have been entirely his idea. Although there must have been a great deal of early intermarriage in India, nowhere did such an Indo-European social system become as rigid a system of *birth* as there. The rigidity may well be due to the influence of the idea of *karma*, that poor birth is morally deserved. According to the *Laws of Manu*, when the twice born come of age, they enter into the four *ashramas* or "stages of life."

1. The first is the *brahmacharya*, or the stage of the student (*brahmacharin*). For boys, the student is supposed to go live with a teacher (*guru*), who is a Brahmin, to learn about Sanskrit, the Vedas, rituals, etc. The *dharma* of a student includes being obedient, respectful, celibate, and nonviolent. "The teacher is God." For girls, the stage of studenthood coincides with that of the householder, and the husband stands in the place of the teacher. Since the boys are supposed to be celibate while students, Gandhi used the term

brahmachari to mean the celibate practitioner that he thought made the best *Satyagrahi*, the best nonviolent activist.

2. The second stage is the *garhastya*, or the stage of the householder, which is taken far more seriously in Hinduism than in Jainism or Buddhism and is usually regarded as mandatory, like studenthood, although debate continued over the centuries whether or not this stage could be skipped in favour of a later one. This is the stage where the principal *dharma* of the person is performed, whether as priest, warrior, etc., or for women mainly as wife and mother. Arjuna's duty to fight the battle in the *Bhagawad Gita* comes from his status as a householder. Besides specific duties, there are general duties that pay off the "three debts": (1) a debt to the ancestors that is discharged by marrying and having children; (2) a debt to the gods that is discharged by the household rituals and sacrifices; and (3) a debt to the teacher that is discharged by appropriately teaching one's wife, children, and, for Brahmins, other students. The three debts are sometimes associated with the three Gods of the Trimurti—the ancestor debt with Brahma, the gods debt with Vishnu, and the teacher debt with Shiva.
3. The third stage is the *vanaprastya*, or the stage of the forest dweller. This may be entered into optionally if (ideally) one's hair has become gray, one's skin wrinkled, and grandchildren exist to carry on the family. Husbands and wives may leave their affairs and possessions with their children and retire together to the forest as hermits. This does not involve the complete renunciation of the world, for husbands and wives can still have sex (once a month), and a sacred fire still should be kept and minimal rituals performed. This stage is thus not entirely free of *dharma*. The Forest Treatises were supposed to have been written by or for forest dwellers, who have mostly renounced the world and have begun to consider liberation. I am not aware that forest dwelling is still practiced in the traditional way. The

modern alternatives seem to consist of the more stark opposition between householding and becoming a wandering ascetic. Nevertheless, forest dwelling is an institution that doesn't really develop as such in Jainism and Buddhism. The idea that husbands and wives would engage in ascetic practices together, without celibacy, would appear extraordinary. In those terms, it is an unfortunate loss if the institution does not continue in modern Hinduism.

4. The fourth stage is the *sannyasa*, or the stage of the wandering ascetic, the *sannyasin* (or *sadhu*). If a man desires, he may continue on to this stage, but his wife will need to return home; traditionally she cannot stay alone as a forest dweller or wander the highways as an ascetic. The *sannyasin* has renounced the world completely, is regarded as dead by his family (the funeral is held), and is finally beyond all *dharma* and caste. When a *sannyasin* enters a Hindu temple, he is not a worshipper but one of the objects of worship. Not even the gods are *sanyasins* (they are householders), and so this is where in Hinduism, as in Jainism and Buddhism, it is possible for human beings to be spiritually superior to the gods. It has long been a matter of dispute in Hinduism whether one need really fulfil the requirements of the *Laws of Manu* (gray hair, etc.) to renounce the world. The Mahabharata says that Brahmins may go directly to Renunciation, but it also says that the three debts must be paid—and the debt to the ancestors could only be paid with husbands and wives living together either as householders or, if renunciates, as forest dwellers (indeed, the Pandavas are all born in that way). There are definitely no such requirements in Jainism or Buddhism. The Buddha left his family right after his wife had a baby, which would put him in the middle of his *dharma* as a householder. Buddhism and Jainism thus developed *monastic* institutions, with monks and nuns, but these did not really develop as such in Hinduism: While

wandering ascetics are rather like mendicant monks, we lack monasteries and nuns, and the ascetics are, traditionally, supposed to have already lived something like a normal, lay life..

The four stages of life may, somewhat improbably, be associated with the four parts of the Vedas: the samhitas with the stage of the student, who is particularly obligated to learn them; the Brahmans with the stage of the householder, who is able to regulate his ritual behaviour according to them; the aranyakas with the stage of the forest dweller, who regulates his ritual behaviour according to them and who begins to contemplate liberation; and finally the upanishads with the stage of the wandering ascetic, who is entirely concerned with meditation on the absolute, *Brahman*.

The twice born may account for as much as 48% of Hindus, though I have now seen the number put at more like 18%—quite a difference but more believable. The Shudras (58% of Hindus) may represent the institutional provision that the Arya made for the people they already found in India. The Shudras thus remain once born, and traditionally were not allowed to learn Sanskrit or study the Vedas—on pain of death. Their *dharma* is to work for the twice born. But even below the Shudras are the Untouchables (24% of Hindus), who are literally "outcastes," without a varna, and were regarded as "untouchable" because they are ritually polluting for caste Hindus. Some Untouchable sub-castes are regarded as so polluted that members are supposed to keep out of sight and do their work at night: They are called "Unseeables."

In India, the term "Untouchable" is now regarded as insulting or politically incorrect (like *Eta* in Japan for the traditional tanners and pariahs). Gandhi's *Harijans* ("children of God") or *Dalits* ("downtrodden") are preferred, though to Americans "Untouchables" would sound more like the gangster-busting federal agent Elliot Ness from the 1920's. Why there are so many Untouchables is unclear, although caste Hindus can be ejected from their jatis and become outcastes and various tribal or formerly tribal people in India may never have been properly integrated into the social system. When Mahatma

Gandhi's sub-caste refused him permission to go to England, as noted above, he went anyway and was ejected from the caste.

After he returned, his family got him back in, but while in England he was technically an outcaste. Existing tribal people as well as Untouchables are also called the "scheduled castes," since the British drew up a "schedule" listing the castes that they regarded as backwards, underprivileged, or oppressed.

The Untouchables, nevertheless, have their own traditional professions and their own sub-castes. Those professions (unless they can be evaded in the greater social mobility of modern, urban, anonymous life) involve too much pollution to be performed by caste Hindus: (1) dealing with the bodies of dead animals (like the sacred cattle that wander Indian villages) or unclaimed dead humans, (2) tanning leather, from such dead animals, and manufacturing leather goods, and (3) cleaning up the human and animal waste for which in traditional villages there is no sewer system.

Mahatma Gandhi referred to the latter euphemistically as "scavenging" but saw in it the most horrible thing imposed on the Untouchables by the caste system. His requirement on his farms in South Africa that everyone share in such tasks comes up in an early scene in the movie *Gandhi*. Since Gandhi equated suffering with holiness, he saw the Untouchables as hallowed by their miserable treatment and so called them "Harijans" (*Hari=Vishnu*). Later Gandhi went on fasts in the hope of improving the condition of the Untouchables, or at least to avoid their being politically classified as non-Hindus.

Today the status of the Shudras, Untouchables, and other "scheduled castes," and the preferential policies that the Indian government has designed for their advancement ever since Independence, are sources of serious conflict, including suicides, murders, and riots, in Indian society.

Meanwhile, however, especially since economic liberalization began in 1991, the social mobility of a modern economy and urban life has begun to disrupt traditional professions, and oppressions, even of Untouchables. Village life and economic stasis were the greatest allies of the caste system, but both are slowly retreating before modernity in an India that finally gave up the Soviet paradigm of economic planning.

Varna, Caste, and Other Divisions

Although many other nations are characterized by social inequality, perhaps nowhere else in the world has inequality been so elaborately constructed as in the Indian institution of caste. Caste has long existed in India, but in the modern period it has been severely criticized by both Indian and foreign observers. Although some educated Indians tell non-Indians that caste has been abolished or that "no one pays attention to caste anymore," such statements do not reflect reality.

Caste has undergone significant change since independence, but it still involves hundreds of millions of people. In its preamble, India's constitution forbids negative public discrimination on the basis of caste. However, caste ranking and caste-based interaction have occurred for centuries and will continue to do so well into the foreseeable future, more in the countryside than in urban settings and more in the realms of kinship and marriage than in less personal interactions.

Castes are ranked, named, endogamous (in-marrying) groups, membership in which is achieved by birth. There are thousands of castes and sub-castes in India, and these large kinship-based groups are fundamental to South Asian social structure. Each caste is part of a locally based system of interdependence with other groups, involving occupational specialization, and is linked in complex ways with networks that stretch across regions and throughout the nation.

The word *caste* derives from the Portuguese *casta*, meaning breed, race, or kind. Among the Indian terms that are sometimes translated as caste are *varna*, *jati*, *jat*, *biradri*, and *samaj*. All of these terms refer to ranked groups of various sizes and breadth. *Varna*, or colour, actually refers to large divisions that include various castes; the other terms include castes and subdivisions of castes sometimes called sub-castes.

Many castes are traditionally associated with an occupation, such as high-ranking Brahmans; middle-ranking farmer and artisan groups, such as potters, barbers, and carpenters; and very low-ranking "Untouchable" leatherworkers, butchers, launderers, and latrine cleaners. There is some correlation between ritual rank on the caste hierarchy and economic prosperity. Members of higher-ranking castes tend, on the whole, to be more prosperous than members of lower-ranking castes. Many lower-caste people live in conditions of great poverty and social disadvantage.

According to the Rig Veda, sacred texts that date back to oral traditions of more than 3,000 years ago, progenitors of the four ranked *varna* groups sprang from various parts of the body of the primordial man, which Brahma created from clay. Each group had a function in sustaining the life of society—the social body. Brahmans, or priests, were created from the mouth. They were to provide for the intellectual and spiritual needs of the community. Kshatriyas, warriors and rulers, were derived from the arms. Their role was to rule and to protect others. Vaishyas—landowners and merchants—sprang from the thighs, and were entrusted with the care of commerce and agriculture. Shudras—artisans and servants—came from the feet. Their task was to perform all manual labour.

Later conceptualized was a fifth category, "Untouchable" menials, relegated to carrying out very menial and polluting work related to bodily decay and dirt. Since 1935 "Untouchables" have been known as Scheduled Castes, referring to their listing on government rosters, or schedules. They are also often called by Mohandas Karamchand (Mahatma) Gandhi's term Harijans, or "Children of God." Although the term *Untouchable* appears in literature produced by these low-ranking castes, in the 1990s, many politically conscious members of these groups prefer to refer to themselves as Dalit, a Hindi word meaning oppressed or downtrodden. According to the 1991 census, there were 138 million Scheduled Caste members in India, approximately 16 percent of the total population.

The first four *varnas* apparently existed in the ancient Aryan society of northern India. Some historians say that these categories were originally somewhat fluid functional groups, not castes. A greater degree of fixity gradually developed, resulting in the complex ranking systems of medieval India that essentially continue in the late twentieth century.

Although a *varna* is not a caste, when directly asked for their caste affiliation, particularly when the questioner is a Westerner, many Indians will reply with a *varna* name. Pressed further, they may respond with a much more specific name of a caste, or *jati*, which falls within that *varna*. For example, a Brahman may specify that he is a member of a named caste group, such as a Jijotiya Brahman, or a Smartha Brahman, and so on. Within such castes, people may further belong to smaller sub-caste categories and to specific clans and lineages. These finer designations are particularly relevant when marriages are being arranged and often appear in newspaper matrimonial advertisements.

Members of a caste are typically spread out over a region, with representatives living in hundreds of settlements. In any small village, there may be representatives of a few or even a score or more castes.

Numerous groups usually called tribes (often referred to as Scheduled Tribes) are also integrated into the caste system to varying degrees. Some tribes live separately from others—particularly in the far northeast and in the forested centre of the country, where tribes are more like ethnic groups than castes. Some tribes are themselves divided into groups similar to sub-castes. In regions where members of tribes live in peasant villages with nontribal peoples, they are usually considered members of separate castes ranking low on the hierarchical scale.

Inequalities among castes are considered by the Hindu faithful to be part of the divinely ordained natural order and are expressed in terms of purity and pollution. Within a village, relative rank is most graphically expressed at a wedding or death feast, when all residents of the village are invited. At the home of a high-ranking caste member, food is prepared by a member of a caste from whom all can accept cooked food (usually by a Brahman). Diners are seated in lines; members of a single caste sit next to each other in a row, and members of other castes sit in perpendicular or parallel rows at some distance.

Members of Dalit castes, such as Leatherworkers and Sweepers, may be seated far from the other diners—even out in an alley. Farther away, at the edge of the feeding area, a Sweeper may wait with a large basket to receive discarded leavings tossed in by other diners. Eating food contaminated by contact with the saliva of others not of the same family is considered far too polluting to be practiced by members of any other castes. Generally, feasts and ceremonies given by Dalits are not attended by higher-ranking castes.

Among Muslims, although status differences prevail, brotherhood may be stressed. A Muslim feast usually includes a cloth laid either on clean ground or on a table, with all Muslims, rich and poor, dining from plates placed on the same cloth. Muslims who wish to provide hospitality to observant Hindus, however, must make separate arrangements for a high-caste Hindu cook and ritually pure foods and dining area.

Castes that fall within the top four ranked *varnas* are sometimes referred to as the "clean castes," with Dalits considered "unclean." Castes of the top three ranked *varnas* are often designated "twice-born," in reference to the ritual initiation undergone by male members, in which investiture with the Hindu sacred thread constitutes a kind of ritual rebirth. Non-Hindu castelike groups generally fall outside these designations.

Each caste is believed by devout Hindus to have its own dharma, or divinely ordained code of proper conduct. Accordingly, there is often a high degree of tolerance for divergent lifestyles among different castes. Brahmans are usually expected to be nonviolent and spiritual, according with their traditional roles as vegetarian teetotaller priests. Kshatriyas are supposed to be strong, as fighters and rulers should be, with a taste for aggression, eating meat, and drinking alcohol. Vaishyas are stereotyped as adept businessmen, in accord with their traditional activities in commerce. Shudras are often described by others as tolerably pleasant but expectably somewhat base in behaviour, whereas Dalits—especially Sweepers—are often regarded by others as followers of vulgar life-styles. Conversely, lower-caste people often view people of high rank as haughty and unfeeling.

The chastity of women is strongly related to caste status. Generally, the higher ranking the caste, the more sexual control its women are expected to exhibit. Brahman brides should be virginal, faithful to one husband, and celibate in widowhood. By contrast, a Sweeper bride may or may not be a virgin, extramarital affairs may be tolerated, and, if widowed or divorced, the woman is encouraged to remarry. For the higher castes, such control of female sexuality helps ensure purity of lineage—of crucial importance to maintenance of high status. Among Muslims, too, high status is strongly correlated with female chastity.

Within castes explicit standards are maintained. Transgressions may be dealt with by a caste council, meeting periodically to adjudicate issues relevant to the caste. Such councils are usually formed of groups of elders, almost always males. Punishments such as fines and outcasting, either temporary or permanent, can be enforced. In rare cases, a person is excommunicated from the caste for gross infractions of caste rules. An example of such an infraction might be marrying or openly cohabiting with a mate of a caste lower than one's own; such behaviour would usually result in the higher-caste person dropping to the status of the lower-caste person.

Activities such as farming or trading can be carried out by anyone, but usually only members of the appropriate castes act as priests, barbers, potters, weavers, and other skilled artisans, whose occupational skills are handed down in families from one generation to another. As with other key features of Indian social structure, occupational specialization is believed to be in accord with the divinely ordained order of the universe.

The existence of rigid ranking is supernaturally validated through the idea of rebirth according to a person's karma, the sum of an individual's deeds in this life and in past lives. After death, a person's life is judged by divine forces, and rebirth is assigned in a high or a low place, depending upon what is deserved. This supernatural sanction can never be neglected, because it brings a person to his or her position in the caste hierarchy, relevant to every transaction involving food or drink, speaking, or touching. In past decades, Dalits in certain areas (especially in parts of the south) had to display extreme deference to high-status people, physically keeping their distance—lest their touch or even their shadow pollute others—wearing neither shoes nor any upper body covering (even for women) in the presence of the upper castes.

The lowest-ranking had to jingle a little bell in warning of their polluting approach. In much of India, Dalits were prohibited from entering temples, using wells from which the "clean" castes drew their water, or even attending schools. In past centuries, dire punishments were prescribed for Dalits who read or even heard sacred texts.

Such degrading discrimination was made illegal under legislation passed during British rule and was protested against by pre-independence reform movements led by Mahatma Gandhi and Bhimrao Ramji (B.R.) Ambedkar, a Dalit leader. Dalits agitated for the right to enter Hindu temples and to use village wells and effectively pressed for the enactment of stronger laws opposing disabilities imposed on them. After independence, Ambedkar almost single-handedly wrote India's constitution, including key provisions barring caste-based discrimination. Nonetheless, discriminatory treatment of Dalits remains a factor in daily life, especially in villages, as the end of the twentieth century approaches.

In modern times, as in the past, it is virtually impossible for an individual to raise his own status by falsely claiming to be a member of a higher-ranked caste. Such a ruse might work for a time in a place where the person is unknown, but no one would dine with or intermarry with such a person or his offspring until the claim was validated through kinship networks. Rising on the ritual hierarchy can only be achieved by a caste as a group, over a long period of time, principally by adopting behaviour patterns of higher-ranked groups. This process, known as Sanskritization, has been described by M.N. Srinivas and others. An example of such behaviour is that of some Leatherworker castes adopting a policy of not eating beef, in the hope that abstaining from the defiling practice of consuming the flesh of sacred bovines would enhance their castes' status.

Increased economic prosperity for much of a caste greatly aids in the process of improving rank.

The Indenture System

In the colonies of the British, French and the Dutch, exploitation in one form or the other stalked the Indian indentured labourers. The Coolies who arrived to work in the sugar estates in the West Indies were marched to their barracks known as 'Nigger Yard.' It was the same in Mauritius--only the language was different, 'camps des Noirs' or the backbreaking work in the canefields.

In 1843 the first shipload of 217 Indian labourers arrived in Port of Spain in Trinidad in the Caribbean. And in the same decade, others were taken to British Guiana in South America, and Mauritius off the coast of Africa; in the 1860's to the British colony of Natal in South Africa; in the 1870's to the Dutch colony of Surinam; in the 1880's to Fiji. By 1917-20 the indenture system was abolished but not before 1.5 million Indian bonded labourers had been induced move to remote parts of the globe in the service of British capitalism.

In South Africa they worked from daybreak to nightfall, from four in the morning to seven in the night, and far beyond their capacity. They were strictly confined to the limits of their master's estate. Beating and flogging was part of the regular routine in the plantations. In the West Indies the cattle whip was employed; in Malaya it was the cane, and in South Africa it was the rawhide cattle lash. One callous estate manager reportedly said "As long as the coolie is working for you, you have the right to do what you like with him-that is, short of killing".

Some Caribbean planters solved the problem of the sick by abandoning them to fate. In Grenada the majority of the 2000 Indians were kicked off the estates when they became ill and allowed to die on the road. The editor of a Jamaica newspaper wrote in 1863: 'One must see these wretched hungry, houseless and outcast specters picking up in the streets a chance bone or any putrid offal.... and so crippled, nude, skeletoned before their death, they live on, no parish authority taking them in'.

Unlike the Chinese and the Blacks, the Indians were also wary of the penchant for proselytizing among white missionaries who were on the lookout for 'heathen converts'. Indians were always branded as the dregs of their country, low-born, even criminal. Inspite of this, the Europeans managed to take Indian women for sexual purposes-usually the daughter of a coolie.

Dave Freedholm teaches world religion and philosophy at a nationally recognized independent college preparatory school in the US. and a practitioner of Hindu spirituality for some years, says: 'Caste' was used to justify Christian proselytizing and for continued domination over the Indian population, and this continues to be the case today. Also, the ills of contemporary Indian society (poverty, caste, etc.), which were exacerbated in part due to centuries long foreign occupation, exploitation and domination, are blamed primarily on Hindu thought. Thus, some Western scholars, ignoring the historic subversion of Indian society and Hinduism by the West, align themselves with the 'oppressed' against the 'evils' of Hinduism. The victim is made to feel guilty and hence the 'Hindu shame' I find amongst some Hindus.

Most Christians today (and most scholars of religion) would be scandalized if the feudal system, slavery, capitalist exploitation or anti-Judaism were used to define the essence of Christianity. They would understand these things to be historically and socially bound and not part of Christian universal ideals. In short, descriptions of Christianity in textbooks would distinguish the core or essence of Christian theology from specific social, historical and political contexts. However, Hinduism is not treated in the same way.

It does seem that the caste system, as understood today, was foisted on Indian society by its Western (Christian) oppressors, the British. Efforts within Hindu society to reform itself, and to provide a new vision of Hinduism, are too often ignored or downplayed.

Sociology of Groups in Ancient India

The whole philosophy of Indian social organization may be summarized in one word, varna-ashrama-dharma, which may be appropriately translated as Social Federalism. This principle of social integration or synthesis was understood as early as the times of the Samhitas in the Vedic age. The Vedic seers realized that the best and surest way of saving society from frequent suicidal chaos was to divide its members into specific groups, with well-defined functions and privileges or rewards for each.

The first group was that of the Brahmans, the teachers and the priests. They were the custodians of the social and spiritual heritage of the group and were to pass it on to the succeeding generations. They were to preserve the purity of idealism, point the way to the Eternal discovered by them through study and meditation, while their fellowmen were busy with life's daily tasks which left little leisure. The Brahman was a man of intellect; he came from the mouth of Brahma.

The second group was that of the Kshatriya. They were men of action. They were the guardians of the race. They were soldiers, sailors, civil servants and legislators. They kept the peace and order within the group and protected it from alien aggression. Theirs was a life of service and sacrifice; they came from the arms of Brahma.

The third group was that of the Vaishyas, the merchants. They attended to the distribution of the necessities of life. The vaishya was the merchant who made wealth; he was a man of desire. He was born from the thighs of Brahma.

The fourth and last group was that of the Sudras. The shudra was engaged in producing life's necessities, food, clothing and shelter, so that the physical organism of the group was kept in good health. On this group of working men depended the physical welfare of the whole community, its industries, its prosperity. This working class was psychologically, a group of undefined aptitudes, un-evolved, men of mechanical temperament, the common men. They came from the feet of Brahma. Look where we will, whether it be a primitive community or a modern nation, its population falls easily into these four categories. According to Manu, there are no other groups.

Integration of Various Factors

This division of men into four types, the teacher, the warrior, the merchant and the labourer, is based on sound psychology, ethics, biology and economics. Some men are intellectually by temperament, some are active, some acquisitive and others undefined, none of these. To each are assigned the task true to its type, in conformity with its inherent temperament, svadharma. All together formed an organic whole. Under an arrangement such as this, there is conservation of social energies; there is no necessity of trial and error method.

All are not equally endowed with equal physical and mental capacities, but every one should be given an opportunity for putting to use the faculties with which he has been endowed. Man should be treated as man, and not as an economic hand. Danger of exploitation of one group by another can be eliminated. Social harmony and conscious cooperation were made the chief characteristics of human association.

The ideal was to evolve a functional and not an acquisitive society. It is this varna dharma that has been the bulwark of Indian civilization and saved it from wreckage of time. Each group had its duties and its own rewards or compensation. The labourer had to work, but he was to be looked after as a younger member of a family. The man of desire, the vaishya, was to acquire wealth; power and authority was vested in the Kshatriya, while all these were to honour the teacher, to obey his religious and spiritual injunctions and accept his guidance. The teacher was to be supported by the gifts of the other three groups.

It was with the aid of this mechanism that India sought to solve her racial problem. The Aryans did not resort to the short cut of annihilating the primitive people with whom they came into contact as the European races have done whenever they have occupied lands in America, Asia, Africa and Australia, but they gave them a place in their body-politic, assigning to them the task befitting their intelligence and subordinate status. Observant scholars of the West have not failed to notice the spiritual significance of the varna-ashrama-dharma and given it its due praise.

Writing of this varna-ashrama-dharma, Auguste Comte (1798-1857) the great French sociologist, wrote in his book Systeme de philosophie positive or Positive Society: "No institution has ever shown itself more adopted to honour, ability to various kinds than this polytheistic organization...In a social view, the virtues of the system are not less conspicuous. Politically, its chief attribute was stability...As to the influence on mortals, this system was favourable to personal morality, and yet more to domestic, for the spirit of caste was a mere extension of the family spirit....As to social morals, the system was evidently favourable to respect for age and homage to ancestors."

These principles formed the background of the Indian social organization; on them was built a superstructure of social institution, such as education, marriage, family and the state. It was realized by the Indian sociologists that both the individual and the group could find self-expression and fulfilment only in and through a complex of social institutions, based on dharma, cooperation, mutual aid, integration, synthesis, the vision of the whole. Balance, orderly progress of individual and group, harmonious relationship between both, was the ideal aimed at by the Indian sociologist.

Castes and Traditional Economics

The traditional world had three or four castes. In India, they were the brahmana, kstriya, Vaishya, and Shudra. They corresponded, roughly, to the European feudal classes of clergy, nobility, burghers, and servants. More primitively, however, the priestly and warrior functions were united in a single caste. The caste system establishes natural justice; everyone "decides" before birth to incarnate the qualities that make them fit for one caste rather than another. Those in the lower castes were connected to the transcendent by their loyalty to their superiors. Note that this was not personal devotion; traditional loyalty is impersonal, just as the transcendent is nonhuman. The form provided by the caste system is an instance of "creative limitation." The decay of the system is one of the marks of the Kali Yuga.

Work in traditional societies was not work in our sense of the term. All activities, from the sacred sciences to the inferior professions, had their mysteries, anagogic elements that looked upward. The mysteries were preserved by guilds, which eschewed competition and monopoly. The only people who "worked' were slaves, whose activities had no transcendent element. That was what "work" meant. By this definition, the modern West is the civilization of slavery par excellence.

Rigvedic Brahmans and their Social Status

Since the early Rigvedic stage, Brahmans, undoubtedly, had already fixed ritual status: they were the priests, who had a wide circle of duties during soma sacrifices. They were also considered as the assistants of the gods at creation of the world, as the duty of "delivery" of the victim to the gods had been assigned to them.

In time the ritual duties of Brahmans began more and more detail, their universality and the cosmogonic abilities were moved gradually to the second plan in favour of their knowledge of the technical aspects of ritual.

By the end of Rigvedic period this process has resulted in rather precise codification of particular brahmanic qualities and duties, which were based on their personal abilities and skills. Because of that process Brahmans have gradually turned to an independent social class inside the Rigvedic society. Brahmans did not form the triad with Arya-and dasa-/dasyu-nor regarding the recognizable set of ritual and religious attributes, neither as the opposition of each varna at the Cosmic level. It means that they were not considered as the separate varna. However, already during the Rigvedic period the special social status of Brahmans has been realized de facto. It means, that the Rigvedic society knew some sort of social structure, which had been parallel to the varna one for some time.

It is very well known, that Brahmans were the supreme varna of Ancient Indian society since at least late Rigvedic period. However, most of the modern researchers consider, that Rigvedic Brahmans, like other Rigvedic realities, may not be characterized on the basis of more recent sources, as the former may be of very big time difference from the latter. This is why we consider, that the most productive way of researches of the Brahman subject is to define it with the help of each source as detail as possible and then to compare the results. So, this paper is the Brahman description as they were inside Rigveda.

Of course, this subject has been already searched by scholars and it has brought ahead several points of view.

1. Initially Brahman was one of the four priests (together with hotar, udgatar and adhvaryu), who had supervised over the ceremony with doing nothing else. This position goes from two issues: (a) there are many words for priests in Rigveda, (b) there are Rigvedic passages, that mention Brahmans as connected to "the way of ration" but not with "the way of speech".
2 Initially Brahman was the priest, who had read hymns to Indra during soma sacrifice, later his functions had been enlarged and he had become the chief of the entire process of sacrifice and also of all the cult procedures. This position is based on some Rigvedic passages which describes Brahman as a functional priest during soma sacrifice.
3. It has been since Rigvedic time Brahmans formed a separate social group of strata, different from Kshatriya and Vaishya, they were very honoured, read hymns and drank soma. The very word of "Brahman" mivemeant "class of priests-sacrificers". This comes mostly from some passages of non-family Rigvedic hymns (f. e. RV I 108,7).
4. Social meaning of Brahmans passed three stages inside the Rigvedic society. Initially they were poets, who had created hymns, and also wise men, then, it had been any functional priest, and after that Brahmans had formed their own social class. That vision was put ahead by J. Gonda in early 1970s, and was based on detail analysis of considerable number of Rigvedic texts of different mandalas.

Except for historians, "Brahman" subject was researched also by linguists who had created their own theories. We marked only two main ones here.

1. Brahmans formed separate social class since the time of the Indo-European unity, and they preserved their position inside all the historical Indo-European societies, including the Rigvedic one. The theory was based on results of comparative mythology, put ahead in 1950s, and has been under serious critics since that time.
2. Brahmans were those, who provided following of strictly formulated rituals. The concept runs from comparative linguistic studies, mostly of Iranian and Indian languages. It is of the most accepted for now.

So, all those positions we consider as of too fragmented or subjective, as the former come from language data only, and the latter-from few Rigvedic texts without real consideration of the correlation of the mentioned concepts inside Rigveda.

To overcome this situation, we consider to research "Brahman" subject as the Rigvedic one only (*i.e.* as a sphere of Rigvedic society). Only after this way being covered, one can determine their place and role inside the social structure of Rigvedic society. Here are the results of that vision.

Brahman goes, probably, to verb root barh-/brh-, which forms two semantic fields:

1. barh-/brh-"to grew", "to encrease", "to strengthen". This variant has been put ahead, for instance, by A. Macdonell and M. Mayrhofer.
2. barh-/brh-"to speak". This version of Brahman formation adherents O. Boehtlingk and R. Roth.

We consider, that these both variants form the same semantic field. The reasons for this admittance are: (a) goddess vac possessed cosmological (creative) functions, (b) in spite of the recognition of Brahman origin from two semantically different verb roots, both sides give the same semantics for the very Brahman. Let us overlook this more detail.

It is well known, that the word Brahman occurs as of neutral so of masculine gender. It was the stress that had probably made that difference: Brahman (n.) and Brahman (m.). In Vedic language semantically that stress moving meant formation of actor (m.) from action (n.), i. e. action "praying", "life power", "form of religious ceremony" gives actor "poet, singer, form creator", "ritual performer, priest", "the one, who performs the ritual in strictly fixed form".

So, according to the etymology there is no doubt, that Vedic concept of Brahman was the act of verbal putting in order of strengthen; and according to semantics to define the meaning of Brahman as the name of actor one should primarily outcome from Brahman as the name of action.

And one more thing. It is known that there are few words of the same root in Rigveda beside Brahman. Brahman, which one can find in family mandala, is formally the same as Brahman. This paper regards Brahman as the derivatives of Brahman (m.), the Brahman and Brahma-as the derivative of Brahman (n.), and the author does not differ those ones from the base form during the analysis.

All the things told above demonstrates very clear, that there was a tendency of transformation of social status of brahmas during the time of Rigveda. Initially they were functional priests, who had wide enough obligations during soma sacrifice.

They also played a role of assistants of gods during creation of the world, the duty of "the delivery" of sacrifice to gods and of dialogue with them was assigned to them. Eventually brahmanic ritual duties began to be specified more and more, their universality was being lost, and their cosmological abilities gradually began to be fixed for "the former" Brahmans. "Present" Brahmans turned more and more to narrow specialized experts-professionals of ritual, which became more and more detailed technically. All that became the basis for brahmanic social allocation from Aryan environment. By the end of Rigvedic times that process has led to rather precise codification of particular brahmanic qualities and duties based on their personal abilities and skills. That was, in our opinion, a doubtless attribute of gradual transformation of Brahmans to an independent social class inside Rigvedic society.

In spite of all the said above, Brahmans did not formed their own varna in Rigvedic society before its very end, because they had not formed any opposition with Arya or dasa/dasyu. However, Brahman had his special social status since very beginning of Rigvedic period, his functions were very important both for that time society and for every Aryan.

In time that status was fixed and became formally recognizable by the entire society. By the end of Rigvedic period Aryans had recognized, that they had Brahmans as the special social class de facto. Their next step was to form new social opposition, which had been to become the new basis of cosmological structuring. And it has been done by the time of Purusha sukta. New and the most known varna system has appeared.

Purpose of Varn Vyavastha

Brahman, Kshatriya, Vaishya and Shoodr are 4-Varn that Bhagavan Shri Krishna spoke about. There was a definitive purpose behind 4-Varn System in Hindu society. Necessary occupational training would come from the family itself, and each ancient Hindu village would be self-dependant. There would be No need for migration, like today; self-sufficiency and self-dependence would be the motto of Hindu 4-Varn System.

Brahman parents would provide the child with an environment to grow up as teachers to the society. Kshatriya parents would provide the child with an environment to grow up as protectors of life and land of the society. Vaishya parents would provide the child with an environment to grow up as suppliers of necessities of life to the society. Shoodr parents would provide the child with an environment to grow up as provider of all services to the society.

The necessary training that each would receive would come from the family itself. For instance, son would learn necessary skills from his father. The system would operate in a cyclic pattern from one generation to other. The necessary training would be passed on from one generation to another, by father to the son, and thus ensure continuity of self-sufficiency and self-dependence of each village unit.

The Hindu society would live in small units called villages, and each village would be self-sufficient in respect of its needs with regard to its education, administration, supplies and services. Towns would be few, and the number of those living in towns would be minuscule in comparison to the whole nation.

To ensure that, each village administration would be self-sufficient and self-dependant. It would have Brahman priests and teachers, Kshatriya administrators and defenders, Vaishya producers and agriculturists, and Shoodr service providers with all types of artisans. Here is the documented evidence.

The village communities are composed of those who cultivate the land, the established village-servants, priest, blacksmith, carpenter, accountant, washer-man (whose wife is ex officio midwife of the little village community), potter, watchman, barber, shoemaker, etc. Max Muller, p 255 referring to old Hindu system.

There would be no need for migration of people from one village to another, except by marriages. Thus, women would come from nearby villages, while sons would remain on the soil. For instance, in ancient Hindu society, a child of a barber would learn necessary skills from his father watching his father do the job when the child comes up a certain stage.

Case of India's 'Untouchables'

More than one-sixth of India's population, some 160 million people, live a precarious existence, shunned by much of society because of their rank as "untouchables" or Dalits-literally meaning "broken" people-at the bottom of India's caste system. Dalits are discriminated against, denied access to land, forced to work in degrading conditions, and routinely abused at the hands of the police and of higher-caste groups that enjoy the state's protection. In what has been called India's "hidden apartheid," entire villages in many Indian states remain completely segregated by caste. National legislation and constitutional protections serve only to mask the social realities of discrimination and violence faced by those living below the "pollution line."

For most of the world caste remains an ancient cultural artefact and untouchability a long eradicated practice. This paper attempts to shift the debate on caste and on broader issues pertaining to socially institutionalised discrimination. It begins with a brief description of the characteristics and mechanisms of caste discrimination and a summary overview of the Indian government's response. It then attempts to dismantle those misperceptions that have allowed the system to survive, and comments on the barriers that keep the international community from effectively intervening against a practice that relegates millions of people to a lifetime of segregation, discrimination, and violence.

India's caste system is perhaps the world's longest surviving social hierarchy. A defining feature of Hinduism, caste encompasses a complex ordering of social groups on the basis of ritual purity. A person is considered a member of the caste into which he or she is born and remains within that caste until death, although the particular ranking of that caste may vary among regions and over time. Differences in status are traditionally justified by the religious doctrine of karma, a belief that one's place in life is determined by one's deeds in previous lifetimes. Traditional scholarship has described this more than 2,000-year-old system within the context of the four principal varnas, or large caste categories. In order of precedence these are the Brahmins (priests and teachers), the Ksyatriyas (rulers and soldiers), the Vaishyas (merchants and traders), and the Shudras (labourers and artisans). A fifth category falls outside the varna system and consists of those known as "untouchables" or Dalits; they are often assigned tasks too ritually polluting to merit inclusion within the traditional varna system.

Within the four principal castes, there are thousands of sub-castes, also called jatis; endogamous groups that are further divided along occupational, sectarian, regional, and linguistic lines. Collectively all of these are sometimes referred to as "caste Hindus" or those falling within the caste system. The Dalits are described as varna-sankara: they are "outside the system"-so inferior to other castes that they are deemed polluting and therefore "untouchable." Even as outcasts, they themselves are divided into further sub-castes and practice untouchability against those ranked below; the discrimination is wholly internalised. Although "untouchability" was abolished under Article 17 of the Indian constitution, the practice continues to determine the socioeconomic and religious standing of those at the bottom of the caste hierarchy. Whereas the first four varnas are free to choose and change their occupation, Dalits have generally been confined to the occupational structures into which they are born.

With little land of their own to cultivate, Dalit men, women, and children numbering in the tens of millions work as agricultural labourers for a few kilograms of rice or less than US$1 a day. Most live on the brink of destitution, barely able to feed their families and unable to send their children to school or break away from cycles of debt bondage that are passed on from generation to generation. At the end of day they return to a hut in their Dalit colony with no electricity, kilometres away from the nearest water source, and segregated from all non-Dalits, known as caste Hindus. They are forbidden by caste Hindus to enter places of worship, to draw water from public wells, or to wear shoes in caste Hindu presence. They are made to dig the village graves, dispose of dead animals, clean human waste with their bare hands, and to wash and use separate tea tumblers at neighbourhood tea stalls, all because-due to their caste status-they are deemed polluting and therefore untouchable.

In November 1999, after a cyclone slammed into the eastern state of Orissa, killing thousands and rendering millions homeless, the government brought in 200 Dalit manual scavengers from New Delhi, and planned to bring 500 more from other parts of Orissa, to load animal carcasses onto hand-drawn carts and take them away to be burned. Government officials had offered local upper-caste residents more than the daily minimum wage for each animal burned but they refused citing the decayed conditions of the carcasses and the fact that the task was beneath them: they had "some self-respect left." Even in times of natural disaster, the laws of purity and pollution prevail and the government moves quickly to accommodate the prejudice. At all levels, and under all circumstances, the discrimination is institutionalised.

Dalit women face the triple burden of caste, class, and gender. Dalit girls have been forced to become prostitutes for upper-caste patrons and village priests. Sexual abuse and other forms of violence against women are used by landlords and the police to inflict political "lessons" and crush dissent within the community. According to a Tamil Nadu state government official, the raping of Dalit women exposes the hypocrisy of the caste system as "no one practices untouchability when it comes to sex." Like other Indian women whose relatives are sought by the police, Dalit women have also been arrested and tortured in custody as a means of punishing their male relatives who are hiding from the authorities.

Any attempt to defy the social order is met with physical or economic retaliation. According to the most recent figures available, between 1994 and 1996 a total of 98,349 cases were registered with the police nationwide as crimes and atrocities against Dalits. Given that Dalits are both reluctant and unable (for lack of police cooperation) to report crimes against themselves, the actual number of abuses is presumably much higher. Whether the clashes are social, economic, or political in nature, they are premised on the same basic principle: any attempt to alter village customs or to demand land, increased wages, or political rights sets off a chain of events and leads to social boycotts and acts of retaliatory violence on the part of those most threatened by changes in the status quo.

Dalit communities as a whole are summarily punished for individual transgressions; Dalits are cut off from their land and employment, women endure physical attacks, and letter of the law is rarely enforced. Most of the conflicts take place within very narrow segments of the caste hierarchy, between the poor and the not so poor, the landless labourer and the marginal landowner. The differences lie in the considerable amount of leverage that the higher-caste Hindus or non-Dalits are able to wield over local police, district administrations, and even the state government. A theme that is almost universal in its application, it illustrates a crucial aspect of identity politics: one's identity as a person belonging to a certain caste is perceived not only by one's absolute rank but also by the relative treatment meted out to communities that are ranked below.

Building on constitutional provisions, the government of India has pursued a two-pronged approach to narrowing the gap between the socioeconomic status of the Dalit population and the national average. The first approach involves regulatory measures designed to ensure that relevant legal provisions are adequately implemented, enforced, and monitored; the second focuses on increasing the self-sufficiency of the Dalit population through financial assistance for self-employment activities and through development programs to increase education and skills.

The protective component of this two-pronged strategy includes the implementation of legal provisions contained in state and central government legislation, and reservations or quotas in the arenas of government employment and higher education. India's policy of reservations is an attempt by the central government to remedy past injustices related to low-caste status. To allow for proportional representation in certain state and federal institutions, the constitution reserves 22.5 percent of seats in federal government jobs, state legislatures, the Lower House of parliament, and educational institutions for scheduled castes and scheduled tribes.

Though some have benefited the reservation policy has not been successfully implemented and has yet to achieve its desired effect. Moreover, most of the landless and illiterate Dalits in the country are not in a position to avail themselves of any of their constitutional privileges. Controversy over the reservations scheme has also allowed the debate to predictably stagnate around the distribution of privilege, taking the focus away from violations of basic rights. India's policy of economic liberalisation is also having an effect on Dalits and their livelihood.

As the public sector shrinks due to privatisation, the reservations model is affecting-and able to assist-fewer people, inasmuch as government-related jobs are being drastically reduced. Globalisation has also led to coastal lands increasingly being acquired by multinationals (via the central government) for aquaculture projects. Dalits are the main labourers and tenants of coastal land areas and are increasingly being forced to leave these areas-to live as displaced people, for the most part-as foreign investment rises.

The persistence of caste-based prejudices and the denial of access to land, education, and political power have all contributed to an atmosphere of increasing intolerance. Violence against Dalits, which has steadily climbed since 1994, is only the most extreme form of that intolerance. In 1989 the Scheduled Castes and Scheduled Tribes (Prevention of Atrocities) Act was enacted to prevent and punish caste-based abuses, to establish special courts for the trial of such offences, and to provide for victim relief and rehabilitation. Its enactment represented an acknowledgement on the part of the government that abuses, in their most degrading and violent forms, were still perpetrated against Dalits decades after independence.

A look at the offences made punishable by the act provides a glimpse into the retaliatory or customarily degrading treatment Dalits may receive. They include forcing members of a scheduled caste or scheduled tribe to drink or eat any inedible or obnoxious substance; dumping excreta, waste matter, carcasses or any other obnoxious substance in their premises or neighbourhood; forcibly removing clothes and parading them naked or with painted face or body; interfering with their rights to land; compelling a member of a scheduled caste or scheduled tribe into forms of forced or bonded labour; corrupting or fouling the water of any spring, reservoir or any other source ordinarily used by scheduled castes or scheduled tribes; denying right of passage to a place of public resort; and using a position of dominance to exploit a scheduled caste or scheduled tribe woman sexually.

The potential of the law to bring about social change has been hampered by institutional prejudice and police corruption, with the result that many offences are not registered. Ignorance of procedures or a lack of knowledge of the act itself has also affected implementation. Even when cases are registered, the absence of special courts to try them can delay prosecutions for up to three to four years. Some state governments dominated by higher castes have even attempted to repeal the legislation altogether. Much like other "social welfare" legislation in India, the act remains a paper tiger with little actual effect.

The existence of constitutionally mandated quotas and a large body of legislation and administrative agency mandates assigned exclusively to deal with the plight of Dalits is held up by the government as a panacea to problems of discrimination. These so-called remedies have also shifted attention away from the institutional nature of caste prejudice. It would be difficult to convince the Dalits of Dholapur district, Rajasthan, that after over fifty years of independence, government intervention had made a difference.

In April 1998, a Dalit of the area was assaulted by an upper-caste family who forcibly pierced his nostril, drew a string through his nose, paraded him around the village, and tied him to a cattle post-all because he refused to sell bidis (hand-rolled cigarettes) on credit to the nephew of the upper-caste village chief. The message sent from the judiciary on caste discrimination is equally grim: in July 1998 in the state of Uttar Pradesh, an Allahabad High Court judge had his chambers "purified with Ganga jal" (water from the River Ganges), because it had earlier been occupied by a Dalit judge.

India's distinction as the "world's largest democracy" also helps to mask the abuses. For Dalits throughout the country who suffer from de facto disenfranchisement, democracy has not been a self-fulfilling prophecy. During elections, those unpersuaded by typical electioneering are routinely threatened and beaten by political party strongmen in order to compel them to vote for certain candidates. Already under the thumb of local landlords and police officials, Dalit villagers who do not comply have been murdered, beaten, and harassed.

Dalits who have contested political office in village councils and municipalities through seats that have been constitutionally "reserved" for them have been threatened with physical abuse and even death in order to get them to withdraw from the campaign. In Tamil Nadu in June 1997, a newly elected Dalit village council president was beheaded by caste Hindus displaced from their once secure elected positions. In 1999, a Dalit woman from Uttar Pradesh considered contesting elections. She was gang-raped and subsequently beaten and murdered as a lesson to other villagers not to disturb the status quo. As with most cases of violence against Dalits, the culprits have yet to be convicted.

Political mobilisation that has resulted in the emergence of powerful interest groups and political parties among middle- and low-caste groups throughout India since the mid-1980s has also largely bypassed Dalits. Dalits are courted by all political parties but generally forgotten once elections are over. The expanding power base of low-caste political parties, the election of low-caste chief ministers to state governments, and even the appointment of a Dalit as president of India in July 1997 all signal the increasing prominence of Dalits in the political landscape but cumulatively have yet to yield any significant benefit for the majority of Dalits. Laws on land reform and protection for Dalits remain unimplemented in most of India's twenty-five states.

Political parties have frequently fashioned their manifestos and campaign slogans around the need for "upliftment" of these marginalised sectors, while political leaders, mostly drawn from higher castes, offer the promise of equal status and equal rights. However, the laws have benefited very few and, due to a lack of political will, development programs and welfare projects designed to improve economic conditions for Dalits have generally had little effect. Dalits rarely break free from bondage or economic exploitation by upper-caste landowners.

Equally insidious, though not as apparent, is the fact that Dalits are denied their place in the public consciousness. The plight of India's "untouchables" elicits only sporadic attention within the country. Public outrage over large-scale incidents of violence or particularly egregious examples of discrimination fades quickly, and the state is under little pressure to undertake more meaningful reforms. Despite ambitious calls for action by central and state governments in the aftermath publicity of massacres and police raids, the Indian authorities have shown little commitment to resolving the root causes of caste conflicts. Society as a whole has turned a blind eye to the institutional character of caste-based abuse and discrimination. Laws are openly flouted, police allegiance is routinely up for sale, and society continues to sanction what the legislature defines as crimes. In the eastern state of Bihar, for example, the first person to be convicted under a decadesold law combating child labour was in 1998.

A loss of faith in the state machinery and increasing intolerance of their abusive treatment has led many Dalit communities into organised movements to claim their rights. In response, state and private actors have engaged in a pattern of repression to preserve the status quo. Unable to find sustainable alliances within, and in an effort to counter their invisibility at home, Dalit movements have from time to time turned outward to look for parallels in struggles abroad. During the 1970s, for example, the Dalit Panthers emerged outside the framework of recognised political parties and aligned themselves ideologically to the Black Panther movement in the United States. During the same period, Dalit literature, painting, and theatre challenged the very premise and nature of established art forms and their depiction of society and religion. Many of these new Dalit artists formed the first generation of the Dalit Panther movement that sought to wage an organised struggle against the varna system. Dalit Panthers visited atrocity sites, organised marches and rallies in villages, and raised slogans of direct militant action against their upper-caste aggressors.

The determined stance of the Dalit Panthers served to arouse and unite many Dalits, particularly Dalit youth and students. The defeat of ruling party candidates and the boycott of elections in some areas forced the government to take notice of the movement: Panther leaders were often harassed and removed from districts for speaking out against the government and Hindu religion. They also became frequent targets of police brutality and arbitrary detentions. Disagreements over the future of the movement and inclusion of other caste groups ultimately led to a dispersal of Dalit Panther leadership. The former aggressiveness and militancy of the Dalit Panthers has for the most part dissipated, though small splinter groups or groups that have adopted the name still survive.

In the 1960s, leftist guerrilla organisations with Marxist, Leninist, and Maoist orientations began advocating the use of violence to achieve land redistribution. By 1970, these so-called Naxalites had initiated a series of peasant uprisings to seize land, burn property records, and assassinate exploitative landlords and others identified as "class enemies" in large areas of the countryside stretching from West Bengal to the southern state of Kerala.

Although the Naxalite insurgency was brought to an end in most parts of the country by a brutal police crackdown designed to eliminate the militants and their supporters, the movement continues to survive, albeit with some splits and regroupings, in the rural areas of West Bengal, Orissa, Andhra Pradesh, and Bihar. Higher-caste landlords in Bihar have organised private militias to counter the Naxalite threat. These militias, or senas, also target Dalit villagers believed to be sympathetic to Naxalites. Senas are believed responsible for the murders of many hundreds of Dalits in Bihar since 1987.

Though offshoots of militant movements still thrive in many parts of the country, the strategy for the actualisation of rights has in the past fifteen years undergone a major shift. Beginning in the 1980s, a handful of Dalit organisations began turning to the United Nations as a possible forum for the mobilisation of international support and condemnation of caste-based abuses. However, the difficulty of slotting caste-based abuses into standard categories of human rights violations, and the prevalence of constitutional and legislative protections at the national level, has allowed these abuses to escape international scrutiny. The government of India has consistently asserted that the caste issue does not fall within the mandate of various "race"-based UNHCHR bodies. The government has also refused to allow relevant working groups and special rapporteurs to gain access to the country.

In turn, the response of the international community has been superficial at best. Dalit activists now find themselves struggling to overcome their invisibility abroad. Though caste identity is used as a justification for segregation and exploitation, the discrimination is so entrenched that the victims' shared membership in lower-caste communities is often ignored by upper-caste families and international bodies alike.

While the world was united in its condemnation of increasing attacks on India's Christian community this past year, for example, it ignored a significant underlying cause: a majority of Christians in India are Dalits and tribals for whom conversion offers a partial escape from untouchability and exploitation. Conversions are therefore threatening to the social and economic status quo.Like evaluating the symptoms without diagnosing the disease, most international interventions have also overlooked the fact that Dalits, numbering in the tens of millions, comprise the majority of those driven to bonded labour, manual scavenging, and forced prostitution, under conditions that violate national law and their basic human rights.

Despite their mandate of reaching the "poorest of the poor," international development institutions have yet to understand that for those at the bottom of its hierarchy, caste is a determinative factor for the attainment of social, political, civil, and economic rights.

Which strategies then are likely to be effective in reforming socially institutionalised discrimination? Part of the answer lies in supporting the work of grassroots Dalit and human rights activists throughout the country who for many years have assumed many state-like functions and have stepped in where the administration has failed. The second part is to involve the international community in forcing the government to remedy its failures.

In 1998, the National Campaign for Dalit Human Rights was born out of an initiative of grassroots Dalit activists in eight Indian states. Many of these activists were involved in the drafting of over forty recommendations to the government of India and the international community that are contained in a Human Rights Watch report on caste violence released earlier this year. The campaign, which has since expanded to include fourteen states and eleven countries, seeks to mobilise a national coalition that operates at the grassroots level while eliciting the participation of the international community in its struggle. Still, there are other prejudices to be overcome before such participation can be ensured. Internationally, the cyclone in India received little attention in comparison to other recent tragedies of similar or lesser magnitude. Like disparities in responding to crises in Europe and Africa, the "otherness" of those most vividly affected by violence, disaster, or day-to-day deprivation, eases the decision not to respond. When the victims of attacks, even massacres, are non-Christian Dalits, the news barely breaks into international headlines.

Interventions on caste discrimination, if any, have been limited to inquiries regarding the mechanisms of protection offered by the state, without asking for evidence of their effective implementation (which, generally speaking, is a recurring problem in the nature of international intervention on race and ethnicity matters).

The Indian government needs to place a priority on strengthening institutional mechanisms aimed at addressing issues of violence and discrimination. But it also needs the active support of-and pressure from-the United Nations, multilateral financial institutions, trading partners, and national and international non-governmental organisations to eradicate the pervasive problem of caste-based abuse. Will the international community respond or even apply the necessary pressure to stimulate domestic political will? Or will it continue to deny Dalits and others their place in the public consciousness? Entrenched forms of discrimination stemming from the world's longest surviving system of social hierarchy may offer some lessons as we prepare for a global forum on modern day "racism." The first and most obvious is to look beyond race as the only arbiter of rights.

The second is to look beyond democracy, affirmative action, and the existence of domestic legislation as sufficient guarantors of basic freedoms. The third is to recognise the resilience and adaptability of ancient custom to contemporary global trends. The fourth is to scrutinise the discrimination inherent in the international community's decision to act, and more importantly, in its failure to respond.

Varnasrama Social System

There is a natural system of social organization which can bring about a peaceful society where everyone is happy. This system is described in the timeless Vedic literature of India and it is called Varnasrama dharma.

The purpose of the Varnasrama social system is to provide a structure which allows people to work according to their natural tendencies and to organize society so that everyone, regardless of their position, makes spiritual advancement.

People can only work with a cooperative spirit if there is a central point. Over the years proponents of many different political ideologies have tried to unite society by providing such a central point, however, these attempts have all ultimately failed.

Generally people work for their own pleasure and this is sometimes extended to working for the family, the nation or even the whole world. Because the aims and aspirations of the members of society are so varied it is practically impossible to achieve a peaceful situation as everyone is working to fulfil his own personal goals. The only universal central point around which everyone can work is God. He provides an absolute, eternal centre for all our activities. If we try to make something else the central point the resulting society is doomed to fail.

The Varnasrama system recognizes there are many different types of people who may not be spiritually inclined. The society is organized under the direction of qualified Brahmans and is divided into four occupational and four spiritual divisions in such a way that everyone is serving God simply by performing their occupational duties. As the entire society is arranged to please God, anyone working within the society also pleases God.

The Structure of Varnasrama Society: The practical application of the Varnasrama system is to divide the society according to four occupational and four spiritual orders of life.

The Varnasrama system recognizes the natural talents and abilities of each person and provides work according to a persons qualities. There are four qualities of work, the Brahmans are the intellectual and priestly class, the Kshatriyas are the government, the military and the administrative classes, the Vaishyas are farmers and businessmen, and the sudras are workers.

There are also four spiritual divisions, brahmacary, student life, grhastha, married life, vanaprasta, retired life and sunnyasa, renounced life. If this system is properly implemented under the direction of qualified Brahmans the result will be peace and prosperity throughout the world.

The Corrupt Indian "Caste" System: The Varnasrama social divisions are based on qualities and work. If someone has the qualities of a brahmana and if they work as a brahmana they are accepted as a qualified brahmana. This system should not be confused with the corrupt "caste" system of India.

In India people claim to be Brahmans simply because they are born in a brahmana family even though they do not possess the qualifications or qualities of a brahmana and in most cases they are not working as Brahmans either..

The result of the corruption of the original system has been the destruction of the entire social structure in India and the "caste" system is now being used by the rich to exploit and oppress the poor.

Divisions According to Qualification: In Varnasrama society all members are equally important. An analogy comparing the social body to the human body is given to explain this. The Brahmans are the head of the body as they possess the intelligence and give directions to the other parts of the body. The Kshatriyas are likened to the arms of the body as their business as administrators and the military is to protect the social body from threats from outside (attacks from enemies) and disruption from within. (Thieves and rogues).

The Vaishyas are likened to the stomach. The stomach provides energy to the body. The Vaishyas, as the productive class, are the farmers and businessman who produce and distribute food to the social body. The Vaishyas are also responsible for protecting the cows.

The sudras are likened to the legs as they provide the manual labour required by the social body.

We look after our whole body. It is not that we attend to problems affecting the head and neglect problems in the legs. The body works as a coordinated unit and a problem anywhere in the body causes a disruption to the proper functioning of the whole body and is therefore immediately attended to.

The social body should work as a coordinated unit with different members of the society acting in their respective positions as Brahmans, Kshatriyas, Vaishyas and sudras according to their qualities. The result will be a happy, peaceful and efficient society.

The Brahmans: Although all members of the social body are important, as the Brahmans are the intelligent class directing society by giving guidance and advice to the king or government (Kshatriyas), it is vital that they be properly qualified.

If the head of society is not functioning properly the whole social body is in trouble.

All over the world we are seeing misguided governments make the lives of their citizens hell, simply because they have no qualified Brahmans to give them advice.

The whole planet has become very unfortunate and disturbed due to such unqualified leadership.

The brahmana's position is that of an unpaid adviser to the king or government. The business of the brahmana is to understand the Vedic Scriptures and be expert in applying them in different places and at different times.

The Vedic system doesn't require the creation of any new rules or legislation The perfect laws have been given by Manu, the father of mankind in the Manu Samhita, and the qualified brahmana simply implements these timeless laws. There is no need for imperfect man made laws.

The qualities of a brahmana are given in the Bhagawad Gita as peacefulness, self control, austerity, purity, tolerance, honesty, knowledge, wisdom and religiousness and all of these qualities must be actually manifest before someone can be accepted as a brahmana.

Giving Charity to the Brahmans: On special days such as the birth of a child, marriage and other auspicious occasions it is customary for the Kshatriyas and Vaishyas to give in charity to the Brahmans. The Kshatriya king is wealthy because in return for giving the citizens protection he levies taxes. The Vaishya farmers and businessmen are wealthy because of their farming and trading activity. The brahmana takes whatever small amount is required to maintain himself and his family and he distributes the rest of the charity he receives for the benefit of the people in general.

Because the brahmana is intelligent and an expert in spiritual matters he can understand how best to distribute charity. It is for this reason in Vedic society charity is given to the Brahmans. It is not very intelligent to give charity to unqualified persons, for they will simply squander it. For example if you give a drunkard money, it will be used for purchasing alcohol, not food. Such charity is charity in the mode of ignorance and is not very auspicious.

The Kshatriyas: The Kshatriyas take the positions of king or politicians and the military. They administer society according to the directions and advice of the Brahmans.

Their qualities are given in the Bhagawad Gita as heroism, power, determination, resourcefulness, courage in battle, generosity and leadership.

The Perfect King: A good Kshatriya king is strong and just, he acts according to the advice of the Brahmans, he is loved by the law abiding citizens and feared as death personified by the thieves and rogues.

In a country ruled by a qualified Kshatriya king the citizens are protected and thus they develop good qualities and are peaceful and happy. Because the king is strong and honest the citizens have no fear of being disturbed by thieves and rogues or by attacks from invading armies. They also have no fear of being plundered by unfair or exorbitant taxation or dishonest government officers, as such a strong king will quickly correct any corruption within his own ministry. The lives of many saintly kings are described in Srimad Bhagavatam and we recommend those interested m hearing more about the qualities and activities of such great souls study the Srimad Bhagavatam.

The Problem With Modern Government: In modern governments we find many politicians and government officers who are simply interested in a good salary and a comfortable life. They achieve this for themselves and their colleagues by levying exorbitant taxes and creating an ineffectual and bureaucratic top heavy government.

The citizens under the rule of such an unqualified government are most unfortunate. They are not protected from thieves and rogues from within the country. Instead they are exploited by the governments taxation system. Excessive taxation is levied to maintain the ineffectual top heavy bureaucratic system. No one can be happy in such a difficult position.

Selection of Members of the Government: Unless a person has the qualities of a Kshatriya he should not be given the position of king, president, Prime Minister, minister or a military man. If the men in these positions do not have the qualities of a Kshatriya (heroism, power, determination, resourcefulness, courage in battle, generosity and leadership) then the government becomes unworkable and the society suffers due to lack of protection. Currently, all over the world, the people in general are suffering because the governments of the world are full of unqualified persons who have no idea of the process of creating a fair society and maintaining law and order.

The Vaishyas: The Vaishyas are responsible principally for the production food and the protection of the cows. It is the duty of the Brahmans to understand the Vedic Scriptures and give guidance to the Kshatriya government and military who, in turn give directions to the Vaishyas and the sudras.

The qualities of a Vaishya are given in the Bhagawad Gita as farming, cow protection and business and they work to provide the society with the required food, clothing and other goods.

The Sudras: The sudras have little intelligence and must therefore be engaged in the service of one of the other three classes. Their occupation is to perform manual labour, give service and to engage in arts and craftsmanship. The sudras are unable to support themselves independently therefore they must take shelter of an employer who can direct and provide for them. It is described in this age of Kali almost everyone is a Shudra. We can actually see society is now so degraded that practically everyone must work as a Shudra by serving an employer.

Only the sudras take such employment, the Brahmans simply depend on God and this way they get everything required. They receive charity from members of the other divisions of society. The Kshatriya has some land and collects taxes from the citizens and the Vaishya makes some money by trading farm produce and doing business. Only the sudras depend on someone else for their maintenance.

If proper education is provided then the sudras who have the capacity to learn can be elevated to higher positions in the social structure. A society of sudras means a society of chaos as sudras don't have the intelligence to organize society, therefore, there is great need to train qualified Brahmans to re-establish the "head" of the social body. If this is done there is certainly hope for the future.

Caste is a Variety of Race

Ever Since Dalit groups have started mobilising themselves to fight their centuries old discrimination, the ruling elite have begun to hit back. In recent days, there have been articles in major newspapers on how caste discrimination is very different from race discrimination and that is why it is outside the purview of the U.N. Conference on Racial Discrimination. And all those who have articulated themselves including Andre Beteille, social anthropologist of repute, (in The Hindu of March 10, 2001) have backed the irrational position of the present government and other forces of vested interest.

What is however forgotten in the whole course of the arguments by the ruling elite is their own location in the social hierarchy. Our relationship to other human beings and society depends on our own social location and subjectivity. One can quote from authors and scholars to legitimise one's position and strengthen one's case. Unfortunately, the ground realities are experiential.

To be fair to discriminated groups none of the elites who have been part of the oppressive structure should have any business to talk on their behalf since they have not experienced the reality of discrimination. The language and ideas of the ruling elite have been one of subjugation and exploitation since it is purely centred on concepts evolved in ivory towers. The objective of such knowledge is to preserve one's class interests. More than theory, knowledge must be constructed from experience. This position is unlikely to be acceptable to our noble theoreticians, academicians, the politicians and the bureaucrats since this class has benefited through subjugation of certain social groups in the name of caste.

The principle of equality is a fundamental component to the U.N. mechanism of promotion and protection of human rights. Article 1 of the Universal Declaration of Human Rights states that "All human beings are born free and equal in dignity and rights. They are endowed with reason and conscience and should act towards one another in a spirit of brotherhood." As we step into 21st century we need to ask ourselves as a nation whether our social and institutional structures are based on discrimination or not. And if there is discrimination what is it based on?

Endogamy: Whether it is caste or race, the status is entirely ascribed, the status one obtains at birth. Segregation exists in both the systems. Outcasts still remain outcastes. Even in the midst of the recent worst human tragedy that hit the country in the form of an earthquake in Gujarat, the whole institutional mechanism of the state did not move into the Dalit areas and belts while the benefits of relief went to the upper castes as fast as possible. This is no concoction. Papers have reported it. Parliament has discussed it. The Congress party has highlighted it and NGOs have testified to it. In both caste and race those in the lowest rung are not only discriminated against but cursed to do menial jobs. Endogamy is another feature of both. Marriages are rare and few both among different racial and caste groups. Both are stratifications, a hierarchical ordering of social categories, supported by social institutions. Inequality is intergenerationally transmitted in caste and race. Prejudice and discrimination are both a part of race and caste. And what is worse is that such prejudice and discrimination are not merely personal but institutional, a part of the structure and processes of whole society.

In both caste and race theories, there is an attitude of the so-called higher or superior groups that their culture is superior to all other cultures and all the other groups should be judged according to their culture. What is the difference in the claims made by the white race in Europe and the upper castes in India? In any racial or caste society the access to the society's resources including power is proportionately larger to the pure in comparison to the impure or polluted. Take the example of the Dalits in India.

The Constitution has made caste illegal and abolished it in 1950. Affirmative action programme was introduced to bring the unequals to the level of equality. Regardless of official policy, the system still permeates Indian life and culture. "When we are working, they ask us not to come near them. At canteens, we have separate tea tumblers and they make us clean them ourselves and make us put the dishes away. We cannot enter temples. We cannot use upper caste water taps. Our children in schools are not treated as children of the others. We live in colonies of our own"-is a testimony of a scavenger in Ahmedabad. Caste has still limited social advancement, job and marriage choices.

In spite of 50 years of Independence can one still believe that the SC/ST representation in teaching jobs at the level of higher education is a mere 2 per cent at the all India level, when the affirmative action has provided them with 22 per cent. How do those who oppose the linkage of caste with race explain this? Though skin colour or physical differences may not all the time play a significant part in distinguishing caste as in race, social descent and occupation does. Apartheid exists in both. On several counts Dalit oppression is worse than racial discrimination. Over 240 million people of this country have been shunned as outcastes.

In fact, the Government of India's 1996 state report on the Committee on Elimination of all forms of Racial Discrimination (CERD) clearly notes though caste may not be equivalent to race, it falls within the purview of Article 1 of the Convention due to the clause on descent. Why is the government playing a different tune now? Even the U.N. Committee on Civil and Political Rights has observed ``SC/STs continue to endure severe social discrimination and suffer disproportionately from...intercaste violence, bonded labour and discrimination of all kinds." The U.N. bodies have opened up opportunities for Dalit activists, movements and organisations to highlight their oppression in the international forum. When the Indian state has not effectively implemented its constitutional mandate of Dalit Human Rights, what is wrong that the Dalits demand for rights from the World Government, the U.N.? After all, India is a signatory to most of the covenants of the U.N. In the light of India's ratification of CERD in 1969 it is perfectly constitutional, lawful and democratic for the discriminated communities to approach the very body to bring to its notice the discrimination they suffer.

Vested Interests: In spite of ground realities why is our ruling elite thus sound increasingly irrational? The reason is vested interests. It is the same interests that did not permit Ambedkar to raise specific concerns of the Dalits with regard to independence at the Round Table Conference. Once again, it is the very same interests that deny any implementation of affirmative action in the name of efficiency and merit. The caste system has developed a large amount of socioeconomic interests and any change in it affects the existing socioeconomic order. That is why our ruling elite abhor any transformation of the system. What the Dalit cause needs is perception of ground level realities from all concerned and not faithfulness to the position of the state and its academicians. We need to work for the liberation of the marginalisalised based on ground realities as experienced by the discriminated people.

4

Some Thoughts on Caste System

All developed social systems are stratified. No society is a mass of individuals. European society was organized along class, guilds, and religion (Jews and gentiles, Protestants and Catholics, etc.) India had castes, or more properly, jatis.

As a political category, caste is a British invention. The British introduced the category of caste for purposes of counting population in the census that began in 1871. The British began to rank order castes by status and economics. Many petitions were filed by new resurgent groups to seek higher ranking. Caste began to be organized as political movement. In a similar fashion, the counting of people by tribal identity in Africa led to tribalism. Sikhism was defined as a separate religion by the British, and it became so. These points are elaborated in an excellent book by Nicholas Dirks, Castes of Mind: Colonialism and the Making of Modern India, 2001.

Castes in India are different than classes in the West. Castes are not economically structured. Each caste has its own rich and its own poor. There are rich Brahmins and poor Brahmins. As a general rule, Brahmins were among the poorest section of society. This observation runs counter to the prevalent view that Indian society is Brahmin dominated and Brahmin exploited. Different castes in India are like different ethnic groups within the United States. There are rich Italians and poor Italians, rich Irish and poor Irish. Also like caste groups in India, till recently the ethnic groups in America married in their own community, *i.e.* Jews would marry other Jews, the Polish would marry other Polish, and so on. The caste system in ancient times was not static. Castes rose and fell. Castes became static and rigid during extended foreign rule. Under Muslim rule, some caste groups that fought against domination were pushed to the outer edges of the social system. I have been told that among the sweeper castes in India, one finds many Rajput gotras.

Why is caste denied in the West and replaced by 'class'? Why are dowry murders denied when husbands in the West shoot their wives more frequently than dowry murders in India? Why is idolatry denied when Westerners worship celebrities and money and brand names as their idols? Is the American flag not an idol that is worshipped by the Pledge of Allegiance? The third world non Christian phenomenon is always given a separate term so as to be able to demonize it whereas the western equivalent is spared by saying the term does not apply.

This is linguistic sleigh of hand.

"The European colonizers wanted to impose their ideal of equality so profoundly contrary to that of liberty, that the Western peoples sought to impose their ideas, culture, religion, language, and ways of living and thinking on the people of their empires who preferred to live and think differently. Whole races and civilizations have been destroyed by the European conqueror so that he can preserve the illusion of living in a world of justice, equality, and democracy."

"The moneyed elite in the United States have long coveted their neighbours' land, resources, and cheap labour forces. Eager to invade, annex, and exploit, the plutocracy began to disseminate the warped notion of Manifest Destiny in the Nineteenth Century. Purporting to have the unwavering support of the Almighty, the "superior" Anglo-Saxons rationalized slavery, the Native American Genocide, the conquest of half of Mexico, the annexation of Hawaii, and their eradication of over 300,000 "savages" in conquering the Philippines."

Racial and Social inequities continue to plague modern Western industrial societies who claim to be the beacon of Human Rights. Historically, nations in Europe and America have had a similar structure: the class system. A Westerner who has had occasion to witness the rise of the new castes in industrial societies, or status-oriented thinking and bureaucratic hierarchies would not praise the modern or industrial culture. Exploitation exists in all societies-in India, it is caste, while in the West, it is based on class. Casteism in India is a terrible injustice. No thoughtful person will deny that. So is crime, homelessness, social inequality and racism in Western nations. Ancient Hindus have never discriminated against people based on their colour or race. Hindus worship God Krishna and Goddess Kali. Both, Krishna and Kali, means black and are depicted as such as well.

> *"In Europe and America, which are said to be the most democratic and highly individualistic, individual life is least regarded. In the land of liberty, fundamentalism, Ku Klax Klan, and Nordic assaults on all other races and cultures prevail."*

Degeneration of the Varna System

The Varna system was started as analogous to professional guilds, but as a result of exploitation by some priests, and socioeconomic elements of society, this system became hereditary and degenerated over the centuries. The ancient culture of India was based upon a system of social diversification according to spiritual development.

Four orders of society were recognized based upon the four main goals of human beings and established society accordingly. These four groups were the Brahmins, the priests or spiritual class; the Kshatriya, the nobility or ruling class; the Vaishya, the merchants and farmers; and the Shudras or servants. These four orders of society were called "varna", which has two meanings; first it means "colour" and second it means a "veil". As colour it does not refer to the colour of the skin of people, but to the qualities or energies of human nature. As a veil it shows the four different ways in which the Divine Self is hidden in human beings. In ancient India, these divisions were not based on birth but based on qualifications. According to the Bhagawad Gita this Aryan family system broke down in India over three thousand years ago at the time of Krishna. Hence after three thousand years this system of determining natural aptitude has degenerated into the caste system which resembles it now only in form.

As the Varna system became increasingly rigid and based on inheritance, it was enveloped by another system known as the caste system. Thus, this varna system determined the social structure of ancient Hindu society. The caste system could not have been part of Hindu religious philosophy, since it violates fundamental Hindu doctrine, according to which there is no absolute distinction between individuals, since the atman dwells in the hearts of all beings. There is no religious sanction whatsoever to the concept of the caste system in Hinduism.

Swami Sivananda (The Divine Life Society, Rishikesh), in his commentary on Gita, Ch.18, verses 41, and 45 says: "Mankind is organized into the four castes and each man's life is divided into four stages, according to the nature of the Gunas (traits) and the degree of growth or evolution. This is the division of labour for which each caste is fitted according to its own nature. The duty prescribed is your sole support, each devoted to his own duty in accordance with his own nature or caste, and the highest service you can render to the Supreme is to carry it out wholeheartedly, without expectation of fruits, with the attitude of dedication to the Lord.

The caste system is, indeed, a splendid thing. It is quite flawless. But the defect came in from somewhere else. The classes gradually neglected their duties. The test of ability and character slowly vanished. Birth became the chief consideration in determining castes. All castes fell from their ideals and forgot all about their duties."

Varna-Not Racial Colour

Varna was conferred on the basis of the intrinsic nature of an individual, which is a combination of the three gunas. The term, 'Varna', has nothing to do with racial colour. It is related to the three 'gunas' or traits-white (sattva or sagacity), red (rajas or aggressiveness), and dark (tamas or ignorance) which all men and also all living beings possess, albeit in different proportions-varying from species to species, from man to man and even from sibling to sibling.

Alain Danielou has said: "That abusive caste practices were introduced when the administrative power ceased to be in Hindu hands, thus making the repression of abuses legally impossible. Such abuses as there are have been greatly exaggerated in order to justify Western domination and are normally quite local. In most of India, the caste system functions today as it always has; as a harmonious whole in which each is satisfied with his social lot, in which the freedom of each tribe, and religious group to live according to its customs, traditions, and convictions is respected as it is in no other country and no other form of society.

Manu Smrti: Not a Religious Book:

"The Seniority of Brahmans is from Sacred Knowledge, that of Kshatriyas from valour, that of Vaishyas from wealth in grain, but that of Sudras is from age alone." (Manu Smriti II, 155)

"Manu has declared that those Brahmans who are thieves, outcasts, eunuchs, or atheists are unworthy to partake of oblations offered to gods and ancestors." (Manu Smriti III, 150)

" A Brahmin who departs from the Rule of Noble Conduct, does not gain the fruit described in the Veda, but he who duly follows the Rule of Noble Conduct, will obtain the full reward." (Manu Smriti I,109)

" He who possesses faith may receive pure learning even from a man of lower caste, the highest law even from the lowest, and an excellent wife even from a base family." (Manu Smriti II, 238)

Manu Smriti which outlines the scheme of the four varnas (socioeconomic classes) and four ashramas (stages of life of the individual) refuses a provide for the fifth varna. The four classes are adequate to cover all the sections of the society. Manu Smriti is a sociological treatise and not a religious or theological work. It has never been held on par with the Vedas and has never been claimed to be a Holy Book whose authority is unquestionable.

Manu Smriti does not deal with the Absolute, a field specialized in by the Upanishads. Manu Smriti is as this-worldly as the Arthashastra is. Manu was also only a Codifier (Documenter of the then-existing codes) of the Caste System and was not to be interpreted as the creator of the Caste System.

"Only the British administrators and jurists who dominated the scene since 1757 found it expedient for their purposes to present it as a religious code binding all the Hindus. The original text of Manu Smriti has been tampered with is acknowledged by Sir William Jones who introduced it as the law book of the Hindus, as he agrees that ' it is accommodated to the improvements of a commercial age'. The extant text of Manu Smriti is a doctored version, doctored to benefit the commercial class of Britain which had sponsored the East India Company, the company for which he was serving as a judge at Calcutta."

Varnashrama Dharma, said to be the mainstay of the Hindu Social Order has no sanction in the Vedas.

In ancient India, these divisions were not based on birth but based on qualifications. According to the Bhagawad Gita this Aryan family system broke down in India over three thousand years ago at the time of Krishna. Hence after three thousand years this system of determining natural aptitude has degenerated into the caste system which resembles it now only in form.

Manu made it clear that superiority is not by birth but by Conduct. This Principle was further emphasized later by Maharishi Veda Vyasa in Mahabharata. Manu himself says that if there is anything in his Smriti which is not acceptable to the conscience of any person, that person should reject it and act according to his/her own conscience.

> *"For choosing your course of conduct at any time and place, keep in view the instructions given first in Sruti (Vedas), then in Smritis, Itihaas (History of great personalities) and finally you act according to your conscience." (Manu Smriti, 11, 6).*

> *"Just as a wooden toy elephant cannot be real elephant, and a stuffed deer cannot be a real deer, so, without studying scriptures and the Vedas and the development of intellect, a Brahmin by birth cannot be considered a Brahmin. " (Manu Smriti 11-157).*

Louis Francois Jacolliot (1837-1890), who worked in French India as a government official and was at one time President of the Court in Chandranagar, translated numerous Vedic hymns, the Manusmriti, and the Tamil work, Kural. His masterpiece, La Bible dans l'Inde, stirred a storm of controversy.

Manu-Hindu Law: The Hindu law were codified by Manu more than 3,000 years before the Christian era, copied by entire antiquity and notably by Rome, which alone has left us a written law-the code of Justanian, which has been adopted as the base of all modern legislations.

Jurisprudence: "Observe, enpassant, this striking coincidence with French law, that the Hindu wife, in default of her husband's authority may release from her incapacity, by authority of justice. " "The contract made by a man who is drunk, foolish, imbecile or grievously disordered in his mental condition...." Manu further adds; "What is held under comprehension-held by force is declared null."

Would not this be thought a mere commentary on the Code of Napoleon? Of 4-5,000 years after "How far is all this from those barbarous customs of first ages, when every question was solved by violence and force, and what admiration should we feel for a people who, at the epoch at which Biblical fall would date the world's creation, had already reached the extraordinary degree of civilization indicated by laws so simple and so practical."

Caste System and Code of Manu

The Hindus have been an intensely practical people. The magnificence of daring glimpses into the cosmos as their meditations or scientific investigations revealed to them, convinced them beyond doubt that the complexity of earthly existence could be reduced to some order and the march of human progress subjected to some form of control. They embraced in their researches such subjects as astronomy, physics, chemistry, biology, medicine, ethics, logic, psychology, aesthetics, politics, economics, sociology, and metaphysics. Indeed, in sociology alone, they have left us over twenty treatises; and the Code of Manu, the subject of the present study, is only one of them.

Manu, Manas, manava, all have the same philological root, man, to think. Manu's Code, therefore, is a treatise of social relations for human beings. It lays emphasis on reason, the thinking faculty (manas), in the ordering of man's social relations. It stands for a planned society. Manu's social theory is an art of life; it is a technique, not mere congeries of consistent concepts.

An individual's life is divided into four parts—1. studentship, 2. householding 3. partial retirement or hermitage, 4. and complete retirement. Correspondingly, there are four groups: 1. the manual worker, 2. the merchant, 3. the warrior, and 4. the teacher. A unity of function ties each stage of individual life to the corresponding group. This unity, which lays emphasis on harmonious relations, is the dharma, or the ethics of Manu. There are thus presented four social institutions: 1. the educational, 2. the family-economic, 3. the political, 4. and the religious.

Stable Human Societies

Alain Danielou says: "The Hindus assert that their social formula meets the requirements of man's individual and collective nature. The fact that the Hindu civilization has been able to survive over thousand of years, despite disorders caused by invasions, schisms, and internal wars, and has been capable of constant renewal, as demonstrated by one brilliant period after another, merits all our attention in the study of a social system whose longevity is unique in history."

Aryan Invasion Theory and Caste System

Guy Sorman visiting scholar at Hoover Institution at Stanford and the leader of new liberalism in France, writes: "The Invasion theory has today become the standard explanation for the caste system, though it came up only in the 19th century. Besides, all we have to attest the Aryan invasion is a specious interpretation of the Mahabharata, which is like searching the origins of European aristocracy in the works of Homer! In any case, it is doubtful whether a single invasion, which was more likely a slow infiltration of the North, could have succeeded in structuring so perfectly Indian society along ethnic lines for over three thousand years. Finally, in South India the caste system among the dark, skinned Dravidians is as rigid as it is in the North, though the Aryans in all probability never reached there.

The racial origin of caste hypothesis tells us little about India but it does tell us a great deal about the 19th century Westerners who invented the Aryan invasion theory. It was at the same time that Sieyes and Augustin Thierry claimed that the French nobility was of Germanic stock, whereas the lower classes were of Gallic origin; so the 1789 Revolution was a race war rather than a class war! It was also in the 19th century that appeared the myth of the Indo-Europeans being at the source of all Western civilization and for this we have to thank British authors who were taken up with evolutionist theory. Indian historians trained in Europe have fallen victim to this myth but that does not make it any more authentic. Later on, at the beginning of the 20th century, it became fashionable to support the Marxist theory which replaced race with class, though its premises were just as shaky."

Genetic Evidence of Indian Caste

The origins and affinities of the 1 billion people living on the subcontinent of India have long been contested.

This is owing, in part, to the many different waves of immigrants that have influenced the genetic structure of India. In the most recent of these waves, Indo-European-speaking people from West Eurasia entered India from the Northwest and diffused throughout the subcontinent. They purportedly admixed with or displaced indigenous Dravidic-speaking populations. Subsequently they may have established the Hindu caste system and placed themselves primarily in castes of higher rank.

To explore the impact of West Eurasians on contemporary Indian caste populations, we compared mtDNA (400 bp of hypervariable region 1 and 14 restriction site polymorphisms) and Y-chromosome (20 biallelic polymorphisms and 5 short tandem repeats) variation in 265 males from eight castes of different rank to 750 Africans, Asians, Europeans, and other Indians. For maternally inherited mtDNA, each caste is most similar to Asians. However, 20%-30% of Indian mtDNA haplotypes belong to West Eurasian haplogroups, and the frequency of these haplotypes is proportional to caste rank, the highest frequency of West Eurasian haplotypes being found in the upper castes.

In contrast, for paternally inherited Y-chromosome variation each caste is more similar to Europeans than to Asians. Moreover, the affinity to Europeans is proportionate to caste rank, the upper castes being most similar to Europeans, particularly East Europeans. These findings are consistent with greater West Eurasian male admixture with castes of higher rank. Nevertheless, the mitochondrial genome and the Y-chromosome each represents only a single haploid locus and is more susceptible to large stochastic variation, bottlenecks, and selective sweeps.

Thus, to increase the power of our analysis, we assayed 40 independent, biparentally inherited autosomal loci (1 LINE-1 and 39 Alu elements) in all of the caste and continental populations (600 individuals). Analysis of these data demonstrated that the upper castes have a higher affinity to Europeans than to Asians, and the upper castes are significantly more similar to Europeans than are the lower castes.

Collectively, all five datasets show a trend toward upper castes being more similar to Europeans, whereas lower castes are more similar to Asians. We conclude that Indian castes are most likely to be of proto-Asian origin with West Eurasian admixture resulting in rank-related and sex-specific differences in the genetic affinities of castes to Asians and Europeans.

Shared Indo-European languages (*i.e.*, Hindi and most European languages) suggested to linguists of the nineteenth and twentieth centuries that contemporary Hindu Indians are descendants of primarily West Eurasians who migrated from Europe, the Near East, Anatolia, and the Caucasus 3000–8000 years ago (Poliakov 1974; Renfrew 1989a,b). These nomadic migrants may have consolidated their power by admixing with native Dravidic-speaking (*e.g.*, Telugu) proto-Asian populations who controlled regional access to land, labour, and resources (Cavalli-Sforza et al. 1994), and subsequently established the Hindu caste hierarchy to legitimize and maintain this power (Poliakov 1974; Cavalli-Sforza et al. 1994).

It is plausible that these West Eurasian immigrants also appointed themselves to predominantly castes of higher rank. However, archaeological evidence of the diffusion of material culture from Western Eurasia into India has been limited (Shaffer 1982). Therefore, information on the genetic relationships of Indians to Europeans and Asians could contribute substantially to understanding the origins of Indian populations.

Previous genetic studies of Indian castes have failed to achieve a consensus on Indian origins and affinities. Various results have supported closer affinity of Indian castes either with Europeans or with Asians, and several factors underlie this inconsistency. First, erratic or limited sampling of populations has limited inferences about the relationships between caste and continental populations (*i.e.*, Africans, Asians, Europeans).

These relationships are further confounded by the wide geographic dispersal of caste populations. Genetic affinities among caste populations are, in part, inversely correlated with the geographic distance between them (Malhotra and Vasulu

1993), and it is likely that affinities between caste and continental populations are also geographically dependent (*e.g.*, different between North and South Indian caste populations).

Second, it has been suggested that castes of different rank may have originated from or admixed with different continental groups (Majumder and Mukherjee 1993). Third, the size of caste populations varies widely, and the effects of genetic drift on some small, geographically isolated castes may have been substantial. Fourth, most of the polymorphisms assayed over the last 30 years are indirect measurements of genetic variation (*e.g.*, ABO typing), have been sampled from only a few loci, and may not be selectively neutral. Finally, only rarely have systematic comparisons been made with continental populations using a large, uniform set of DNA polymorphisms (Majumder 1999).

To investigate the origin of contemporary castes, we compared the genetic affinities of caste populations of differing rank (*i.e.*, upper, middle, and lower) to worldwide populations. We analysed mtDNA (hypervariable region 1 [HVR1] sequence and 14 restrictionsite polymorphisms [RSPs]), Y-chromosome (5 shorttandem repeats [STRs] and 20 biallelic polymorphisms), and autosomal (1 LINE-1 and 39 Alu inserts) variation in 265 males from eight different Teluguspeaking caste populations from the state of Andhra Pradesh in South India (Bamshad et al. 1998). Comparisons were made to 400 individuals from tribal and Hindi-speaking caste and populations distributed across the Indian subcontinent (Mountain et al. 1995; Kivisild et al. 1999) and to 350 Africans, Asians, and Europeans (Jorde et al. 1995, 2000; Seielstad et al. 1999).

Results: Analysis of mtDNA Suggests a Proto-Asian Origin of Indians MtDNA HVR1 genetic distances between caste populations and Africans, Asians, and Europeans are significantly different from zero ($p < 0.001$) and reveal that, regardless of rank, each caste group is most closely related to Asians and is most dissimilar from Africans. The genetic distances from major continental populations (*e.g.*, Europeans) differ among the three caste groups, and the comparison reveals an intriguing pattern. As one moves from lower to upper castes, the distance from Asians becomes progressively larger. The distance between Europeans and lower castes is larger than the distance between Europeans and upper castes, but the distance between Europeans and middle castes is smaller than the upper caste-European distance. These trends are the same whether the Kshatriya and Vysya are included in the upper castes, the middle castes, or excluded from the analysis. This may be owing, in part, to the small sample size (n = 10) of each of these castes. Among the upper castes the genetic distance between Brahmins and Europeans (0.10) is smaller than that between either the Kshatriya and Europeans (0.12) or the Vysya and Europeans (0.16). Assuming that contemporary Europeans reflect West Eurasian affinities, these data indicate that the amount of West Eurasian admixture with Indian populations may have been proportionate to caste rank.

Conventional estimates of the standard errors of genetic distances assume that polymorphic sites are independent of each other, that is, unlinked. Because mtDNA polymorphisms are in complete linkage disequilibrium (as are polymorphisms on the nonrecom-bining portions of the Y-chromosome), this assumption is violated. Alternatively, the mtDNA genome can be treated as a single locus with multiple haplotypes.

However, even if this assumption is made, mtDNA distances do not differ significantly from one another even at the level of the three major continental populations (Nei and Livshits 1989), the standard errors being greater than the genetic distances. Considering that the distances between castes and continental populations are less than those between different continental populations, the estimated mtDNA genetic distances between upper castes and Europeans versus lower castes and Europeans would not be significantly different from each other. Therefore, to resolve further the relationships of Europeans and Asians to contemporary Indian populations, we defined the identities of specific mtDNA restriction-site haplotypes. The presence of the mtDNA restriction sites

Ddei 10,394 and Alui 10,397 defines a haplogroup (a group of haplotypes that share some sequence variants), M, that was originally identified in populations that migrated from mainland

Asia to Southeast Asia and Australia (Ballinger et al. 1992; Chen et al. 1995; Passarino et al. 1996) and is found at much lower frequency in European and African populations. Most of the common haplotypes found in Telugu-and Hindi-speaking caste populations belong to haplogroup M and do not differentiate into language-specific clusters in a phylogenetic reconstruction. Furthermore, these Indian haplogroup-M-haplotypes are distinct from those found in other Asian populations and indicate the existence of Indian-specific subsets of haplogroup M (*e.g.*, M3). As expected if the lower castes are more similar to Asians than to Europeans, and the upper castes are more similar to Europeans than to Asians, the frequencies of M and M3 haplotypes are inversely proportional to caste rank.

Of the non-Asian mtDNA haplotypes found in Indian populations, most are of West Eurasian origin. However, most of these Indian West-Eurasian haplotypes belong to an Indian-specific subset of haplogroup U, that is, U2i (Kivisild et al. 1999), the oldest and second most common mtDNA haplogroup found in Europe (Torroni et al. 1994). In agreement with the HVR1 results, the frequency of West Eurasian mtDNA haplotypes is significantly higher in upper castes than in lower castes ($p < 0.05$), the frequency of U2i haplotypes increasing as one moves from lower to higher castes. In addition, the frequency of mtDNA haplogroups with a more recent coalescence estimate (*i.e.*, H, I, J, K, T) was fivefold higher in upper castes (6.8%) than in lower castes (1.4%). These haplotypes are derivatives of haplogroups found throughout Europe (Richards et al. 1998), the Middle East (Di Rienzo and Wilson 1991), and to a lesser extent Central Asia (Comas et al. 1998). Collectively, the mtDNA haplotype evidence indicate that contemporary Indian mtDNA evolved largely from proto-Asian ancestors with Western Eurasian admixture accounting for 20%-30% of mtDNA haplotypes.

Y-Chromosome Variation

Confirms: Indo-European Admixture Genetic distances estimated from Y-chromosome STR polymorphisms differer significantly from zero ($p < 0.001$) and reveal a distinctly different pattern of population relationships. In contrast to the mtDNA distances, the Y-chromosome STR data do not demonstrate a closer affinity to Asians for each caste group. Upper castes are more similar to Europeans than to Asians, middle castes are equidistant from the two groups, and lower castes are most similar to Asians. The genetic distance between caste populations and Africans is progressively larger moving from lower to middle to upper caste groups.

Genetic distances estimated from Y-chromosome biallelic polymorphisms differ significantly from zero ($p < 0.05$), and the patterns differ from the mtDNA results even more strikingly than the Y-chromosome STRs. For Y-chromosome biallelic polymorphism data, each caste group is more similar to Europeans, and as one moves from lower to middle to higher castes the genetic distance to Europeans diminishes progressively.

This pattern is further accentuated by separating the European population into Northern, Southern, and Eastern Europeans; each caste group is most closely related to Eastern Europeans. Moreover, the genetic distance between upper castes and Eastern Europeans is approximately half the distance between Eastern Europeans and middle or lower castes. These results suggest that Indian Y-chromosomes, particularly upper caste Y-chromosomes, are more similar to European than to Asian Y-chromosomes. This underscores the close affinities between Hindu Indian and Indo-European Y-chromosomes based on a previously reported analysis of three Y-chromosome polymorphisms (Quintana-Murci et al. 1999b).

Overall, these results indicate that the affinities of Indians to continental populations varies according to caste rank and depends on whether mtDNA or Ychromosome data are analysed. However, conclusions drawn from these data are limited because mtDNA and the Y-chromosome is each effectively a single haploid locus and is more sensitive to genetic drift, bottlenecks, and selective sweeps compared to autosomal loci.

These limitations of our analysis can be overcome, in part, by analyzing a larger set of independent autosomal loci.

Consequently, we assayed 1 LINE-1 and 39 unlinked Alu polymorphisms.

Affinities to Europeans and Asians Stratified

Genetic distances estimated from autosomal Alu elements correspond to caste rank, the genetic distance between the upper and lower castes being more than 2.5 times larger than the distance between upper and middle or middle and lower castes (upper to middle, 0.0069; upper to lower, 0.018; middle to lower, 0.0071). These trends are the same whether the Kshatriya and Vysya are included in the upper castes, the middle castes, or excluded from the analysis (data not shown). Furthermore, a neighbour-joining network of genetic distances between separate castes clearly differentiates castes of different rank into separate clusters.

This is similar to the relationship between genetic distances and caste rank estimated from mtDNA (Bamshad et al. 1998). It is important to note, however, that the autosomal genetic distances are estimated from 40 independent loci. This afforded us the opportunity to test the statistical significance of the correspondence between genetic distance and caste status. The Mantel correlation between interindividual genetic distances and distances based on social rank was low but highly significant for individuals ranked into upper, middle, and lower groups ($r = 0.08$; $p < 0.001$) and into eight separate castes ($r = 0.07$; $p < 0.001$). Given the resolving power of this autosomal dataset, we next tested whether we could reconcile the results of the analysis of mtDNA and Ychromosome markers in castes and continental populations.

Genotypic differentiation was significantly different from zero ($p < 0.0001$) between each pair of caste populations and between each caste and continental population. Similar to the results of both the mtDNA and Y-chromosome analyses, the distance between upper castes and European populations is smaller than the distance between lower castes and Europeans. However, in contrast to the mtDNA results but similar to the Ychromosome results, the affinity between upper castes and Europeans is higher than that of upper castes and Asians. If the Kshatriya and Vysya are excluded from the analysis or included in the middle castes, the genetic distance between the upper caste (Brahmins) and Europeans remains smaller than the distance between the lower castes and Europeans and the distance between upper castes and Asians. Analysis of each caste separately reveals that the genetic distance between the Brahmins and Europeans (0.013) is less than the distance between Europeans and Kshatriya (0.030) or Vysya (0.020). Nevertheless, each separate upper caste is more similar to Europeans than to Asians.

Because historical evidence suggests greater affinity between upper castes and Europeans than between lower castes and Europeans (Balakrishnan 1978, 1982; Cavalli-Sforza et al. 1994), it is appropriate to use a one-tailed test of the difference between the corresponding genetic distances.

The 90% confidence limits of Nei's standard distances estimated between upper castes and Europeans (0.006-0.016) versus lower castes and Europeans (0.017-0.037) do not overlap, indicating statistical significance at the 0.05 level. Significance at 0.05 is not achieved if the Kshatriya and Vysya are excluded. These results offer statistical support for differences in the genetic affinity of Europeans to caste populations of differing rank, with greater European affinity to upper castes than to lower castes.

Discussion: Previous genetic studies have found evidence to support either a European or an Asian origin of Indian caste populations, with occasional indications of admixture with African or proto-Australoid populations (Chen et al. 1995; Mountain et al. 1995; Bamshad et al. 1996, 1997; Majumder et al. 1999; Quintana-Murci et al. 1999a).

Our results demonstrate that for biparentally inherited autosomal markers, genetic distances between upper, middle, and lower castes are significantly correlated with rank; upper castes are more similar to Europeans than to Asians; and upper castes are significantly more similar to Europeans than are lower castes. This result appears to be owing to the amalgamation of two different patterns of sex-specific genetic variation.

The majority of Indian mtDNA restriction-site haplotypes belong to Indian-specific subsets (*e.g.*, M3) of a predominantly Asian haplogroup M, although a substantial minority of mtDNA restriction site haplotypes belong to West Eurasian haplogroups. A higher proportion of proto-Asian mtDNA restriction-site haplotypes is found in lower castes compared to middle or upper castes, whereas the frequency of West Eurasian haplotypes is positively correlated with caste rank, that is, is highest in the upper castes.

For Y-chromosome STR variation the upper castes exhibit greatest similarity with Europeans, whereas the lower caste groups are most similar to Asians. For Y-biallelic polymorphism variation, each caste group is more similar to Europeans than to Asians, and the affinity to Europeans is proportional to caste rank, that is, is highest in the upper castes.

Importantly, five different types of data (mtDNA HVR1 sequence, mtDNA RSPs, Y-chromosome STRs, Ychromosome biallelic polymorphisms, and autosomal Alu polymorphisms) support the same general pattern: relatively smaller genetic distances from European populations as one moves from lower to middle to upper caste populations. Genetic distances from Asian populations become larger as one moves from lower to middle to upper caste populations. It is especially noteworthy that the analysis of Y biallelic polymorphisms, which involved an independent set of comparative Asian, European, and African populations, again indicated the same pattern. Additional support is offered by the fact that the autosomal polymorphisms yielded a statistically significant difference between the uppercaste-European and lower-caste-European genetic distances.

With additional loci, other differences (*e.g.*, the distances between different caste groups and Asians) may also reach statistical significance. The most likely explanation for these findings, and the one most consistent with archaeological data, is that contemporary Hindu Indians are of proto-Asian origin with West Eurasian admixture. However, admixture with West Eurasian males was greater than admixture with West Eurasian females, resulting in a higher affinity to European Y-chromosomes. This supports an earlier suggestion of Passarino et al. (1996), which was based on a comparison of mtDNA and blood group results. Furthermore, the degree of West Eurasian admixture was proportional to caste rank.

This explanation is consistent with either the hypothesis that proportionately more West Eurasians became members of the upper castes at the inception of the caste hierarchy or that social stratification preceded the West Eurasian incursion and that West Eurasians tended to insert themselves into higher-ranking positions. One consequence is that shared Indo-European languages may not reflect a common origin of Europeans and most Indians, but rather underscores the transfer of language mediated by contact between West Eurasians and native proto-Indians.

West Eurasian admixture in Indian populations may have been the result of more than one wave of immigration into India. Kivisild et al. (1999) determined the coalescence (50,000 years before present) of the Indian-specific subset of the West Eurasian haplotypes (*i.e.*, U2i) and suggested that West Eurasian admixture may have been much older than the purported Dravidian and Indo-European incursions. Our analysis of Indian mtDNA restriction-site haplotypes that do not belong to the U2i subset of West Eurasian haplotypes (*i.e.*, H, I, J, K, T) is consistent with more recent West Eurasian admixture.

It is also possible that haplotypes with an older coalescence were introduced by Dravidians, whereas haplotypes with a more recent coalescence belonged to Indo-Europeans. This hypothesis can be tested by a more detailed comparison to West Eurasian mtDNA haplotypes from Iran, Anatolia, and the Caucasus. Alternatively, the coalescence dates of these haplotypes may predate the entry of West Eurasians populations into India. Regardless of their origin, West Eurasian admixture resulted in rank-related differences in the genetic affinities of castes to Europeans and Asians. Furthermore, the frequency of West Eurasian haplotypes in the founding middle and upper castes may be underestimated because of the upward social mobility of women from lower castes (Bamshad et al. 1998).

These women were presumably more likely to introduce proto-Asian mtDNA haplotypes into the middle and upper castes.

Our analysis of 40 autosomal markers indicates clearly that the upper castes have a higher affinity to Europeans than to Asians. The high affinity of caste Y-chromosomes with those of Europeans suggests that the majority of immigrating West Eurasians may have been males. As might be expected if West Eurasian males appropriated the highest positions in the caste system, the upper caste group exhibits a lower genetic distance to Europeans than the middle or lower castes.

This is underscored by the observation that the Kshatriya (an upper caste), whose members served as warriors, are closer to Europeans than any other caste (data not shown). Furthermore, the 32-bp deletion polymorphism in CC chemokine receptor 5, whose frequency peaks in populations of Eastern Europe, is found only in two Brahmin males (M. Bamshad and S.K. Ahuja, unpubl.). The stratification of Y-chromosome distances with Europeans could also be caused by malespecific gene flow among caste populations of different rank. However, we and others have demonstrated that there is little sharing of Y-chromosome haplotypes among castes of different rank (Bamshad et al. 1998; Bhattacharyya et al. 1999).

The affinity of caste populations to Europeans is more apparent for Y-chromosome biallelic polymorphisms than Y-chromosome STRs. This could be attributed to the use of different European populations in comparisons using STRs and biallelic polymorphisms.

Alternatively, it may reflect, in part, the effects of high mutation rates for the Y-chromosome STRs, which would tend to obscure relationships between caste and continental populations. A lack of consistent clustering at the continental level has been observed in several studies of Y-chromosome STRs (Deka et al. 1996; Torroni et al. 1996; de Knijff et al. 1997). The autosomal Alu and biallelic Y-chromosome polymorphisms, in contrast, have a slower rate of drift than Ychromosome STRs because of a higher effective population size, and their mutation rate is very low. Thus, the Y-chromosome biallelic polymorphisms and autosomal Alu markers may serve as more stable markers of worldwide population affinities.

Our analysis may help to explain why estimates of the affinities of caste groups to worldwide populations have varied so widely among different studies. Analyses of recent caste history based on only mtDNA or Y-chromosome polymorphisms clearly would suggest that castes are more closely related to Asians or to Europeans, respectively. Furthermore, we attempted to minimize the confounding effect of geographic differences between populations by sampling from a highly restricted region of South India. Because of the ubiquity of the caste system in India's history, it is reasonable to predict similar patterns in caste populations living in other areas. Indeed, any genetic result becomes more compelling when it is replicated in other populations. Therefore, comparable studies in caste populations from other regions of India must be completed to test the generality of these results.

The dispersal and subsequent growth of Indian populations since the Neolithic Age is one of the most important events to shape the history of South Asia.

However, the origin and dispersal route of the aboriginal inhabitants of the Indian subcontinent is unclear.

Our findings suggest a proto-Asian origin of the Indian-specific haplogroup-M-haplotypes. Haplogroup-M-haplotypes are also found at appreciable frequencies in some East African populations-18% of Ethiopians (Quintana-Murci et al. 1999a) and 16% of Kenyans (M. Bamshad and L.B. Jonde, unpubl.). A comparison of haplogroup-M-haplotypes from East Africa and India has suggested that this southern route may have been one of the original dispersal pathways of anatomically modern humans out of Africa (Quintana-Murci et al. 1999a). Together, these data support our previous suggestion (Kivisild et al. 1999) that India may have been inhabited by at least two successive late Pleistocene migrations, consistent with the hypothesis of Lahr and Foley (1994). It also adds to the growing evidence that the subcontinent of India has been a major corridor for the migration of people between Africa, Western Asia, and Southeast Asia (Cavalli-Sforza et al. 1994).

It should be emphasized that the DNA variation studied here is thought to be selectively neutral and thus represents only the effects of population history.

These results permit no inferences about phenotypic differences between populations. In addition, alleles and haplotypes are shared by different caste populations, reflecting a shared history. Indeed, these findings underscore the longstanding appreciation that the distribution of genetic polymorphisms in India is highly complex. Further investigation of the spread of anatomically modern humans throughout South Asia will need to consider that such complex patterns may be the norm rather than the exception.

Methods

Sample Collection: All studies of South Indian populations were performed with the approval of the Institutional Review Board of the University of Utah, Andhra University, and the government of India. Adult males living in the district of Visakhapatnam, Andhra Pradesh, were questioned about their caste affiliations and surnames and the birthplaces of their parents. Those who were unrelated to any other subject by at least three generations were considered eligible to participate.

We classified caste populations based upon the traditional ranking of these castes by varna, occupation, and socioeconomic status. According to various Sanskrit texts, Hindu populations were partitioned originally into four categories or varna: Brahmin, Kshatriya, Vysya, and Sudra (Tambia 1973; Elder 1996).

Those in each varna performed occupations assigned to their category. Brahmins were priests; Kshatriya were warriors; Vysya were traders; and Sudra were to serve the three other varna (Tambia 1973; Elder 1996). Each varna was assigned a status; Brahmin, Kshatriya, and Vysya were considered of higher status than the Sudra because the Brahmin, Kshatriya, and Vaishya are considered the twice-born Bamshad et al. castes and are differentiated from all other castes in the caste hierarchy. This is the rationale behind classifying them as the upper group of castes (Tambia 1973).

The Kapu and the Yadava are called once-born castes that have traditionally been classified in the Sudra, the lowest of the original four varna. However, the status of the Sudra was actually higher than that of a fifth varna, the Panchama. This fifth varna was added at a later date to include the so-called untouchables, who were excluded from the other four varna (Elder 1996). The untouchable varna includes the Mala and Madiga. The position of the Relli in the caste hierarchy is somewhat ambiguous, but they have usually been classified in the lower caste group. Therefore, prior to the collection of any data, males from eight different Telugu-speaking castes (n = 265) were ranked into upper (Niyogi and Vydiki Brahmin, Kshatriya, Vyshya [n = 80]), middle (Telega and Turpu Kapu, Yadava [n = 111]), and lower (Relli, Madiga, Mala [n = 74]) groups (Bamshad et al. 1998). This ranking has been used by previous investigators (Krishnan and Reddy 1994).

After obtaining informed consent, 8 mL of whole blood or 5 plucked scalp hairs were collected from each participant. Extractions were performed at Andhra University using established methods (Bell et al. 1981).

DNA Polymorphisms

The mtDNA data consisted of 68, 116, and 73 HVR1 sequences and 79, 159, and 72 restriction-site haplotypes from largely the same individuals in upper, middle, and lower castes, respectively. These data were compared to data from 143 Africans (15 Sotho-Tswana, 7 Tsonga, 14 Nguni, 24 San, 5 Biaka Pygmies, 33 Mbuti Pygmies, 9 Alur, 18 Hema, and 18 Nande), 78 Asians (12 Cambodians, 17 Chinese, 19 Japanese, 6 Malay, 9 Vietnamese, 2 Koreans, and 13 Asians of mixed ancestry), and 99 Europeans (20 unrelated males of the French CEPH kindreds, 69 unrelated Utah males of Northern European descent, and 10 Poles) (Jorde et al. 1995, 1997).

In addition to our samples, the phylogenetic analyses also included data from 98 published HVR1 sequences from two castes (48 Havlik and 43 Mukri), and a tribal population (7 Kadar) living in south-western India (Mountain et al. 1995) and restriction-site haplotypes from one caste (62 Lobana) from

Northern India, three tribal populations from Northern (12 Tharu and 18 Bhoksa) and Southern (86 Lambadi) India, and 122 individuals from various caste populations in Uttar Pradesh (Kivisild et al. 1999). Phylogenetic relationships of HVR1 sequences assigned to haplogroupMwere estimated for Indians (this study), Turks (this study), Central Asian populations (Comas et al. 1998), Mongolians (Kolman et al. 1996), Chinese (Horai et al. 1996), and Japanese (Horai et al. 1996; Seo et al. 1998).

The mtDNA HVR1 Sequence was Determined by Fluorescent: Sanger sequencing using a Dye terminator cycle sequencing kit (Applied Biosystems) according to the manufacturer's specifications (Bamshad et al. 1998). Sequencing reactions were resolved on an ABI 377 automated DNA sequencer, and sequence data were analysed using ABI DNA analysis software and SEQUENCHER software (Genecodes). To identify mtDNA haplotypes and haplogroups (a group of haplotypes that share some sequence variants), major continent-specific genotypes (Torroni et al. 1994, 1996; Wallace 1995) for the following polymorphic mtDNA restriction sites were determined: Hpai 3592, Ddei 10394, Alui 10397, Alui 13262, Bamhi 13366, Alui 5176, Haeiii 4830, Alui 7025, Hinfi 12308, Acci 14465, Avaii 8249, Alui 10032, Bstoi 13704, and Haeii 9052.

Y-Chromosome and Autosomal Polymorphisms

Y-chromosome-specific STRs (DYS 19, DYS 288, DYS 388, DYS 389A, DYS 390) were amplified using published conditions (Hammer et al. 1998). PCR products were separated on an ABI 377 automated sequencer and scored using ABI Genotyper software. Y-chromosome STR data were collected from 622 males including 280 South Indians, 200 Africans (Seielstad et al. 1999; this study), 40 Asians, and 102 Europeans. Autosomal data were collected from 608 individuals including 265 South Indians, 155 Africans, 70 Asians, and 118 Europeans.

The Y-chromosome-specific biallelic polymorphisms tested included: DYS188792, DYS194469, DYS 211105, DYS 221136, DYS 257108, DYS 87, M3, M4, M9, M12, M15, SRY 4064, SRY

10831.1, SRY 10831.2, p12f2, PN1, PN2, PN3, RPS 4Y711, and Tat (Hammer and Horai 1995; Hammer et al. 1997, 1998, 2000; Underhill et al. 1997; Zerjal et al. 1997; Karafet et al. 1999). All individuals tested negative for the Y Alu insert (DYS287). A complete description of the Ychromosome STR loci can be found in Kayser et al. (1997).

For the Y-chromosome biallelic dataset, comparisons were made to a different set of worldwide populations including: East Asians from Japan, Korea, China, and Vietnam (n = 460); Western Europeans from Britain and Germany (n = 77); Southern Europeans from Italy and Greece (n = 148); and Eastern Europeans from Russia and Romania (n = 102) (M.F. Hammer, unpubl.). The complete dataset of Indians consisted of 55 Brahmin, 111 Yadava and Kapu, and 74 Relli, Mala, and Madiga.

Statistical Analysis

Genetic distances for Y-chromosome STRs were estimated using the method of Shriver et al. (1995), which assumes a stepwise mutation model. Genetic distances for mitochondrial and autosomal markers were calculated as pairwise FST distances, using the ARLEQUIN package (Schneider et al. 1997).

For autosomal polymorphisms, Nei's standard distances and their standard errors were estimated using DISPAN; and 90% confidence intervals were estimated by multiplying the standard error by 1.65. The significance of the FST distances between populations was estimated by generating a null distribution of pairwise FST distances by permuting haplotypes between populations. The p-value of the test is the proportion of permutations leading to an FST value larger than or equal to the observed one. Genotypic differentiation was estimated using GENEPOP (Raymond and Rousset 1995) vers. 3.2. The null hypothesis tested is that there is a random distribution of K different haplotypes among r populations.

Estimates of significance for the correlation between interindividual caste rank differences and interindividual autosomal genetic distances were made by forming two n-n matrices, where n is the number of individuals. For the first matrix, interindividual genetic distances were based on the proportion of Alu insertions/deletions shared by each pair of individuals. To form the second matrix, each individual was assigned a score according to his rank in the caste hierarchy for caste groups (*i.e.*, upper caste = 1, middle caste = 2, lower caste = 3) and also for separate castes (*i.e.*, Brahmin = 1, Kshatriya = 2, Vyshya = 3, Kapu = 4, Yadava = 5, Relli = 6, Mala = 7, and Madiga = 8). An interindividual matrix of score distances was formed by comparing the absolute value of the difference between the scores of each pair of individuals. The matrix of genetic distances was compared to 10,000 permuted matrices of score distances using a Mantel matrix comparison test (Mantel 1967).

To illustrate phylogenetic relationships we constructed reduced median (Bandelt et al. 1995) and neighbour-joining networks (Felsenstein 1989). Coalescence times were calculated as in Forster et al. (1996), using the estimator, which is the average transitional distance from the founder haplotype.

Acknowledgments: We thank all participants, the faculty and staff of Andhra University for their discussion and technical assistance, as well as Henry Harpending for comments and criticisms. We acknowledge the contributions of an anonymous reviewer who suggested that the Kshatriya and Vyshya be analysed separately from the other upper castes. Genetic distances between STRs were estimated by the program DISTNEW, kindly provided by L. Jin. This work was supported by NSF SBR-9514733, SBR-9700729, SBR-9818215, NIH grants GM-59290 and PHS MO1-00064, the Estonian Science Fund (1669 and 2887), and the Newcastle University small grants committee. The publication costs of this article were defrayed in part by payment of page charges. This article must therefore be hereby marked "advertisement" in accordance with 18 USC section 1734 solely to indicate this fact.

5

Caste and the Woman

Hindu Family Dharma

Hindu value system placed very high degree of importance to morality where a woman does not accept the seed form anyone other than her husband. We are talking of normal circumstances of life. We speak of rules not exceptions!

Family Structure and Allocation of Powers and Responsibilities: Each family would have a head known as Karta whose decision would be final in case of family disputes and disagreements. This authority would be vested in the Karta with the responsibility to be just and fair to all in the family, and not to base crucial decisions on personal preferences. In all his visible judgments and decisions, he would be expected to demonstrate justice and fairness.

Children of the family would grow up 'learning to value' these qualities of justice and fairness. This process of living through just and fair dealings, would inculcate those qualities in them, through the course of their growing up process.

This was a living reality of Hindu social life.

This was a living reality of Hindu social life or else, different visitors from different nations over different centuries would not have mentioned so consistently of this quality among Hindus.

Now, it is quite true that during the two thousand years which precede the time of Mahmud of Ghazni, Bhaarat Varsh has had but few foreign visitors, and few foreign critics; still it is extremely strange that whenever, either in Greek, or in Chinese, or in Persian, or in Arab writings, we meet any attempts at describing the distinguishing features in the national character of the Bhartiyas (*Hindus), regard for truth and justice should always be mentioned first. Max Muller, p 50

Hindu Joint Family Structure of Earlier Times and its Strengths: Returning to the Hindu family structure of earlier days, Karta would normally be the able-bodied able-minded eldest male member of the family. Position of authority and responsibility would be distributed in a hierarchical manner in the sense that elder the member greater the authority coupled with greater responsibility. Younger members would be groomed on the same pattern to learn to assume the authority as well as discharge corresponding responsibility, as they would grow up in the hierarchy.

The respect for the elders would be an unwritten law, and it would be expected of all to observe it without any reservation. With that elders would have the equal amount of responsibility to stay worthy of such respect by their thoughts and actions. This would be the balancing factor for maintaining necessary equilibrium in the family.

Adult male members of the family would have the responsibility of earning for the family to meet its needs, and to provide shelter and protection to the female members and children of the family. Female members would have the responsibility of taking care of the in-house needs of male members of family, and raising the kids in line with the culture and traditions of the family. Elder female members of the family would have the responsibility of grooming up the younger female members of the family in the desired direction.

Each new generation would learn the family values from their mothers and grandmothers, and in this manner the female members of the family would play the crucial role through the formative years of growing children. Spirituality would be an essential part of the family values, and women folk would be the custodian and deliverer of these values to each next generation through their growing up process.

Single spouse system and fidelity would be the norm. Exceptions would be found in the context of political marriages where a king would offer his daughter to another king and thus, the two ruling families would unite and not be threat to each other.

Such marriages would primarily be conducted for maintaining power-balance and political equilibrium. These would be exceptions not rule, and we have references to many kings having only one wife. How Hindu family structure changed so drastically that now we hardly see any evidence of our earlier system.

The whole system, however, changed after brutal onslaught of Islam and its direct interference in Hindu way of family life through forced conversions and forced marriages of Hindu girls and Hindu women into Muslim powerful families. This is when family values started deteriorating substantially though it did preserve a lot of it, as we can see from the testimonies of Sir Thomas Munro as presented below, even after thousand years of inhumane oppression that Max Muller called an inferno and wondered "how any nation could have survived such an inferno without being turned into devils themselves."

If a good system of agriculture, unrivalled manufacturing skill, a capacity to produce whatever can contribute to either convenience or luxury, schools established in every village for teaching, reading, writing, and arithmetic, the general practice of hospitality and charity amongst each other, and above all, a treatment of the female sex full of confidence, respect, and delicacy, are among the signs which denote a civilized people- then the Hindus are not inferior to the nations of Europe, and if civilization is to become an article of trade between England and Bhaarat Varsh, I am convinced that England will gain by the import cargo. Sir Thomas Munro, quoted in Mill's History, vol. i. p. 371, re-quoted by Max Muller, p 57 p 231

The True Culprits have remained unidentified all along. There was so much of beauty left even until early 19th century that the eminent Governor of the then Madras Presidency wrote:

If civilization is to become an article of trade between England and Bhaarat Varsh, I am convinced that England will gain by the import cargo.

This would mean that real downfall has occurred during past 170 years. All factors remaining constant the only variable has been Christian English education system forcibly imposed on the Hindus by systematic elimination of ancient Hindu education system [documentary evidence in Hidden face of Christianity].

Hindu Family Values were totally transformed by the Christian English Education system, which was predominantly guided by the values propagated by Jesus Christ in the Christian Bible.

Oxford Dictionary p 1249, p 792, p 1143 New Testament is the second part of the Christian Bible; Gospel is the record of Christ's life and teachings in the first four books of the New Testament; St. Matthew was an Apostle, and the author of the first Gospel; p 1099 St. Luke was an evangelist, and the author of the third Gospel; p 1928, p 77 St. Thomas was an Apostle; Each of the twelve chief disciples of Jesus Christ is an Apostle.

Christian Bible New Testament Matthew 10:34 Think not that I am come to send peace on earth: I came not to send peace, but a sword. 10:35 For I am come to set a man at variance against his father, and the daughter against the mother, and the daughter in law against her mother in law. 10:36 And a man's foe shall be they of his own household. 10:37 He that loveth father or mother more than me is not worthy of me. 12: 30 He that is not with me is against me.

Christian Bible New Testament Luke 12:51 Suppose ye that I am come to give peace on earth? I tell you, Nay; but rather division: 12:52 For from henceforth there shall be five in one house divided, three against two, and two against three. 12:53 The father shall be divided against the son, and the son against the father; the mother against the daughter, and the daughter against the mother; the mother in law against her daughter in law, and the daughter in law against her mother in law. 14:26 If any man come to me, and hate not his father, and mother, and wife, and children, and brethren, and sisters, yea, and his own life also, he cannot be my disciple. [Nay a negative answer Oxford Dictionary p 1237]

Gospel of Thomas 16 Jesus said: Perhaps men think that I came to cast peace on the world; and they do not know that I came to cast division upon earth, fire, sword, war. For five will be in a house; there will be three against two and two against three, the father against the son and the son against the father. And they will stand because they are single ones. 56 Jesus said: He who will not hate his father and his mother cannot be my disciple. And he who will not hate his brothers and sisters, and carry his cross as I have, will not become worthy of me. [Gospel of Thomas as quoted in The Myth of Saint Thomas and Mylapore Shiva Temple, p 76 n]

To understand Jesus's agenda, as documented in the pages of Christian Bible, you may want to study Christianity in a different Light. Christian missionary educators taught the Hindus for past six generations and media experts created the image in the minds of the Hindus that ancient Hindu Joint Family structure was essentially an evil social structure. This paved the way for promoting Split Family structure which has now been refined to such levels that gradually Single Parent system is becoming the norm in the Christian World that we mistakenly identify as Western world, and aping them faithfully we too are rapidly following their footsteps.

Marriages under Hindu Joint Family System

Marriage was one of the most significant aspects of Family Dharm. Marriage was not considered simply as union of two bodies. Marriage was a significant social event. It was union of two families and family traditions.

Marriages were decided with great care. Several aspects were considered. Not only boy and girl were important, but their parents were also important; so were family lineage, parental characters, parental nature, their values, their traditions, their health, their history and so many things.

Today boy and girl argue, why we need to look at parents, and what character and values they represent; we do not have to marry parents, we have to marry each other. Fine as it sounds, and nice as it feels, we tend to forget 'science' that we are so proud of, which has started understanding a little bit of the relevance of genes in human behavioural pattern.

The hereditary attributes play their role in the long run and we find these lovebirds start splitting after a while. Few years ago, I looked at divorce rates in North America exceeding 50%, while these statistics did not tell us the full story, for they covered only those who were legally married, and such couples often find separation and divorce process pretty demanding, considering future of children involved and therefore, not all broken marriages result in legal divorce.

A very large segment of married couple in North America (I speak of Canada, and assume it would be same in USA) are those called common-law where the boy and girl live together like husband and wife, have children, file tax returns as common-law spouses, for most purposes they are like married couple except they are not legally married.

Most of them are youngsters who have not yet planned children, and these marriages break fairly easy as compared to legal marriages, for all they need is to split, and start living separate. These are high ratio cases. Thus, if we were to take these into account, then total divorces (where divorce would mean essentially all failed marriages), would probably exceed 75%. What a great system it is that does not stand the test of time, that does not stand the test of success in the desired venture that fails and fails, and finally gets reduced to multiple experiments with life! This, we call modern social structure, and we gloat at its supposedly advanced nature.

There is lot to learn from the systems of olden days that we look down upon thinking we have progressed! Have we? Except that we satisfy our ego by consoling ourselves with such inflated self-estimates! The Secret of Stable Hindu marriages of yesteryears—a meticulous system of mathematics applied to human lives.

We may have occasionally heard about extraordinary accomplishments of Hindu mathematics. The Christian World, however, prefers to attribute them to the Greeks and (pre-Islamic) Arabs who basically imported the knowledge from the Hindus and then popularized with the people of Europe.

The foundation of Family Dharm was on the premises of the institution of marriage. Arranged marriages demonstrated great stability and reflected high success rate.

This was ensured by a meticulous system of mathematics applied to human lives. Based on time and place of birth of a human being, it could calculate with fair amount of accuracy the life span of the individual. This helped match-making in a manner that one of the spouses does not have to live very long without the other. The system could calculate the ego development of the marrying partners. This helped match-making with due caution to conflicting egos between the boy and the girl in consideration.

The system could calculate with fair amount of accuracy the degree of magnetic control or amenability either spouse will have on the other. This helped match-making with a view to harmony between the two. The system could calculate with considerable accuracy the sexual compatibility between the boy and girl in question. This helped match-making with regard to this very essential factor in a satisfying marriage.

The system considered sexual compatibility in physical as well as emotional context. It may be difficult for modern people to visualize that a mathematical system could be capable of ascertaining such details without reference to medical and psychological systems.

Well, that difficulty in perception is natural because modern education system has not tried to evolve mathematical modules applied to human lives. It has not tried so because the modern Christian education system is based on an inflated ego that it has nothing to learn from ancient Hindu systems. More significantly, the modern education system is based on knowledge base of the Christian World, which would not want to entertain the thought that Hindu world could have had better developed modules for social, economical, judicial and other processes.

Returning to the mathematical system we have been referring to, it had developed the capability of determining the psychological dispositions of the intended couple. This helped in (a) ascertaining mental qualities and (b) estimating likely affection for each other, this being very significant element in matchmaking. Then the system calculated the temperament and character of the couple concerned where compatibility of temperament was looked at for a satisfactory marriage union.

Finally, system looked at nervous energy indicating the physiological and to certain extent hereditary factors. This helped matchmaking with a view to the children that would be borne of such couple, for a marriage was not meant only for the present generation but also for the future generation of the society to come.

All these factors could be translated into mathematical module because the Creation and maintenance of this Universe itself works on a mathematical module of high precision. The method was widely followed and its results have shown over thousands of years of its application.

In modern times its use has dwindled, for an image has been successfully created that whatever modern Christian education system does not teach us is essentially superstitious. The result of our modernity has already started showing on our present day family structure.

The technique was not an end in itself.

Here, you need to understand another fundamental relating to this Creation. That is: nothing is stand alone in isolation to the exclusion of everything else. Do not think that any one aspect of esoteric knowledge would suffice for you to understand the entire gamut of complexities involved in the process of Creation.

Simply put you need to understand that the module I spoke of ~ applied mathematics to human lives ~ is not stand alone. Its well understood application does ensure substantially a stable married life but in itself, it is not the only means to that end.

Election of the right partner at the initial stage by application of that mathematical module can ensure a stable beginning and a stable journey but then that needs to be complemented with some other equally significant modules relevant to human lives. You cannot ignore other modules and expect the entire fruit by sticking to only one. There are several aspects of esoteric knowledge that have not only remained limited within the boundaries of Science but graduated beyond to the State of Art where they have become relevant to human lives in manners that you may not begin to think because your Christian English educators have systematically buried them over the past two centuries. I am not going to discuss them here but I will return with them someday.

In today's circumstances this clarification is all the more necessary because it is the age of quick fix where every one tends to look for an allopathic medicine for every headache ~ a pill that would instantly relieve you of the headache not bothering to fix the root problem. Besides, the close association with and total dependence on Christian English education system for six generations has made us not only forget those essentials but also treat them as meaningless superstitions because an ignorant education system can give you no better knowledge ~ a culture that cares not to understand Mother Nature but only attempts to conquer it like all arrogant fools do can give you no better understanding of matters that truly affect your lives. All they do is whole lot of trial and errors and give them impressive names like psychiatry and various derivatives of those kinds which are nothing but a huge money making racket in the name of scientific education.

How we lost all that.

Christian British systematically destroyed ancient Hindu education system. They withdrew all governmental support to any form of education that remotely related to Hindu system. Through Christian English education system they filled the minds of Hindu children that all of Hindu system of knowledge was nothing but superstition. Through six generations of Christian English education you have learned to think of them as superstition. Superstition is something that you believe in blindly. Aren't you doing the same thing? Didn't you believe blindly what those ignorant Christian British educators told you. Neither did they examine the validity of Hindu branches of knowledge, nor did you examine them. And, you blindly believed them all to be superstition. This belief of yours ~ isn't it a superstition by itself?

They killed our knowledge base, they let it get lost. If few kept it alive through generations without adequate support system and if they lost most of it, you call them quacks. Who is responsible for the degeneration of Hindu knowledge base? Are these whom you call quacks? Or, are those who methodically wiped it out over the period of time?

Sati was Started for Preserving Caste

With the much discussed subject, now in India, about a so called "sati" of Charanshah, in village Satpura in Uttar Pradesh, some information about this evil in Hindu social system, may be not only informative but also educative to the masses who wish to build a new India on new values.

Condition of Widows in Ancient India

In India, the condition of women in general, was made more dreadful than that of a slave, but the lot of widows was always very hard and they were forced to lead a horrible life of torture, disfigurement, tonsure and deprivation, with an enforced strict ban on remarriage. They were compelled to undergo sex with other men for procreation under the system of Niyoga. As if this was not enough, a peculiar system existed in India, whereby widows were burnt alive on the funeral pyre of their dead husbands. The practice existed among the higher castes mainly, though it was given a honourable and prestigious outlook among the masses by various means adopted by the Brahmins.

Why this system started in India? It was for maintaining the caste, which was very important for the welfare of those, who are benefited by it. And as the caste system grew more rigid, the sati become more strict. Notable example is Bengal, where it was enforced more strictly because of "Kulin system", where any of the hundreds of disgruntled young wives could easily poison the old man.

Position of Women

Ms. Shakuntala Rao Shastri, in her "Women in Sacred Laws" very aptly describes the pitiable condition of women before the Britishers came to India:

"True it is that anyone who has witnessed the pathetic condition of women in India at the dawn of British rule cannot but be shocked at it: the enforced child marriage, the exposure of female children, putting to death female children by throwing them at the junction of the Ganges and the sea, the violence used to make women follow the Sati rite and thus end their miserable existence, the shameful treatment accorded to a widow, the (in)famous kulinism which made marriage a profession rather than a sacrament, made woman not only an object of pity but many a woman sighed in the secret recess for her heart and wished that she had never been born a woman in this unfortunate country." [Shastri Shakuntala Rao, "Women in Sacred Laws" p. 171]

The situation described by the learned Vedic Scholar is at the time of dawn of British occupation, but since how long it was in existence? The reply is that this was the situation since the fall of Buddhism around tenth century AD. That the women enjoyed high position in Buddhist period can be judged by a mere glance at the Buddhist law being practiced in India before tenth century AD and which is practiced in all the Buddhist countries even now.

Today after passing of Ambedkar's Hindu Code, piece meal, the Hindu Laws of Marriage, Adoption, Succession, and other related Laws have been changed to a great extent. But prior to 1956, the Old Hindu Brahmanic Law was in force, under which the condition of women was pitiable. To get some idea of how these laws were made more and more cruel is seen if one considers that original law of India was Buddhist Law. BUDDHIST LAW WAS THE NATIONAL LAW OF INDIA, BECAUSE FROM THE HISTORICAL PERIOD, THE

RELIGION OF INDIA WAS BUDDHISM. IT WAS THE MAIN STREAM. The Brahmins succeeded in causing the fall of Buddhism, at the cost of women and Shudras. They had to bear the brunt of all evils, to maintain the supremacy of the Brahmins.

Epigraphic Evidences of Sati

Ms. Shakuntala Rao Shastri describes the "Memorial stelae". They are small stone uprights sculptured with figures and inscriptions, and are called Devli, and are found in abundance in Rajputana. They are erected in commemoration of women immolating themselves on funeral pyres of their husbands. The earliest one found in Jodhpur state at Gatiyala is dated 890 AD. The earliest of these stelae is found in Eran in Sagar District in M.P. and is dated 510 A. D. Thus the practice of Sati was coming to vogue in sixth century AD. [Shastri Shakuntala Rao, Ibid. p. 130]

The Annals of Kashmir by Kallahna of 12th century, mentions some instances where, in addition to wife / wives others like concubines, slaves, mother nurse, friends and followers also practiced Anumaran. Earliest mentioned was in 902 King Samkaravarman, in 1081 King Ananta, in 1161 King Malla, and the last one mentioned was in 12th century of King Sussala. [Shastri Shakuntala Rao, Ibid. p.130]

Not only it was practiced in North, West and Central India, the examples of Inscriptions from Epigraphica Carnataka show that the custom existed in South India also. Anumarana was practiced after deaths of various kings like-in 1130 AD Kadamba King Tailapa, Ganga King Nitimarga, and Satyavakya Kongunivarman Lord of Nandagiri, both of whom lived in 915 AD, in 1220 AD King Ballala, and in 1180 King Bammarasa. [Ibid. p. 132 ff.]

When a Tomar King in Gujrath died, his 90,000 queens were requested not to commit sati. They consulted their Kula-brahmana, who advised them to commit sati as Veda verse 18/877 mentions "Agne" and not "Agre", just for the sake of golden coins, thus condemning these 90,000 women to flames. 3000 queens committed sati with king of Vijaynagar. On conquest of Jaselmere by Muslims, 24 thousand queens committed sati.

Old cremation place has got inscriptions mentioning names of those committing sati. 112 queens of king Amarsing of Bundi, 88 queens of Keshosing, Jagirdar of Dharampur, 78 queens of Surendrasing of Palitana. Some social reformists tried to prevent sati of 95 queens of Bharatpur, but they had to commit sati. [Francis D'Souza, Loksatta, 3.12.99]

Why Sati was Started: Thus we find that excepting the solitary instance mentioned by Diodoras, which occured in a foreign land, and the persons involved were perhaps from foreign tribes settled in India during those times, the practice started from the time of decline and ultimate fall of Buddhism after seventh century. Still we find Banabhatta (7th century) in the court of Harshavardhana and later Medhatithi (9th century) condemning the practice.

The more important question is why this system started, developed and why it attained such a high respect. Sati custom in India has to be considered in combination with other customs of Child girl marriage with an elderly man and prohibition of widows to remarry. All these customs were imposed by the Brahmins in order to prevent transgression of caste rules. This was explained by Dr. Ambedkar as early as in 1919, ["Castes in India", W&S. vol. I, p. 5 ff.] while dealing with genesis and mechanism of Castes. The following are the salient points from it.

Endogamy is the only characteristic peculiar to caste. No civilized society in today's world shows more survivals of primitive times than Indian society. One such primitive practice is of exogamy long given up by the world but is still favoured in India. Though there are no clans in India, clan system is savoured, as there is prohibition on not only "sapinda" marriages but also on "sagotra" marriages among the Hindus. The various gotras and other totemic organizations have always been exogamus. When endogamy was superimposed over sagotra exogamy, a caste was formed.

To preserve and maintain this caste, inter caste marriages were banned. In case of death of a spouse, the other spouse was likely to marry outside the caste. To prevent this happening various means were adopted. These are:

1. Sati or burning of a widow on the funeral pyre of her deceased husband.
2. Enforced widowhood by which she is forced not to marry and
3. Girl marriage with an aged man.

All the medieval Brahmanic texts eulogize these customs in very glamourous language but give no reasons for them. Dr. Ambedkar, who calls all this eulogy as a sugar coating of the barbarous pill, gives the reasons:

> "... *Sati, enforced widowhood and girl marriage are customs that were primarily intended to solve the problem of the surplus man and surplus woman in a caste and to maintain its endogamy. Strict endogamy could not be preserved without these customs, while caste without endogamy is a fake.*" *[Ibid., p.14]*

The Brahmins enclosed themselves into a caste, thus forcing others to be the other caste. This was divided and further subdivided into multiple non-Brahmin castes and the institution of castes spread through the length and breadth of India. This spread was due to the tendency of imitation of Brahmins by the others. As these customs were very harsh and barbarous, the imitation was imperfect and we find that nearer a caste is to Brahmins more strictly it insisted on observance of these customs. Example of Kulinism in Bengal, which also was a movement to preserve the Caste and ensure supremacy of Brahmins, is discussed elsewhere. That the reason, these customs had to be enforced strictly in Bengal following Kulinism, was to prevent any one among the hundreds of dissatisfied wives of a kulin man from easily poisoning him, could be easily appreciated.

6

Brahminical Religious Text and Caste System

Varna Ashram and Hindu Scriptures

Introduction: The 'Varna' popularly known as the 'Caste system' is perhaps the most explosive topics in Hinduism, which so often gives handle to Non-Hindus to bash Hinduism. Popular misconceptions say that the Vedic religion encourages division of human beings based on one's birth. As a result, some people have beer kept backward and uneducated while others have abused this misconceptions and misinformation for personal gains. Much of this misconception can be attributed to the use of the words 'Varna' and 'Jati' interchangeably. A closer analysis will reveal just how wrong these misconceptions are.

Caste: "The word caste is not a word that is indigenous to India. It originates in the Portuguese word casta which means race, breed, race or lineage. However, during the 19th century, the term caste increasingly took on the connotations of the word race. Thus, from the very beginning of western contact with the subcontinent European constructions have been imposed on Indian systems and institutions. The caste system had been a fascination of the British since their arrival in India.

Coming from a society that was divided by class, the British attempted to equate the caste system to the class system. As late as 1937 Professor T. C. Hodson stated that: "Class and caste stand to each other in the relation of family to species. The general classification is by classes, the detailed one by castes. The former represents the external, the latter the internal view of the social organization."

The difficulty with definitions such as this is that class is based on political and economic factors, caste is not. Caste was seen as the essence of Indian society, the system through which it was possible to classify all of the various groups of indigenous people according to their ability, as reflected by caste, to be of service to the British. It was not until 1872 that a planned comprehensive census was attempted. This was done under the direction of Henry Beverely, Inspector General of Registration in Bengal. The census went well beyond counting heads or even enquiring into sex ratios or general living conditions. Among the many questions were enquiries regarding nationality, race, tribe, religion and caste." (from The Indian Caste System and the British, by Kevin Hobson).

Varna: The root word for Varna is 'Vri' which means one's occupation. The Varna Dharma was based on division of labour. This division was solely based on the attitude of an individual and his/her propensity for performing certain duties according to Gunas (qualities). There are three Gunas-Sattva (white), Rajas (red), and Tamas (black).

Jati: The Root word for 'jati' is 'jan', which means Birth.

The Issue: The issue of Varna Dharma is highly misunderstood. There are many issues and reasons for the decline of Varna Dharma. A key point in the Varna Dharma is the definition and Gunas associated with various classes of Varnas. This paper deals with following two main issues;

- Definition and duties of the Varna Dharma
- Basis of division-Gunas or birth

Supremacy of Vedas

First part in the understanding of Varna Dharma is to accept supremacy of Vedas in all the Hindu scriptures. As Swami Vivekananda said "The Vedas are our only authority, thus says the Shukla Yajur Veda (XXVI, 2). The Smritis, Puranas, Tantras-all these are acceptable as far as they agree the Vedas; and wherever they are contradictory, they are to be rejected as unreliable".

Even Manu Smriti declares that the Vedas are the supreme authority. The knowledge of the sacred law is prescribed for those who are not given to the acquisition of wealth and to the gratification of their desires; to those who seek the knowledge of the sacred law the supreme authority the revelation (Sruti).

What Constitutes Vedic Knowledge

The second part in the understanding of Varna Dharma is what constitutes Vedic knowledge.

Nirukta says on this topic; "He, who reads the Vedas even with proper accents, but does not know their meanings, is like a tree weighed down by its fruit, branches, leaves and flowers, or like a beast of burden carrying on its back grain which it can not eat. But he, who understands their meanings and acts up to their teachings by avoiding sin and leading a virtuous life, enjoys perfect happiness in this world, and eternal bliss hereafter in consequence thereof", Nirukta 1, 18.

Once supremacy of Vedas and the meanings of Vedic education are understood, all the doubts about Varna Dharma will evaporate. There is no division in Vedic knowledge. The division is in our ignorance.

Origin of Varnas

The first reference to the origin of Varna Dharma comes from the Rig Veda and subsequently explained in the Gita and Smritis (*e.g.* Manu, Prashar etc.).

Rigveda: The Purusa Sukta has the first reference to the origin of four groups. The Brahmana (spiritual wisdom and splendour) was His Mouth; the Kshatriya (administrative and military prowess) His Arms became. His Thighs the Vaishya (commercial and business enterprise) was; of His Feet the Sudra (productive and sustaining force) was born. (by Swami Krishnananda The Divine Life Society Sivananda Ashram, Rishikesh, India)

Gita: The Gita elaborates on the origin of Varnas. "The fourfold order was created by Me according to the divisions of quality (Guna) and work (karma); though I am its creator, know Me to be incapable of action or change." (from The Bhagawad Gita by S. Radhakrishnan)

Definition and Duties of Varnas

Brahman (the Supreme Reality) is not known to those who are possessed of avarice, delusion, fear, egotism, lust, anger, and sin or possessed of (unable to bear) heat and cold, hunger and thirst, or mental resolve and indecision, or pride of birth in a Brahmin (priest) family, or vanity in having read a mass of books on Mukti (liberation or salvation).

Gita: "There is no being on earth, or again in heaven among the gods, that is liberated from the three qualities (Sattva, Rajas, and Tamas) born of Nature." "Of Brahmans, Kshatriyas and Vaishyas, as also the Sudras, O Arjuna, the duties are distributed according to the qualities born of their own nature."

"Serenity, self-restraint, austerity, purity, forgiveness and also uprightness, knowledge, realization and belief in God are the duties of the Brahmans, born of their own nature."

"Prowess, splendour, firmness, dexterity and also not fleeing from battle, generosity and lordliness are the duties of Kshatriyas, born of their own nature."

"Agriculture, cattle-rearing and trade are the duties of the Vaishya merchant class), born of their own nature; and action consisting of service is the duty of the Sudras, born of their own nature." (All meanings from Srimad Bhagawad Gita by Swami Chinmayananda)

Varna by Birth: The next issue in the Varna system is to understand the order and how to belong to one Varna. Is it by birth or by 'guna'.

Channdogaya Upanishad: The following story (Channdogaya Upanishad, 4.1.4) reveals that Brahminhood does not depend on birth but on character and Gunas.

"Satyakama, the son of Jabala, addressed his mother and said "I wish to become a brahmacharin, mother. Of what family am I?" She said to him: I do not know, my child, of what family thou art. In my youth, when I had to move about much as a servant, I conceived thee. So I do not know of what family thou art. I am Jabala by name. Thou art Satyakama. Say that thouart Satyakama Jabala."

He going to Gautama, the son of Haridrumat, said to him: I wish to become a brahmacharin with thee, Sire. May I come to you?

He said to him, "Of what family art thou, my friend?"

He replied: "I do not know, Sire, of what family I am. I asked my mother, and she answered: "In my youth, when I had to move about much as a servant, I conceived thee. So I do not know of what family thou art. I am Jabala by name. Thou art Satyakama.' I am therefore Satyakama Jabala, Sire."

He said to him" "No one but a true Brahmin would speak out. Go and fetch fuel, I shall initiate thee. Thou has not swerved from the truth."

Vajra Suchikopanishad: I now proceed to declare the vajrasuuchi-the weapon that is the destroyer of ignorance-which condemns the ignorant and praises the man of divine vision.

There are four castes-the Brahman, the Kshatriya, the vaishya, and the shudra. Even the smritis declare in accordance with the words of the Vedas that the Brahman alone is the most important of them.

Then this needs to be examined. What is meant by the Brahman? Is it a jiva ? Is it a body ? Is it a class? It is Gyana? Is it karma? Or is it a doer of Dharma?

To begin with: is jiva the Brahman? No. Since the jiva is the same in the many past and future bodies (of all persons), and since the jiva is the same in all of the many bodies obtained through the force of karma, there jiva is not the Brahman. Then is the body the Brahman? No. Since the body, as it is made up of the five elements, is the same for all people down to chandalas, etc., since old age and death, dharma and adharma are found to be common to them all, since there is no absolute distinction that the Brahmans are white-coloured, the Kshatriyas red, the vaishyas yellow, and the shudras dark, and since in burning the corpse of his father, etc., the stain of the murder of a Brahman, etc., will accrue to the son, etc., therefore the body is not the Brahman.

Then is a class the Brahman? No. Since many rishis have sprung from other castes and orders of creation-Rishyashringa was born of deer; kaushika, of kusha grass; jaambuka of a jackal; Valmiki of valmika (an ant-hill); Vyasa of a fisherman's daughter; Gautama, of the posteriors of a hare; Vashishtha of Urvasi (a celestial nymph in the court of Indra); and agastya of a water-pot; thus have we heard. Of these, many rishis outside the caste have stood first among the teachers of divine wisdom; therefore a class is not the Brahman.

Is Gyana the Brahman? No. Since there were many Kshatriyas and others well versed in the cognition of divine Truth, therefore Gyana is not the Brahman.

Then is karma the Brahman? No. Since the prarabdha, sanchita, aagami karmas are the same for all beings, and since all people perform their actions impelled by karma, therefore karma is not the Brahman.

Then is the doer of dharma (virtuous actions) the Brahman? No. Since there are many Kshatriyas, etc., who are givers of gold, therefore a doer of virtuous actions is not the Brahman.

Who indeed then is Brahman ? Whoever he may be, he who has directly realised his aatmaa and who is directly cognizant, like the myrobalan in his palm, of his aatmaa, that is without a second, that is devoid of class and actions, that is free from the faults of the six stains (hunger, thirst, grief, confusion, old age, and death) and the six changes (birth, existence etc.), that is of the nature of truth, knowledge, bliss and eternity, that is without any change in itself, that is the substratum of all the kalpas, that exists penetrating all things that pervades everything within and without as aakaash, that is of nature of undivided bliss, that cannot be reasoned about and that is known only by direct cognition. He who by the reason of having obtained his wishes is devoid of the faults of thirst after worldly objects and passions, who is the possessor of the qualifications beginning with saama (dama, uparati, titikshaa, samadhana, sraddha), who is free from emotion, malice, thirst after worldly objects, desire, delusion, etc., whose mind is untouched by pride, egoism, etc., who possesses all these qualities and means-he only is the Brahman. Such is the opinion of the veda, the smritis, the itihasa, and the puranas. Otherwise one cannot obtain the status of a Brahman. One should meditate on his aatma as sachchidananda, and the non-dual Brahman. Yea, one should meditate on his aatma as the sachchidananda Brahman. Such is the Upanishad.

Right to Study Vedas

Contrary to existing view everyone irrespective of caste or sex, has right to read the Veda or hear it read.

Yajur Veda: "As I have given this Word (*i.e.* the four Vedas) which is the word of salvation for all making-Brahmans, Kshatriyas, Vaishyas, Sudras, women, servants, aye, even the lowest of the low, so shoul you all do, *i.e.* teach and preach Veda. Let all men therefore read and recite, teach, and preach the Veda and thereby acquire true knowledge, practice virtue, shun vice, and consequently being freed from all sorrow and pain, enjoy true happiness." 26,2 (translated from Sayarth Prakash, Ch 3, page 78).

Atharva Veda: "Just as boys acquire sound knowledge and culture by the practice of Brahmacharya and then marry girls of their own choice, who are young, well educated, loving and of like temperament, so should a girl practice Brahmacharya, study the Veda and other sciences and there by perfect her knowledge, refine her character, give her hand to a man of her own choice, who is young, learned and loving." (Xl, xvi, 3, 18.)

Brahma-Sutras: "Apasudradhikaranam: Topic 9 (Sutras 34-38) The right of the Sudras to the study of Vedas discussed Sugasya tadanadarasravanat tadadravanat suchyate hi I.3.34 (97) Suk: grief; Asya: his; Tat: that, namely that grief;

Anadarasravanat: from hearing his (the Rishi's) disrespectful speech; Tada: then; Adravanat: because of going to him i.e, to Raikva; Suchyate: is referred to; Hi: because. (King Janasruti) was in grief on hearing some contemptuous words used about him by the sage in the form of a swan; owing to his approaching Raikva, overwhelming with that grief, Raikva called him Sudra; for it (the grief) is pointed at by Raikva.

The Purvapakshin says: The Sudras also have got bodies and desires. Hence they are also entitled. Raikva refers to Janasruti who wishes to learn from him by the name of Sudra. "Fie, necklace and carriage be thine, O Sudra, together with the cows" Chh. Up. IV-2 & 3. But when he appears a second time, Raikva accepts his presents and teaches him. Smriti speaks of Vidura and others who were born from Sudra mothers as possessing highest knowledge. Therefore the Sudra has a claim to Brahma Vidya or knowledge of Brahman. This Sutra refutes the view and denies the right to the study of the Vedas for Sudra. The word 'Sudra' does not denote a Sudra by birth which is its conventional meaning, because Janasruti was a Kshatriya king. Here we will have to take the etymological meaning of the word which is, "He rushed into grief (Sukam abhi dudrava) or as "grief rushed on him" or as "he in his grief rushed to Raikva". The following Sutra also intimates that he was a Kshatriya.

Kshatriyatva: the state of his being a Kshatriya; Avagateh: on account of being known or understood; Cha: and; Uttaratra: latter on in a subsequent part of the text; Chaitrarathena: with Chaitraratha; Lingat: because of the indicatory sign or the inferential mark.

And because the Kshatriyahood (of Janasruti) is known from the inferential mark (supplied by his being mentioned) later on with Chaitraratha (who was a Kshatriya himself).

An argument in support of Sutra 34 is given. Janasruti is mentioned with the Kshatriya Chaitraratha Abhipratarin in connection with the same Vidya. Hence we can infer that Janasruti also was a Kshatriya because, as a rule, equals are mentioned together with equals. Hence the Sudras are not qualified for the knowledge of Brahman.

Samskaraparamarsat tadabhavabhilapacca (I.3.36) (99) Samskara: the purificatory ceremonies, the investiture with sacred thread; Paramarsat: because of the reference; Tat: that ceremony; Abhava: absence; Abhilapat: because of the declaration; Cha: and. Because purificatory ceremonies are mentioned (in the case of the twice-born) and their absence is declared (in the case of the Sudra).

The discussion on the privilege of Brahma Vidya on the part of Sudras is continued. In different places of the Vidyas the Upanayana ceremony is referred to. The Upanayana ceremony is declared by the scriptures to be a necessary condition for the study of all kinds of knowledge or Vidya. We read in Prasna Up. I-1 "Devoted to Brahman, firm in Brahman, seeking for the highest Brahman they, carrying fuel in their hands, approached the venerable Pippalada, thinking that he would teach them all that." Upanayana ceremony is meant for the higher castes. With reference to the Sudras on the other hand, the absence of ceremonies is frequently mentioned in the scriptures. "In the Sudra there is not any sin by eating prohibited food, and he is not fit for any ceremony" Manu X-12-6. A Sudra by birth cannot have Upanayana and other Samskaras without which the Vedas cannot be studied. Hence the Sudras are not entitled to the study of the Vedas. The next Sutra further strengthens the view that a Sudra can have no Samskara.

And on account of the prohibition in Smriti of (the Sudras) hearing, studying and understanding (the Veda) and performing Vedic rites (they are not entitled to the knowledge of Brahman).

Note: Sutras 34-38 of Brahma-Sutras disqualify the Sudras for the Knowledge of Brahman (Supreme Reality) through the study of the Vedas. But it is possible for them to attain that Knowledge through the Puranas and the epics (Ramayana and the Mahabharata)."

"Wherever it is declared (in the books of Rishis) that the Sudras are debarred from the study of the Veda, the prohibition simply amounts to this that he, that does not learn anything even after a good deal of teaching, being ignorant and destitute of understanding, is called a Sudra. It is useless for him to learn and for others to teach him any longer." Satyarth Prakash, chapter 3, 78.

Inter Movement in Varna

Can people by their actions move from one Varna to another? The answer is YES, which is another argument in favour of Varna not based on birth.

Gita: "By following his qualities of work, every man can become perfect. Now please hear from Me how this can be done. (By A. C Bhaktivedanta Swami Prabhupada)."

From Whom is the evolution of all beings, by Whom all this is pervaded, worshipping Him with one's own duty, man attains Perfection. (by Swami Chinmayananda)

Better is one`s own duty (though) destitute of merits, than the duty of another wellperformed. He who does the duty ordained by his own nature incurs no sin. (by Swami Chinmayananda)

One should not give up the work suited to one's nature, O Son of Kunti (Arjuna), though it may be defective, for all enterprises are clouded by defects as fire by smoke. (The Bhagavadgita by S. Radhakrishnan).

Apastamba Sutras: "A low Class man may, by leading a virtuous life, rise to the level of a higher Class man and should be ranked as such. In like manner a high Class man can by leading a sinful life, sink down to the level of a Class lower than his, and should be considered as such." (Translation from Stayarth Prakash, chapter 4, page 100)

Manu Smriti

The scriptures are quoted out of context as if they are stand alone political statements. Manu Smriti is not very entertaining for Sudras is true, only when not understood properly. People take pride in quoting from Manu Smriti to show their knowledge and understanding, and also to put down Varna Dharma. A careful reading will give a different picture. Manu Smriti is very infamous for treatment of Sudras by popular belief. There are shlokas in Manu Smriti that debars a Sudra from learning any Vedic knowledge when read in isolation and not as one part of a scripture. The maximum damage to Varna Dharma was caused by piece meal acquisition and application of knowledge. Manu Smriti deals with all the four Varnas and not only Sudras. The first issue with Manu Smriti is what Vedic knowledge is and what different Varnas are.

Definitions and Duties of Varna: "The study of true sciences, the practice of Brahmacharya, the performance of Homa, the acceptance of truth and rejection of untruth, the dissemination of true knowledge, leading a virtuous life as enjoined by the Veda, the performance of seasonal Homa, the reproduction of good children, faithful discharge of the Five Great Daily Duties, and doing such other good works as are productive of beneficial results to the community, such as developing technical arts, association with the good and the learned, truthfulness in word, deed and thought, and devotion to public good and like, all these things go to make a Brahma.

To Brahmans he assigned teaching and studying (the Veda), sacrificing for their own benefit and for others, giving and accepting (of alms).

Inter Movement of Varnas: "As the son of a Sudra may attain the rank of a Brahmin if he were to possess his qualifications, character and accomplishments, and as the son of a Brahmin may become a Sudra, if he sinks to his level in his character, inclinations and manners, even so must it be with him who springs from a Kshatriya; even so with him who is born of a Vaishya.

In other words, a person should be ranked with the Class whose qualifications, accomplishments, and character he possesses.

> *"A Dwija as well his children who, instead of studying the Veda, wastes his time in doing other things soon goes down to the level of a Shudra." Manu Smriti 2, 168*
>
> *"A twice-born man who, not having studied the Veda, applies himself to other (and worldly study), soon falls, even while living, to the condition of a Sudra and his descendants (after him)." Manu Smriti 2, 168.*

Special Treatment for Brahmans!: It is true that not very complementary and rude things were said about Sudras in Manu Smriti. But as shown in Manu Smriti (discussed in the definition section) that the position of Brahmin's was full of responsibility and not privileges. In (a case of) theft the guilt of a Sudra shall be eightfold, that of a Vaishya sixteen fold, that of a Kshatriya two-and-thirty fold, 8,337

That of a Brahmana sixty-fourfold, or quite a hundredfold, or (even) twice four-and-sixtyfold; (each of them) knowing the nature of the offence. 8,338 Guna or Birth-The Deciding Factor.

"A Brahmana who departs from the rule of conduct, does not reap the fruit of the Veda, but he who duly follows it, will obtain the full reward. (Manu Smriti 1,109)."

"Declares out Manu: Take the jewel of a woman for your wife, though she be of inferior descent. Learn supreme knowledge with service even from the man of low birth; and even from the Chandala, learn by serving him the way to salvation."

Is Breakdown in Varna Unexpected?

Prashar Smriti: Smriti created by sage Parashar and known by his name as 'Parashar Smriti, is the most benevolent for the modern Kali Yuga. Parashar has himself said:

Krite Tu Manavo Dharmastretayaam Gautamo Smritah | |

Dwapare Shankhalikhitaa Kalau Parasharah Smritah | |

Meaning-Manu Smriti was most relevant in Satya Yuga. In Treta, Smriti created by Gautam had most relevance whereas in Dwapar, Shankh's Smriti was mostly recognized. But in Kali Yuga, it is Parashar Smriti that by and large shows the way to the ignorant people.

Sri Ramacharitamanasa: Sri Ramacharitamanasa, Uttar-kanda, verses 97-98, explains very clearly that what happened and happening to Varna Dharma.

"No one follows the duties of one's own caste, and the four Dharms or stages of life also disappear. Every man

and woman takes delight in revolting against the Vedas. The Brahmans sell the Vedas; the kings bleed their subjects; no one respects the injunction of the Vedas. The right course for every individual is that which one takes a fancy to; a man of erudition is he who plays the braggart.

Whoever launches spurious undertakings and is given over to hypocrisy, him does everyone call a saint. He alone is clever, who robs another of his wealth; he who puts up false appearances is an ardent follower of established usage. He who is given to lying and is clever at joking is spoken of as a man of parts in the Kali age. He alone who is a reprobate and has abandoned the path of the Vedas is a man of wisdom and dispassion in the Kali age. He alone who has grown big nails and long locks of matted hair is a renowned ascetic in the Kali age. (1-4)"

What went Wrong?: Swami Dayananda Saraswati (founder of Arya Samaj) has discussed this issue (downfall of Varna Dharma) very nicely in Satyarth Prakash and it states as:

"When the Brahmans became destitute of knowledge, there could be no talk of the ignorance of the Kshatriyas, Vaishyas and Shudras. Even the ancient practice of the study of the Vedas and other Shastras with their meanings died away. The Brahmans only learnt the Vedas by note-just enough to enable them to earn their livelihood. Even that much they did teach to the Kshatriyas, and others.

As the ignorant became the teachers of the people, deceitfulness, fraud, hypocrisy, and irreligion began to increase among them. The Brahmans thought that they should make some arrangement for their livelihood. They held a council among themselves and agreed to preach to the Kshatriyas and others: "We alone are the object of worship to you. You could never enter Heaven or obtain salvation except by serving us. Should you not serve us, you shall fall into an awful Hell."

The Vedas, and the Shastras written by the Vedic sages and seers have declared men of learning and as Brahmans and worthy of respect; but here they, who were ignorant, lascivious, deceitful, licentious, lazy and irreligious, declared themselves as Brahmans and worthy of homage.

But how could the sterling virtues of the righteous, learned and truth-loving Brahmans be found in them. When the Kshatriyas and others became absolutely destitute of Sanskrit learning, whatever cock and bull stories the Brahmans concocted, the simpletons believed. They ensnared all in their net of hypocrisy, brought them under thorough control and began to teach:-"Whatever a Brahman declares is as infallible as words falling from Divine lips."

Conclusions: The most important issue in the understanding of Varna Dharma is to understand the definitions of the various Varnas as explained in Hindu scriptures. The rules of the groups prescribe the duties to society. The duties for various Varnas were based on the 'guna' of an individual and were dependent on the capacities of individuals. Therefore the division of labour, which broadly falls into 'the four orders of human beings' is based upon "guna and karma" of each individual.

"The complete definition of the Varna not only removes our present misunderstanding but also provides us with some data to understand its true significance. Not by mere birth is man a Brahmana (Brahmin); by cultivating good intentions and noble thoughts alone can we ever aspire to Brahmana-hood; nor can we pose as Brahmana merely because of our external physical marks, or bodily actions in the outer world. The definition insists that he alone is a Brahmana, whose thoughts are as much Sattvik, as his actions are. A Kshatriya is one who is Rajasik in his thoughts and actions. A Sudra is not only one whose thoughts are Tamasik, but he who lives a life of low endeavours, for satisfying his base animal passions and flesh-appetites. The scientific attitude in which this definition has been declared, is clear from

the exhaustive implications of the statement: "According to the differentiation of 'guna' and 'karma'."

As discussed earlier, there was no exclusion of any Varna to read Vedic Knowledge in the Veda. Later on restriction were put on people because of with Tamsic Guna. There was a structured and step-wise approach to learning which everyone was supposed to follow.

All Dwij's were following that system of learning. No Vedic knowledge was given even to Dwij's who do not follow the process of learning. With time this (not learning Vedas) became a rule in the society which led to consolidation of Vedic knowledge in very few peoples hand. If a tumbler is full of dirt, grease and other impurities, then it is an unfit receptacle for holding pure water. The mind is the container and if it is filled with Tamasic qualities, then it is an unfit receptacle for receiving pure spiritual knowledge.

"It is written in Chhandogya Upanishad that Gragee and other women of yore have read the Veda, and even Janshruti, a Sudra by birth, has studied the Veda under Raikyamuni" Satyarth Prakash, chapter 11.

Brahma Sutras and Manu Smriti discuss that Sudras can not study Veda. But the important issue is to know who Sudra is. Why he can not study the Vedas. As explained in the section on "Inter-movement in Varna Dharma" section, when Sudra can become a Brahman then he has all the right to study the Veda. The restriction placed on the study of Vedas is because of absence of the process (character, capability, and/or prerequisite) to study the Vedas.

The issue is not whether Varna Dharma is based on birth or not, nor whether Brahmans are higher Varna than any other. These may be important but not sufficient. If Sudras are not Sudra by birth then Brahmans are not Brahmans by birth alone too. This must be an important aspect in the equation in any meaningful discussion about Varna Dharma.

There was no pecking order (higher or lower) in the society according to scriptures. Individuals were identified by their knowledge. The reverence given to a person in society (based on his knowledge) was a responsibility and not a privilege. All men are not equally wise or equally intelligent. Each one is trying to grapple with problems of life with whatever degree of wisdom each possesses. Hinduism provides for the highly evolved as well as those not so evolved or least evolved and even those not at all evolved in distinct categories of Brahimn, Kshatriya, Vaishya and Sudra with distinct Svadharma (assigned duties) suited to their individual state of evolution.

Realisation is not dependent on birth or book-learning as has been repeatedly demonstrated in the lives of saints, from the very earliest times to our own day (Comments by Swami Madhavananda, Advaita Ashrama).

"Who are Rishis? Vatsyayana says, He who has attained through proper means the direct realization of Dharma, he alone can be a Rishi even if he is a Mlechcha by birth"

Many great Rishis were born in lower castes (*e.g.*) Vashishtha was the son of a prostitute; VYASA was born of a fisher woman; PARASARA's mother was a chandala; Nammalwar was a Sudra. Similarly Valmiki, Vishvamitra, Agastya were Brahmins inspite of their non-Brahmin origin. Swami Vivekananda is one of the most revered Hindu worldwide and was a non Brahmin. All these Hindus prove that birth was not a major player in attaining Brahminhood. It is the intellectual and spiritual level that differentiates people.

Swami Sivananda (The Divine Life Society, Rishikesh), in his commentary on Gita,Ch.18, verses 41,and 45 says: "Mankind is organised into the four castes and each man`s life is divided into four stages, according to the nature of the Gunas and the degree of growth or evolution. This is the division of labour for which each caste is fitted according to its own nature.

The duty prescribed is your sole support, each devoted to his own duty in accordance with his own nature or caste, and the highest service you can render to the Supreme is to carry it out wholeheartedly, without expectation of fruits, with the attitude of dedication to the Lord. The caste system is, indeed, a splendid thing. It is quite flawless. But the defect came in from somewhere else. The classes gradually neglected their duties. The test of ability and character slowly vanished. Birth became the chief consideration in determining castes. All castes fell from their ideals and forgot all about their duties."

Scriptures treated all the Varnas as same and none was higher than the other. And nobody belongs to any Varna by birth. Vajra Suchikopanishad clearly states that one cannot be a Brahmin either by its being, birth, physical equipment of body and colour or by wisdom and knowledge or by religious action even The basis of Varna was guna and not birth. Vajra suchikopanishad of Sama Veda defines the word Brahmin in most unambiguous terms thus: One is a Brahmin not because of his birth or caste or heredity or colour or profession or acquisition of worldly knowledge or mere observation of social and moral codes, but because of his spiritual knowledge, his abidance in the Supreme Reality, his state of self-realization.

This is the conclusion of all Veda, Srutis, Puranas, Itihasas and of all great men of India.

According to 'Guru Bala Prabodhika' a commentary on Amara Kosa, the ancient Sanskrit lexicon, a Brahmin is one who knows Brahman (Supreme God), not one who is borne into a caste. (Brahmin Parabrahmani nishtatwat Brahmana).

One of the main reasons for confusion about Varnas is that there is a vast amount of scriptures in the Hindu Dharma. People do not always know the order of the scriptures. Even when the order is known, the scriptures are not easily interpreted since all scriptures are written in Sanskrit. Even the people who can interpret the scriptures not necessarily understand them. The confusion is not what is written originally in Sanskrit but in the misunderstanding of the Sanskrit translations. The first issue in understanding of Varna Dharma is to understand the order of the scriptures. The Vedas are the ultimate authority in Hindu Dharma. The second issue is to understand that Varna Ashram is evolutionary in nature.

A key issue in understanding of Varna lies in knowledge of Sanskrit. There was and is no misunderstanding about Varnas as written in Sanskrit. The Varna Ashram started falling apart when the original Sanskrit work is translated in to English, especially by the people who do not have command over both languages (Sanskrit and English) and with limited knowledge about the scriptures.

There are many words and terms in Sanskrit which have no equivalent in English language-Dharma and Varna are two examples. The closest meaning in English is a force fit and not necessarily the right choice. The right approach in understanding Vedic concepts starts with learning of Sanskrit. As Swami Sivananda said "Varnasrama pertains to body alone, but not to the pure, allpervading, immortal soul or Atman. Attain Knowledge of the Self and become an Ativarnasrami like Lord Dattatreya. Hear what he says:-

Mahadadi jagat sarvam

Na kinchit pratibhati me

Brahmaiva kevalam sarvam
Katham varnasramasthitih

"The whole world, from Mahat downwards, does not shine in Me. Everything is Brahman only. Where then is Varnasrama?"

Vedic Vocations

Rather coincidentally, at the dawn of civilization, as the people gathered and lived in clans or tribes (Visha), they collectively-irrespective of their undertakings within Visha (such as in agriculture, woodworking, trade and other vocations)-came to be known as the Vaishya (meaning-belonging to Visha).

To meet the liturgical needs of the society, the Vaishya-from among themselves-would select, on the basis of skills in elocution, the Brahmins (students or orators of the Vedas-compiled knowledge). Similarly, for administrative purposes, Vaishya with qualities of leadership would be selected as Kshatriya (sovereign, tribal chieftain, administrator of Kshatar-dominion or tribal area / town). Furthermore, a Visha (tribe)-in addition to having the Vaishyas (including Brahmins, Kshatriya, cowherders and woodworkers etc.)-also embodied people known as Shudra (meaning-not of tribe) representing all the newcomers (immigrants) to that particular tribe. They included persons from other tribes (such as the vanquished foes and the migrants) and the children born out of inter-tribal unions.

Being somewhat new into that tribe and encountering unfamiliar rules, regulations and customs, a Shudra was limited in his vocational options and was generally relegated to providing service and assistance to members of the host tribe. But over time, like a modern day immigrant, he would surpass the tribal or social barriers so as to fully assimilate in that society and pursue other professions. Thus, all the responsibilities related to a Visha could be grouped into four sub-categories: Brahmin, Kshatriya, Vaishya and Shudra; the duties and skills involved with each of them are indicated in the following Sections.

Note also that, in old times, there was no concept of money or cash. People produced things and bartered (traded) them for other goods and services. A producer or trader belonging to Vaishya would include people such as farmer producing grains and milk etc., blacksmith (Lohar) making iron implements, leather-worker (Charmar or Chamar, charm meaning leather) manufacturing shoes, and so on. Thus, for subsistence, a Brahmin would do worship (puja) in a 'Vaishya' farmer's house and get grains and milk in return. Similarly, a Chamar would exchange shoes for food items from a farmer, iron implements from a Lohar, and so on. Similarly, a 'Shudra' servant might work or help in a farmer's field for food in return. If he were to help a Lohar, then Lohar would provide him with food items. Moreover, all these people would give a share of their goods (produce) and services to the Kshatriya (tribal chief) for administration of Visha (tribe or society). Society was basically managed through bartering system.

Background and Discussion

Various Social and Cultural Issues: The ancient society recognized the importance of all. Irrespective of one's skill or background, there was a place for him / her to participate actively and make useful contribution. The ceremonial rites, though conducted by the learned priest, were open to all. People used prayers for atonement and benediction for all. Everyone sent their "heroes" (sons) to the battles for Visha or to protect and assist the Sovereign. A number of important aspects of the ancient society can be further clarified by considering the following passages (with references to one God or BRAHMAN+, and manifesting as Agni, Indra or Savitar) from Vedas& (ancient Hindu texts).

From the Rigveda:

"What God shall we adore with our oblation?...He is the God of gods and none beside Him...O Father, thou Creator of Heaven and Earth, by eternal Law ruling-protect us...O Almighty, the Lord of beings, you alone pervade all the created beings..." (Book 10, Hymn: 121.8-10) / p. 98

"We all possess various thoughts and plans and diverse are the callings of men. The carpenter seeks out that which is cracked, the physician the ailing, the priest the worshipper......." (Book 9, Hymn 112.1) / p. 84

"I am a bard, my father is a physician, my mother's job is to grind the corn......" (Book 9, Hymn 112.3) / p. 84

"The man who has awakened to the knowledge, becomes perfect. Let him speak for us to the gods..." (Book 5, Hymn 65.1) / p. 49

"May they, our Fathers who in their skill belong to the lowest order, attain higher one, those of midmost may attain the highest. May they who have attained a life of spirit, the knower of sacrifice, the guileless, help us when called upon...." (Book 10, Hymn 15.1-2) / p. 87

"Let gods lead us, let there be a stable union of the wife and husband... May authority be ever yours (i.e., wife's) in speech. Happy be you and prosper with your children, and be ever watchful to rule the household. Unite yourself with this man your husband. So authority will be yours

in speech.. May the kinsman of the bride thrive well.." (Book 10, Hymn 85.26-28) / p. 94

"May the gods grant riches to the men more liberal than the terrifying..." (Book 1, Hymn 185.9) / p. 26

From the Yajurveda:

"May gods anoint this man to be without rival, for mighty rule, for mighty dominion and for great splendour. This man, son of such a person, such a woman, of such a clan, is anointed king, O you subjects... He is your lord...He is also sovereign of our learned Brahmins...Let all men protect him." (Kanda 1, Prapathaka 8, Hymn i.8.10.c) / p. 54

"O Agni, may all mortals seek your friendship, the guide of all. May all solicit you for glory, riches and fame. May all of us prosper as you do." (Kanda 1, Prapathaka 3, Hymn i.4.46.a-c) / p. 64

"O Agni, grant glory to our Brahmins, set luster in our Kshatriyas, luster in our Vaishyas, luster in our Shudras.." (Kanda 5, Prapathaka 7, Hymn v.7.6.d) / p. 102

"O god Savitar.. strengthen the life of subjects, strengthen the subjects..." (Kanda 1, Prapathaka 3, Hymn i.3.6.m-n) / p. 34

"O Agni...each fault done in a village or in forest, in society or mind, each sinful act that we have committed to Shudra or Vaishya or by preventing a religious act, even of that sin, you are the expiation..." (Kanda 1, Prapathaka 8, Hymn i.8.3.d) / p. 111

"He who knows well both knowledge and Nescience simultaneously, overcoming death by knowledge attains life immortal." (Isa Upanishad-verse 11) / p. 159

From the Samveda:

"May our subjects be rich and strong with the favour of Indra. May we be wealthy in food, rejoice with them..." (Part Second, Book 4, Ch. 1, Hymn 14) / p. 74

From the Bhagawad Gita:

As a part of God's creation (work), the four vocations are subgrouped according to people's guna (skills) and karma (assignments). Know that all work is for Him, even though He is beyond work, in Eternity. (Ch. 4-verse 13)

Ignorant men, but not the wise, say that Sankhya (variously as: Jnana Yoga, Sanyasa or Surrender, Path of Vision or Wisdom) and Yoga (variously as: Karma Yoga, Tyaga or Renunciation, Path of Action, Bhakti or devotional service, Japaa or Silence, Dhayana or Contemplation / Meditation, Brahamcharya or Austerity, Vaanprastha or Hermitlike) are different paths; but he who gives his self (soul) to one reaches the end of two. (Ch. 5-verse 4)

Even if the greatest sinner worships God with all his soul, he must be considered righteous because of his righteous will. (Ch. 9-verse 30)

And he shall soon become pure and reach everlasting peace. For this is His covenant that he who adores Him is not lost. (Ch. 9-verse 31)

God is one in all, but it seems as if he were many; He (as Vishnu / preserver) supports all beings: from Him (as Rudra / destroyer) ensues end, and from Him (as Brahma / creator) ensues beginning. (Ch. 13-verse 16)

The duties involving Brahmin, Kshatriya, Vaishya and Shudra are grouped according to people's abilities and skills. (Ch. 18-verse 41)

The skills for a Brahmin involve serenity, self-harmony, austerity and purity, loving-forgiveness and righteousness; vision, wisdom and faith. (Ch. 18-verse 42)

The qualities needed according to Kshatriya are: a heroic mind, splendor or inner fire, constancy, resourcefulness, courage in battle, generosity and noble leadership. (Ch. 18-verse 43)

Trade, agriculture and rearing of cattle may be tackled by Vaishya; and the background (tenure) of a Shudra is also suited to providing support. (Ch. 18-verse 44)

People attain perfection when they find joy in their work. Hear how a person attains perfection and finds joy in his work. (Ch. 18-verse 45)

A person achieves perfection when his work is-performed with pure feeling of-worship of God, from whom all things come and who is in all. (Ch. 18-verse 46)

The words of vision and wisdom have been conveyed. Ponder them in the silence of your soul, and then in freedom do your will. (Ch. 18-verse 63)

Hindu Dharma (Hinduism): Hinduism is religion based on the Vedas, and also known as the Sanatan Dharma (eternal religion) or Vedic Dharma. In the Vedas, god Bhaga was the bestower of auspicious blessings. It soon became the power of goodness, and he who possessed this power was called Bhagvan. The religion associated with Bhagvan (or Bhagvat) was called Bhagvata Dharma.

Likewise, Indu (Soma-juice or nectar) used to be offered to God as libation in Vedic yajnas (worships), and consumed afterwards by people (Hindu) for health, life, prosperity and progeny. Hindu means as someone propitiated by Indu (the Vedic libation). Note, H--in Hindu, and pronounced as in hut--implies auspiciousness or delight.

Religion belonging to Hindu is called Hindu Dharma.

In response to the misconception that the word Hindu originated as some foreigners stepped into India, note that no one from outside could have come to India and started calling the locals Hindu suddenly if such a word (in Sanskrit--not those foreigners' language) had not already existed there. 'Hindu' also is not related to 'Sindhu'--a word with similar ending and meaning ocean or river, especially in the west of India.

The words Sindhu (ocean or river) and Hindu (expiated by Indu) are linguistically and phonetically different, and Hindu is not derived from Sindhu. Note that Vedic Sanskrit did use the letters (sounds) 's' and 'dh' and therefore would not replace them with 'h' and 'd', respectively, transforming Sindhu into Hindu. In addition, the ancient Greeks reaching India (circa Alexander the great) could have easily pronounced Sindhu without changing it to Hindu by dropping S in favour of H since they were used to pronounce Sigma (an alphabet in Greek, their mother-toungue) which is syllabically somewhat similar to Sindhu.

Furthermore, Muslims entering India for the first time and speaking Arabic or Persian—languages having alphabets Sad and Sin etc. for 's' sounds—would not have to substitute H for S in Sindhu (and thus make it Hindu) to pronounce or use it in their own languages. The word Hindu—not specific to any particular region or area—was already in use when these foreigners arrived in India, and they did not invent it from Sindhu accidentally or due to necessity.

Women's Issues: It seems from the above that the ancient society was quite considerate and respectful to those (both men and women) engaged in various vocations, and people were free to make choices or changes in their careers or skills if the opportunity existed. Vedic prayers also indicate that the women had considerable say in selecting their marriage partners, and were espoused to live in monogamous relationships while enjoying same rights as their husbands. Furthermore, in the Vedas there is little evidence of child marriages, dowry system and the practice of suttee or sati (self-immolation of a woman upon her husband's death).

Similarly, there is no indication of any stigma relating to widowhood or the remarriage of a widow. Note also that the well-educated, scholarly and charismatic women of yore, who also participated in many philosophical debates with men, included Gargi (the daughter of Vachaknu-from the Brihadaranyaka Upanishad) and Vidyottama (wife of the famed poet and writer, Kaalidasa, who started his life as a humble and menial worker in the woods). It is clear that the women or the lowly and humble in the society were neither ignored nor abandoned.

Listed below are a few examples of multi-vocational families and people changing their occupations and life styles.

(a) As indicated in the above, from the Rigveda, the mother of a bard (probably of the scriptures) was working in corn-grinding (an activity usually for a Shudra).

(b) Majority of the Rishis (sages) were both Brahmin and Kshatriya so as to manage their Aashramas (hermitages) effectively.

(c) In the Chandogya Upanishad, Satyakama (the illegitimate, varnasankra, son of a Shudra woman who did not even remember who her son's father was) went on to be accepted and educated for Brahmin work (the Gita: Ch. 18-verse 42). This shows that the people (including the Shudra and of unknown lineage) had the choice of pursuing any occupation (even that of a Brahmin).

(d) Valmiki (given to chanda-meaning impetuosity-in his early days) started life as a robber. But later in life, after performing penance, he studied to become a Brahmin. He went on to become a great Rishi (sage) and wrote the Ramayana in Sanskrit. Thus, going from being a chandaal (meaning-cruel and brutal person) to a great human being not only demonstrates his personal endeavour, but also that the society was quite accepting of such a process and its outcome. In general, as indicated here and in the Vedic passages, the concept of untouchability (with respect to the Shudra or any one else as a dalit / untouchable) did not exist. Any shunning or condemnation of a person was due mainly to his / her engaging in an activity not useful or acceptable to the society. Above all, it is also clear that any type of socially stigmatic situation could be easily improved through penance and by changing one's behaviour. Incidentally, this type of humane rehabilitation of criminals and sinners is a sign of civilized people long ago; and this humane practice exists even today in various countries claiming to be modern and civilized.

(e) In one of the stories from the Ramayana, Rishi Vishvamitra is said to have conducted Yajna (worship) at which the officiating priest was a once Kshatriya and the Yajamaan (worshipper) a Chandaal.

(f) In the Mahabharata, Satyavati (a Shudra-girl whose father was a fisherman), when presented with a marriage proposal from king Shantanu, married him only after he accepted her pre-nuptial agreement. Her own children, in stead of another older heir to the throne, went on to inherit the Kshatriya kingdom as was demanded in the pre-nuptial agreement. This indicates that the intercaste marriages and exchanges were quite prevalent; and that the women and Shudras could make free choices even when there was royalty involved.

(g) *Matrimonial and Vocational Choices:* The evolution of society and customs was mainly due to the individual and collective needs and choices (as indicated also in some of the above Vedic quotes on marriage, vocational activities etc.). In addition, the role and influence of various espoused or suggested proclamations such as involving the varnashrama dharma (casteo-monastic orders) etc.-based on non-scriptural (non-Vedic) writings (such as Manusmriti etc. accredited to Manu et al.)-on the development and progress of society at large (across-the-board) was rather insignificant.

The ancient society (generally modest and homogeneous economically) did not restrict the cross-caste matrimonial and occupational choices. In spite of the socially liberal conditions, though, the change in vocation did not always lead to significant economic gains. In addition, some vocations (*e.g.*, Vaishya and Shudra) were inherently conducive for their young to quickly and easily engage in the family business / profession and settle down (socially and economically) early in life. Consequently, the children from these families found the other vocations (such as the Brahmins and, to some extent, the Kshatriya) to be less rewarding and not worth the preparatory effort, which included living and training (and paying the teacher through labour) for decades in hermitages in harsh and forest-like conditions where the knowledge exchange between the guru and the pupils was usually in the oral tradition since the written manuscripts (on papyrus etc.) were scarce.

On the other hand, the children from the Brahmins and the Kshatriyas families were predisposed (through the natural and continuous exposure to the family business) and were readily inducted by their parents into their traditional professions. Over time, this type of selecting the professions inadvertently gave rise to the tradition of vocation based families all around even though the society had not sought such an outcome. Note that the society in this respect remained flexible and allowed people (including the Shudra, who also engaged in menial and ignoble pursuits) the freedom of choice in their undertakings.

In a similar and related context, it was deemed vocationally advantageous and convenient for a couple to marry if they both had the same background, because they would then be able to get involved in their family occupation quickly and easily without facing any uncertainty or requiring any additional apprenticeship. Moreover, the bride or the groom in this type of wedding arrangement would be less likely to encounter any unexpected, unfamiliar, inhospitable and unwanted post-marital social situations. Note also that, in addition to the weddings involving same type of families, the marriages among people from vastly different backgrounds also frequently took place (as in the case of Satyavati and Shantanu) and the society posed no restrictions.

Thus it was basically an arbitrary social custom which arose over time as a matter of convenience whereby the people stuck to their family professions and also married within same type of families (vocations). Note, the lack of relevant information available in print etc. probably also led to the guru-pupil based disciplic tradition for knowledge/spirituality which would otherwise be not as crucial. In any case, people (of any caste) desiring to not follow these customs or to break away from them simply should go on their own-without any fear of repercussions from the state, society or religion-to learn and pursue new vocations; and in the process they would also be able to find compatible and willing marriage partners for themselves within the society at large. Moreover (as regards to the Gita: Ch. 5-V. 18, Ch. 6-V. 9, Ch. 9-V. 32), the priests and temples that serve (cater to) and admit all (Brahmin, Kshatriya, Vaishya, Shudra including the disadvantaged or Dalit) should be accorded the greatest respect and support.

Illustration of the Rise of Sub-castes within Castes: As humans continued to create and adopt new occupations, move to new places and territories, or encounter unfamiliar surroundings and situations, the four primary vocations (castes: Brahmin, Kshatriya, Vaishya and Shudra) developed or transformed into several secondary sub-castes characterized by peoples' tasks etc. For example, vocationally speaking, if a person-while trying to become a Brahmin-learnt two Vedas, he would be called a Dwivedi, whereas the learner of three Vedas would be known as a Trivedi. It shows that titles (or sub-castes) as Dwivedi and Trivedi basically correspond to certain specific Brahminic pursuits.

Similarly, a Vaishya engaged in forming objects from loha (iron) would be called the Lohar, whereas, the maker of articles from sona (gold) would be called the Sonar. Moreover, if a Sonar's son pursued his father's occupation (business) and was followed by his son, and so on, it would give rise to a sub-caste (lineage) called Sonars within the Vaishya caste. Note that such preference or tradition for family business would occur for several reasons. First, the parents generally found it easy and safe to guide their young towards a familiar and time assured vocation. Second, the familiarity with parents' job made it easy for children to learn and practice that occupation. Third, it might probably help in attaining the familial stability and lead to an easy transfer of accumulated knowledge and expertise between generations.

The influence of migration on sub-castes can be similarly explored. Consider the following example. At some point in history, a certain inhabited area was to be inundated under a new dam and the people had to move and live elsewhere. As they settled in a new area, the locals there would address them as the Damiya (meaning-from the dam). Some of the newcomers might even prefer this new title to that they had before moving to the new place. Moreover, when, for example, a newcomer (migrant or Shudra) started working as Mistree (mason), he would be called a Damiya-Mistree (a Vaishya-usually a person in non-priestly or non-administrative occupation). Similarly, if the person worked as a priest, he would be known as the Damiya-Brahmin. This indicates that the title 'Damiya' had suddenly acquired the status as a sub-caste. More importantly, note that two principal castes (Brahmin and Vaishya) had gained sub-castes with the same name (Damiya) with reference to totally different tasks (as priests and masons).

The above examples illustrate the manner in which the sub-castes are created and the way they relate to the principal castes. Note also that, depending on the circumstances, the newly created sub-castes may either co-exist with the original sub-castes, or replace some or all of the latter. This surely can lead to drastic fluctuations in their numbers. As this process of creating and retaining of sub-castes occurs time and again over vast places and cultures, their numbers remain uncertain and alter frequently making it difficult to keep track of them. Nonetheless, the sub-castes are functional in character and subject to easy transformations.

Vedic/Hindu Tenets: The ancients were in favour of progressive ideas (*e.g.*, about the environment, philosophy / religion and life style) and appear to have conducted their affairs reasonably and democratically. They either shunned or actively opposed the stagnant, blind and baseless practices (rituals) and the intolerant / autocratic persons and beliefs (faiths). The rituals for invocations of the physical, imagery (tales / myths) and the mundane were deemed less rewarding than the meditation of the spiritual, the source (truth / logic) and the divine; (meditation is explained in Ch. 6 of the Gita). Note that the reality expressed in terms of various physical (artistic) forms or through poetry can have different interpretations. For example, in some of the ancient texts, a viman may just be a cart or chariot and not necessarily an airplane or sky-craft.

While considering chatur as four (and bhuj meaning arm, and mukh meaning face or mouth), chatur-bhuj and chatur-mukh are shown as four-armed and four-faced idols. In stead, consider for example, chatur as the skilled one: chatur-bhuj and chatur-mukh will then represent, anthropomorphically (like a human with a face and two arms), a god (deva: friendly and blissful, superior being) who is skilled-armed (or ambidextrous: probably in all the occupations) and skilled-orator (*i.e.*, a fine instructor).

Thus, chatur-bhuj and chatur-mukh are, respectively, symbols of the omnipotence and the omniscience of One God, or reflect His excellence in enterprise (as Vishnu) and instruction (as Brahma). God is One: Braham or Brahman (not the Brahmin caste). When He (as Atman) enters the body (or as spirit unites with nature), life begins, and He is called Brahma. As long as He stays in the body, the life continues, and He is seen as preserving it and is called Vishnu. Once He leaves the body, life ends (or body expires); and His departure is seen as if He has worked as Rudra in bringing an end to life. But, throughout, He remains One: Brahma, Vishnu and Rudra are only His aspects of creation, preservation and termination.

Thus, in regard to man-made symbols for displaying various Divine attributes for the purposes of worship and meditation etc., there should be some correspondence between the attribute and the symbol. For example, if omnipotent God is to be represented 'as meaning Vishnu' in human form, it is sufficient and logical to interpret chatur (in chatur-bhuj) as skilled (even as ambidextrous) in all the tasks. Similarly, if omniscient God is to be represented 'as meaning Brahma' in human form, it is sufficient and logical to interpret chatur (in chatur-mukh) as skilled in oratory and knowledge.

Thus, there is no need to interpret chatur as four in chatur-bhuj or chatur-mukh; and hence it is unnecessary to assume or create various four-headed and four-armed religious symbols for representing God anthropomorphically. Incidentally, note also in Ch. 11 of the Gita, Arjuna-after having realized vision of the Omnipresent encompassing all Creation-wishes (verse 46) to see the lord (mentor) in chatur-bhuj form (holding scepter and circle), which seems to refer only to latter's dexterity. And Arjuna's wish is soon fulfilled (Ch. 11-V. 50) as he is able to see Krishan as a regular (normal looking) person, and there is no suggestion anywhere that the former had an encounter with anyone bearing four arms.

Metaphorically speaking, Shiv-Linga (or Shiv-Lingam) refers only to Shiva-the remover of destruction, *i.e.*, same as the preserver (Vishnu or God), and it necessarily is not a certain special symbol (*e.g.*, shown often in pollex or index form); because in Linga (or Lingam), the word Li (which in second or Object case singular form becomes Lim or Lin with nasal sound ending) means loss or destruction, and ga (or gam) implies removing or going away. Thus, Shiv-Linga (or Shiv-Lingam) symbolizes God's power (attribute) to extricate from destruction or loss.

Note also that the symbol (such as, the pollex, ling or phallus looking), portrayed in various religious rituals (Hindu and elsewhere), has probably the origins in the ancient fire (Agni) sacrifice or worship to God. It appears to be a solid image of jwala (flame) from a yajna (sacrificial fire) and was perhaps introduced long ago as a duplicate for the sacrificial fire. Because creating and lighting of a yajna used to be a very difficult and time-consuming process (as indicated in some of the Vedic hymns also), this image made the worship possible anywhere anytime (*i.e.*, by using it in place of live fire and pouring oblations upon it).

Note that the smearing of the solid symbol with ash also points to a close association with fire worship. Similarly, when this fire (Agni) solid (symbol) is placed under a pitcher from which the libation slowly and continuously flows over it, it appears to give the impression of an unending and uninterrupted active worship even during the absence of worshippers. There, the solid symbol represents the live fire in a yajna and the pitcher (with dripping libation) symbolizes the worshipper pouring oblations into the fire. In addition, it is worth noting that some of the practices in present-day worships appear to relate closely to the original fire sacrifice: the lighting of lamps or candles represents the actual or original fire (flame), and the burning of incense recreates the aroma that would be given off by the oblations (soma etc.) into the live fire.

In this regard, the symbols dedicated to Agni (or Shiv, God) should also correspond to logic and not just to myth or fiction. The identification of Agni symbol (*i.e.*, jwala, or Agni-ling: ling meaning symbol) as a phallus is perhaps due to the confusion that their shapes are similar. Note that the early humans were praying and worshipping for everything. They also prayed to God for children (heroes, sons). In this regard, religiously and psychologically, the Agni symbol 'looking like phallus' became the favourite idol. Unfortunately, over time, people forgot about its association with Agni, and identified it only in terms of biology and procreation. (Note: Since Shiva refers also to the auspicious flame or Agni-jwala, Agni-ling or a similar looking object probably was referred to as Shiv-ling.)

Note, Agni is a manifestation of BRAHMAN or Iswara. Agni in the male aspect is Shiva, and as female is Shakti. The Agni-jwala (flame) is called Shiva. The common symbols (*e.g.*, long or stubby ling or symbol) for Shiva and Shakti are just solid images of Agni (Yajna fire). Incidentally, Shiva and Shakti always appear together--perhaps due to their common association with Agni. Moreover, Agni is also probably the biggest destroyer. Thus the connection between Agni and Shiva as the destroyers can be seen. On the other hand, Shankra is the greatest among Rudras; and Rudras are destroyers. Thus Shiva (through a connection with Agni as the greatest destroyer) probably, in His destructive aspect at least, is also identified with Shankra (the greatest Rudra destroyer). Note, Agni probably also is the origin of a number of other dark coloured gods (idols), where their colour corresponds to dark (black) coloured ash (associated with fire or yajna).

In references to Hanumat or Hanuman, the name appears simply to imply a strong-jawed (or a very strong) person and not necessarily a monkey or monkey-chief. Similarly, Ganesha or Ganapati may simply mean Lord (Isha, Pati) of the people (Gana) and not just an elephant-headed figure (ganika meaning a female elephant).

Thus, it seems that there is a tendency to express and endorse a certain specific divine trait as a whole (entire) phenomenon through recognizable art (shapes and forms) and stories (fictional accounts) to make it more appealing and understandable to the masses. Unfortunately, if such a message is not communicated properly or is lost over time, it will mislead and confuse people and may even wrongly imply that there is more than one real source of divinity. Note, as indicated also in Rigveda (Book 1: Hymn 164 # 46) and the Gita (Ch. 13: Verse 16), the Source basically is, locally and universally, the same and complete in essence and attributes.

Similarly, in the Rigveda, the division of Purusha (Being or Spirit) is indicated to have taken place at the beginning; the implication of which really is the transcendence of the (chaotic) old into the (stable) new in terms of evolution of the society. There, the emergence of Brahmin, Kshatriya, Vaishya and Shudra from the body of Purusha symbolically corresponds, respectively, to their occupations giving the society its voice (arising as if from Purusha's mouth), order (as if through Purusha's arms), form (as if on Purusha's thighs), and change or migration (as if via Purusha's feet).

Furthermore, in the three original (basic to Hinduism) Vedas (Rig, Yajur and Sam) referred to above, little mention or support is shown for astrology; and sorcery, witchcraft, magic and worthless worships are condemned (RV: Book 7, Hymn 104.20, 23-25; Book 10, Hymn 37.4). Similarly (RV: Book 7, Hymn 104.5,7, 13-16), civic or religious (for god or faith) deception (corruption, cheating and wickedness) and exploitation (including coercion, bondage, aggression and plundering) are forbidden and not to be tolerated. Note, the Gita (Ch. 16) reiterates these precepts; and (Ch. 3-V. 26) favours advancing of religion/spirituality peacefully and by example.

Salvation, Karma, Reincarnation and Metamorphosis: It was realized long ago that, irrespective of one's background, attaining the immortality or overcoming the death (or the fear of it) is in understanding oneself (individual life or being)-the union between soul (spirit-real, sat or eternal) and body (matter-unreal, asat or transient)-as part of the Supreme (stated also in Ch. 2, 6, 7 & 9 of the Bhagawad Gita). Symbolically, therefore (as stated in Ch. 8 of the Gita), following the path (or going in the time) of clarity (as in the light of day or the sun) about the self is liberating (Ch. 6); whereas, following the path (or going in the time) of confusion (as in the darkness of night or the moon) about the self brings nothing but fear (morbidity). It is worth noting (the Gita: Ch. 6-verse 45) that, whatever a person's social status or civic duty, the spiritual gains derived from all efforts for achieving the union of one with the One are imminent and cumulative.

In this context, the Karmic principle (*i.e.*, a good or bad action leads to a good or bad outcome) is assumed to influence the course of events taking place during this life and, supposedly, afterwards. Accordingly, each experience or action by a person affects him in body* and soul in the next situation or future. Each experience itself is a life/Janma: its beginning and end symbolically being birth and death. Moreover, according to the Karmic principle, even when the body dies, the soul continues to live and may feel the residual effect of the preceding existence. The reincarnation therefore symbolically represents the extension of this principle during the hereafter.

It is, in other words, a new opportunity or promise to accrue spiritual gains on the basis of actions during previous life. Note also that reincarnation merely presents to a person a new possibility (opportunity) arising out of countless influences, and, depending upon the new surroundings (people, environment etc.) and the future actions by the individual himself, it may or may not fully materialize (the Gita: Ch. 18-verse 14). For example, as indicated above, even though Satyakama started as a Shudra (in a non-Brahmin vocation), he went on, through his own initiative and effort and with the help of his guru, to acquire new skills to become a Brahmin (the profession of choice for him).

Thus, reincarnation-being associated with the soul-appears to be unimportant with regards to the worldly pursuits such as involving vocations (castes) etc. Similarly, salvation (Moksha)-which also relates to the soul-is achievable by all (irrespective of their background), and can be easily attained by uniting (elevating) one's soul with God by practicing good deeds and penance etc. The Gita, to this end, states (in Ch. 2)-in response to a query in Ch. 1 (verse 42) regarding the rituals to ancestors-that God's grace and the good deeds by a person during his own lifetime are important to seek salvation.

The supposed metamorphoses of God as Ram and Krishan etc., heroes of the early civilizations (in epics Ramayana and Mahabharata etc.), should be taken in spiritual/moralistic/ philosophical context. The reverence (mainly ritualistic or for a reward) to them-dedicated according to their physical eminence and existence, and based primarily on the stories which appear to be skewed over time into myths/tales (Pauranic etc.)-thus needs to reduce. Note that God alone is deemed worthy of all worships (the Gita: Ch. 9-V. 24, Chs. 10 & 4) since all the eminence and creation--including even all the gods and goddesses associated with various places, times or events--are ultimately due to Him. Incidentally, when Krishna speaks in the Gita, he is not only speaking as a friend (well-wisher) and charioteer (worker and assistant) of Arjuna, but he is also advising Arjuna in the capacity of a guru. Above all, in essence, Krishna also is both BRAHMAN (Iswara) and Atman in the Gita.

Note also in this regard that the notion of a personal God sometimes results in a very informal devotee-deity relationship. The devotee often uses various preferred salutations, representations and rituals (worships and offerings) to express his unique love and reverence towards the 'kind and caring' deity. But, when many people engaging in this manner-in their own special ways of worships, etc., are viewed collectively, their society is seen to be overly ritualistic and following many gods, even though, in reality the ultimate object of reverence remains One. (Note, the Gita: Ch. 9-V. 26).

Conclusion: The vocational choice long ago was mainly need-based (personal and tribal) and circumstantial (in terms of the availability of labour at a place or time, natural disasters and battles among tribes). It inspired that the societal tasks and responsibilities be dispensed solely in terms of a person's nature or qualification (Guna) and his active undertaking or assignment (Karma). It was a great vision at work that is referred to also in the Bhagawad Gita (as in the original Sanskrit verse 13 of Ch. 4, where the reference is made only to Guna-nature/qualification, and it does not mean born nature). Incidentally, the original vocations seem to have been similar to the present jobs that also require compatibility between the worker's qualifications and the potential assignment.

Inherently, the above system satisfied one and the all. The Gita (Ch. 18-verse 41) further elaborates that all occupations are important and correspond to various needs or segments of the society and are dispensed according to ability (svabhava) on the basis (prabhva) of qualification (guna; which does not mean born nature). The duties relating to each adopted vocation (as explained in the above Introduction: Brahmin, Kshatriya, Vaishya, Shudra) are also listed in the Gita (Ch. 18-verses 42, 43 & 44). It is also indicated in the Gita (Ch. 5-verse 4) that all spiritual paths are applicable and bring same results to people with different vocations.

The Gita (Ch. 16 & 18) stresses that, while it is of utmost importance to recognize and adhere to one's own responsibility or the task at hand, there is no other special advantage or basis (in terms of ritualism or one's heredity) for pursuing a particular undertaking. A socially necessary and useful activity for the physical well-being of person is as important as any worship/puja for his/her salvation (The Gita: Ch. 3-verse 8). The Gita (Ch. 3-verse 35) further notes that taking care of one's own responsibility (purpose/dharma) merits higher than venturing needlessly elsewhere, since keeping one's own obligation (even in a miniscule way) leads to satisfaction that outweighs the trappings, uncertainty and formidableness associated with another's task.

It is also stated in the Gita (Ch. 12, Ch. 18-verses 45 & 46) that, no matter what a person's duty or task (whether shubh-appealing, or ashubh-unappealing), he attains perfection or heavenly bliss if he is fully dedicated to it and performs it with pleasure and interest as if it were a service to the Lord (Transcendent or the Manifest). Lord, God or Hari (Saviour) is expressed (Ch. 17) divinely (in accordance with tattva) as

OM TAT SAT (Creator, Master and the Righteous). (Creation seems to arise from OM during contemplation as the omniscient, TAT is what maintains it through omnipotence, and it has the noble and righteous end according to SAT.) Note also that God is one, yet He can manifest in more ways than one (Ch. 4 & 9); and He dwells in the heart of all (Ch. 18). He is One in all (stated above; the Gita: Ch. 13-verse 16). In addition, one need not be preoccupied about the hereafter (or the heaven and the hell) as long as he understands the good from the bad (Ch. 16 of the Gita) and the redemption (spiritual) through penance (monetarily free and as stated in the Gita: Ch. 9-verses 30 & 31).

Thus, the Vedic religion (Hinduism) is universal and progressive: the Hindu way of life is open to all, and without any discrimination on the basis of gender, race, heredity, beliefs, occupation, social status or background, and the place of origin. It is very logical (promotes knowledge and science / vigyan-the Gita: Ch. 6-verse 8), encourages reasoning (the Gita: Ch. 18-verses 63, 71 & 72), and is quite easy to understand and practice (as indicated in Ch. 3, 9 & 16 of the Gita). It is based on the fundamental principle of 'one to One relationship' or unity between a person and the universal God. In other words (*e.g.* the Gita: Ch. 9-v. 10 & 29), everyone abides identically to the supreme, is significant to the creation, and has the same right to seek and realize the divine. In conclusion and at the personal level, one easily attains perfection and heavenly bliss in any activity (duty) if he / she keeps anger, lust and greed in check (the Gita: Ch. 16); stays mindful of the Lord (the Gita: Ch. 8), such as in the sense of the mantra (sacred words) 'Hari OM TAT SAT' (the universal God is the means of salvation); and through that undertaking (activity) adores/serves Him and His creation (the Gita: Ch. 11 & 18).

Thus it is also clear from the above that one (of any caste or background) need not feel disadvantaged, discriminated, dispossessed or deprived of spirituality as a Hindu if he/she pursues God by own free will in a manner convenient or appropriate to him/her. Remember that everyone is entitled to the same inspiration (guidance) and bliss (love) from God, who (as the source of vision and benediction) is the ultimate (greatest) guru/prophet (the Gita: Ch. 11) and friend / benefactor (the Gita: Ch. 5).

Closing Comment: It is okay for a person-having no one to extend to him objective or satisfactory help and guidance in the matters relating to spiritual fulfilment, prayer and the place to pray-to choose a mode of worship suited to his needs and resources. Incidentally, worthless worships, myths / tales, hate-mongering and evil/corrupt deeds are detrimental to spirituality / faith. It is also worth noting that all-men, women, believers, nonbelievers and others-have the same rights and freedoms and they all deserve equal protection and consideration under a law that is constantly evolving with time and according to the need of the society.

Thus, a contemporary civil legal code-progressive and reflective of the peoples and times-seems preferable to a law that may be perceived as antiquated, dictatorial, discriminatory, cultist or religious.

The notion that a group/nation run by decree will be foremost in freedoms and human rights is misguided. A diverse, pluralistic and progressive society subjected to an autocratic or religious law/rule can quickly drift into a puritanical, singular and regressive system as the dissenting people either run away from it or totally succumb to the ruling dogma to ensure their own safety. Thus, the sectarian territorialization or vision of the world must cease, and any regime adverse to progressiveness should be shunned.

In addition, the practices of casteism (social stratification in terms of vocation or caste), animal abuse, child labour, gender discrimination, dowry, veil (*e.g.* the body and face covering apparel) etc. must stop. It is also in the interest of humanity to rise above various tenets and practices and, while not ignoring the local issues, tackle serious global problems: rapidly deteriorating environment, depleting natural resources, disappearing flora and fauna, and overpopulation-already indicating a population exceeding the reasonable limit of about five billion people worldwide.

History of Social Relations in India

No aspect of Indian history has excited more controversy than India's history of social relations. Western indologists and Western-influenced Indian intellectuals have seized upon caste divisions, untouchability, religious obscurantism, and practices of dowry and sati as distinctive evidence of India's perennial backwardness. For many Indologists, these social ills have literally come to define India-and have become almost the exclusive focus of their writings on India.

During the colonial period, it served the interests of the British (and their European cohorts) to exaggerate the democratic character of their own societies while diminishing any socially redeeming features of society in India (and other colonized nations). Social divisions and inequities were a convenient tool in the arsenal of the colonizers. On the one hand, tremendous tactical gains could be achieved by playing off one community against the other. On the other hand, there were also enormous psychological benefits in creating the impression that India was a land rife with uniquely abhorrent social practices that only an enlightened foreigner could attempt to reform. India's social ills were discussed with a contemptuous cynicism and often with a willful intent to instill a sense of deep shame and inferiority.

Strong elements of such colonial imagery continue to dominate the landscape of Western Indology. A liberal, dynamic West embracing universal human values is posed against an obdurate and unchanging East clinging to odious social values and customs.

It is little wonder, therefore, that India's intellectuals have been unable to either fully understand the historic dynamics and context which gave life to these social practices or find effective solutions for their cure. Many historians and social activists appear to have tacitly accepted the notion that caste divisions in society are a uniquely Indian feature and that Indian society has been largely unchanged since the writing of the Manusmriti which provides formal sanction to such social inequities.

But caste-like divisions are neither uniquely Indian nor has Indian society been as socially stagnant as commonly believed. In all non-egalitarian societies where wealth and political power were unequally distributed, some form of social inequity appeared and often meant hereditary privileges for the elite and legally (or socially) sanctioned discrimination against those considered lower down in the social hierarchy.

In fact, caste-like divisions are to be found in the history of most nations-whether in the American continent, or in Africa, Europe or elsewhere in Asia. In some societies, caste-like divisions were relatively simple, in others more complex. For instance, in Eastern Africa some agricultural societies were divided between land-owning and landless tribes (or clans) that eventually took on caste-like characteristics. Priests and warriors enjoyed special privileges in the 15th C. Aztec society of Mexico as did the Samurais (warrior nobles) and priests of medieval Japan. Notions of purity and defilement were also quite similar in Japanese society and members of society who carried out "unclean" tasks were treated as social outcasts-just as in India.

Amongst the most stratified of the ancient civilizations was the Roman Civilization where in addition to state-sanctioned slavery, there were all manner of caste-like inequities coded into law. Even in the Christian era, European feudalism provided all manner of hereditary privileges for the knights and landed barons (somewhat akin to India's Rajputs and Thakurs) and amongst the royalty, arranged marriages and dowry were just as common as in India. Discrimination against the artisans was also commonplace throughout Europe, and as late as the 19th century-artisans in Germany had to go through a separate court system to seek legal redress. They were not permitted to appeal to courts that dealt with the affairs of the nobility and the landed gentry. (For instance, Beethoven wrote numerous letters to German judicial authorities pleading that he not be treated as a second-class citizen-that as Germany's pre-eminent composer he deserved better treatment.)

A common pattern that seems to emerge from a study of several such ancient and medieval societies is that priests and warriors typically formed an elite class in most medieval societies and social privileges varied according to social rank; in settled agriculture based societies, this was usually closely related to ownership of land.

For instance, we find no evidence of caste-like discrimination in societies where land was collectively owned and jointly cultivated, or where goods and services were exchanged within the village on the basis of barter, and there was no premium assigned to any particular type of work. All services and all forms of human labour were valued equally. Such village communes may have once existed throughout India and some appear to have survived until quite recently-especially in the hills, (such as in parts of Himachal and the North East, including Assam and Tripura), but also in Orissa and parts of Central India. In such societies, we also see little evidence of gender discrimination.

In India, caste and gender discrimination appear to become more pronounced with the advent of hereditary and authoritarian ruling dynasties, a powerful state bureaucracy, the growth of selective property rights, and the domination of Brahmins over the rural poor in agrahara villages. But this process was neither linear nor always irreversible. As old ruling dynasties were overthrown, previously existing caste equations and caste hierarchies were also challenged and modified.

In many parts of India this process may have taken several centuries to crystallize and caste rigidity may be a much more recent phenomenon than has been commonly portrayed. The impression that caste divisions were always strictly enforced, or that there were no challenges to caste rigidity does not seem to square with a dispassionate examination of the Indian historical record.

It should also be emphasized that caste-distinctions were not the only way, or even the most egregious way in which social inequities manifested themselves in older societies. In ancient Greece and Rome, the institution of slavery was at least as cruel a practice, if not worse. (It is therefore quite ironic how the slave-owning Greek states are revered by Western intellectuals as the world's first "democratic" societies but ancient India is denigrated for it's incomprehensible social ills.) Levels and degree of caste discrimination in India have varied with time and there has been both upward and downward mobility of castes and social groups. Going by the strictures outlined in the Manusmriti, one might conclude that caste distinctions were set in stone, rigidly enforced and the possibilities of caste mobility completely circumscribed. But a closer examination of the historical record suggests otherwise.

Already in the Upanishadic period there were tensions between Brahmins and Kshatriyas, and there are explicit parables in the Upanishadic texts illustrating how an enlightened Kshatriya was able to exceed a Brahmin in spiritual wisdom and philosophical knowledge. In the Mahabharatha, there are references to a Brahmin warrior suggesting that caste categories were not entirely inflexible.

There is also criticism of parasitism amongst Brahmins in some of the texts from the Upanishadic period, and social commentators emphasized how those who reneged on their social obligations were undeserving of their caste privileges.

This is an important point because it suggests that there was an implied social contract that involved both privileges and social obligations. The monarch might have enjoyed immense power and prestige, and exacted numerous rights over the common people, but also had the obligation to defend the people- to protect them from invaders, to dispense justice in an unprejudiced manner and assist in the development and preservation of irrigation facilities and roads. Failure to meet such expectations could and did lead to revolts, and dynasties rose and fell within a matter of few generations.

7

The Stages of Brahminical Life

There are four stages of life, *viz.* Brahmachari (student), Grihasta (Householder) Vanaprasta (forest dweller or Hermit in semi retirement) Sannyasi (the renounced one in full retirement) and the Dharma of each is different. The four stages may be said to represent periods of Preparation, Production, Service and Retirement.

"People do not have to be taught to want to be happy, to want to be secure or to want the respect and admiration of their friends and associates—though often they need instruction 'how' to secure these things.

Deeper Hindu thinking suggests, however, that there is also a natural progression of these values so that one should grow toward more fundamental interests.

This movement toward more enduring and satisfying values has been institutionalised in the understanding of the four stages of life known as 'Ashramas".

Brahmacharya (Celibate)

Brahmacharya means Student, usually between 12 and 24 years of age. The first stage is Brahmacharya. The duty of a student is to study. On initiation into Brahmacharya by means of the Upanayana rites, he becomes a 'Dvija' (a twice born). 'Upanayana' means 'bringing near'-the disciple is brought near the Guru for receiving the initiation of mantras.

For the Brahmachari, celibacy is his forte, discipline is his norm, devotion to his Guru is his duty and concentration in studies is his vocation.

In "Gurukula Vasam" (or staying with the preceptor) he learns the nuances and intricate renderings and interpretations of Vedas, Upanishads and Shastras though by means of rote so that when he comes of age the significance of what he learnt would be realised by him in real life situations, which he would be facing in his next Ashrama.

Thus, it is a period of probation, a period of training, in a practical manner without prejudice to the injunctions of Shastras he had so studiously learnt as a Brahmachari. Only when someone consoles we feel relief; only the 'Guru Upadesa' can change our mental attitude. The first lesson of the student is the performance of 'Sandhya Vandanam' at morn, noon and evening, Ablutions, recitation of Gayatri, breath control, sipping and sprinkling of water, pouring libations of water to the Sun-God, etc. were enjoined on the twice-born and they could never be missed.

Grihastaashrama

Grihasta means House-holder usually between 24 and 48 years of age. The next stage is of the householder. After the 'Gurukula Vasa' he graduates himself into the mundane world, taking a wife to assist him in his performance of Dharmic duties.

All Shastras proclaim the importance of the Grihastaasrama as the fulcrum of all other Ashramas. People in the other three Ashramas heavily lean on the Grihasta for support and sustenance required to carry out their respective duties. The Grihasta earns his livelihood by whatever a vocation befitting his being a member of his group, raising children, supporting his own family, kith and kin besides the persons performing their duties in the other three Ashramas.

The life of a Grihasta is therefore, considered a 'Jivayagna'—a lifelong saga of self sacrifice for the benefit of others in society.

Marriage is not meant as a means to satisfy carnal craving. It is regarded as a means to spiritual glory, a sin qua non for the development of lineage—a necessary link between the dead past and an unborn future that must come alive to be undertaken as a part of spiritual duty with devotion (Shraddha) to perpetuate the family tradition. According to Bhagavata Purana, a Griha (house) is not a person for one who has controlled his senses, delights in spirit and is eager for knowledge.

Partners who enter in wedlock are not 'paragons of virtue' as they appear in the first flush of enthusiasm. None is perfect and to seek for perfection in the partner is like seeking a mirage in the desert.

Perfect relationship is created by conscious effort and not discovered all of a sudden. The incompatibilities have to be resolved by a continual mutual adjustment and reconciliation by a willing attitude of 'give and take'.

Marriage is marriage and is not a mere love affair which is but an infatuation. Love affair is a relationship just for the pleasure of the person involved and it has no consideration of the families of the persons. When the pleasure wears out, the affair is gone.

But, marriage is a life commitment. If you make a sacrifice, you are not sacrificing to that person. It is a sacrifice to a permanent relationship. Love bears all, endures all. If the relationship has pains, remember that life is a mixture of joys and sorrows.

The practice in India that a husband and wife could continue to remain as husband and wife till death and also celebrate the Golden jubilee of their wedding at the 60th age of the husband is still very common.

Those that end in divorce or separation are misfits for the marriage life who have no understanding of the marriage and its divinity. They fail in 'making it work' and deserve the real pain, indeed the devastating trauma attaching thereto.

The duties of the Grihasta include the performance of 'Panchmahayagna' (five great sacrifices) laid down in Manu Dharma Shastra.

Deva Yagna: (Deity worship) The daily worship and puja to Ganapathi, Kula devata and Ishta devata. Visiting kula devata temple often or atleast once in a year.

Brahma Yagna: (Seer worship) Each day the householder expresses his debt to the human kind by doing some services to the society. Performing ones own profession/vocation with the standards of ethics itself is a service to the society. Brahma Yagna also includes Guru worship and studying, teaching, repeating and meditating upon the Vedic scriptures. (Vedic rituals)

Pitru Yagna: (Ancestor Worship) Respecting the ancestors, parents of the self and spouse and getting their blessings by making salutations to them by leaning towards their foot. Parentless children should perform Annual Shraddas (Thithi) and observe fasting during new moon days and beginning of months, offer rice balls (pindas) to crows or in holy river. Those persons who do not know the thithi of their parents death should perform thithi on the new moon day of the month "Thai" which usally comes between the second week of January and the second week of February. The thithi given or the fasting observed on thai amavasya constitute a remembrance of ancestors back to the 7th generation.

Bhuta Yagna: Worship of living beings by scattering grains, offering food at the threshold for animals, birds, insects, etc. Loving and watering plants also do constitute bhuta yagna.

Nara Yagna or Purusha Yagna or Manushya Yagna (Guest worship) Obligation to love and honour ties of fellowship with humanity by showing hospitality to fellow humans, friends, relatives or even strangers and beggars. It is to be noted here that a person performing his Panchmahayagna everyday without fail will not be disturbed by kali purusha.

Marriage is an integral part of a Grihasta for it is said that no ritual is efficacious without the presence of the wife, the Sahadharmini.

The wife always accompanies the husband in discharging his duties. Marriage is no doubt, primarily for begetting children but it was also required for the proper performance of worship.

Marriage is not only a contract between individuals but a contract between families.

The difference in the family values as between those obtaining in India and in the West would reveal how different are the expectations about marriage in these two cultures.

The first three nights after marriage, the couple are expected to remain continent to impress that marriage is not a license for sexual pleasures but a holy and irrevocable contract not only between the man and wife but also casts the burden of ensuring it to be so, till the very last, on the community comprising of the families of both sides. The husband is expected to first satisfy the wife's soul and the wife satisfies the husband with her body and gets his soul.

On Abortion, the Shastras are very clearly against it. The foetus is considered to be a living person with consciousness who is required to be protected and reared with care and affection.

Rigveda even goes to the extent of pleading for mercy on behalf of the foetus.

Atharvaveda characterises the killer of a foetus as brunagni, one of the most heinous sins.

Kaushitaki Upanishad equates it to the killing of one's parents.

Gauthama Dharma Shastra advises such persons as having lost their caste status-considered in those days as equal to capital punishment.

Susrutha Samhita the medical treatise, however, permits abortion on purely medical grounds Mudhagarbha which explains the steps to be taken to save both mother and child in case of emergency and advises that if the foetus is alive, every attempt should be made to remove it from the mother's womb alive. If dead, it may be removed in the normal course. Surgical removal (Caesarian) should not be resorted to if it is likely to harm the mother and / or the child. In extreme cases, it permits inducing miscarriage of the foetus if that were the only means to prevent the loss of the mother. Children were loved to the point of becoming spoilt darlings.

Vanaprasta Ashrama (The Anchorite)

Vanaprasta is the third stage of Elder Advisor usually between 48 and 72 years of age. A stage comes when business, family, secular life like the beauties and hopes of youth have exhausted themselves and need to be left behind. The person retires usually from worldly attachments to lead a life of contemplation and meditation alone or with his wife.

What life holds beyond middle age depends in the end not on fancy and imagination but on the realities of the values of life we regard as inviolable. Vanaprasta may be termed as the beginning of a person's real 'adult education' to evaluate his performance thus for as Grihasta and reorder his life in such a way as to discover who he is and what life is all about.

"The time had come for him to probe 'the secret of 'I' with which he has been on such intimate terms all these years yet which remains a stranger, full of inexplicable quirks, baffling surds, irrational impulses."

It is curious to find that many do not wish to venture into this but would like to remain in Grihastashrama even by remarrying if the first spouse predeceases the man.

A playboy of 25 may impress but how could one pose perpetually as the 'prince charming' at 50, 60 or 70 years of age? Look at those who try hard to do this. However hard they might try, they not only fail to receive recognition but also incur the derision of people whom they seek to impress.

Sannyasa Ashrama (The Renounced): Sannyasi is the fourth stage of an Ascetic-Solitaire-usually beyond 72 years of age. This means 'Samyak Nyasa'—'Total detachment' from worldly pleasures including the bare necessities to subsist. This is the last 'Ashrama'. He does not aspire to be recognised as somebody who matters—he wish of the Sannyasi is just to be a 'persona non grata'—one who exists almost without giving any thought to his being-with no desire for name or fame or recognition.

"He no more cares whether his body falls or remains than does a cow what becomes a garland that someone

has hung around her neck—for the faculties of his mind are now at rest in the holy power, the essence of bliss."

"Business, family, secular life, the beauties and hopes of youth and the success of maturity have now been left behind, Eternity alone remains. And, so it is to that— and, not to the tasks and worries of their life, already gone which came and passed like a dream-that the mind is turned."

"The Sannyasi has his spiritual eye on goods that men can't give and cares little for anything that men can take away. Therefore, he is beyond the possibility of either seduction or threat."

Sannyasa is of Four Kinds: 'Vidvat'-born out of real wisdom and is spontaneous 'Vividisha' springing from a yearning for self-realisation through study of the Scriptures and practicing the rigours prescribed Aatura upon one's deathbed when there is no hope in living further, and Markata-embracing Sannyasa as an escape from great misery, disappointment or misfortune that one is not able to face in worldly activities.

No one is encouraged to become a 'Sannyasi' unless one has gone through one's natural impulses through the three previous Ashramas. He who runs away from marriage (Grihastaashrama) is no better than a coward deserting the battle field.

The student's attention is directed inward, preparing for life ahead. In Grihasta and Vanaprasta attention is directed outward-Grihasta supporting the entire society, Vanasprasta sharing his experiences for the good of others. The Sannyasi is again inner directed. Having contributed to society and having received from society what he needed, he prepares himself for the final release.

Sannyasa means renunciation not of life alone but of Kama, Artha and even worldly Dharmas. Sannyasa may be deemed a second phase of Brahmacharya.

The first was a preparation for life; the second a preparation for death. While Brahmacharya and Grihasta show the 'Pravritti Marga (towards the world), Vanaprasta and Sannyasa indicate the 'Nivritti Marga' (away from the world) through introspection and renunciation.

Thus, while 'Varna' is determined by past 'Karma', Ashrama is determined by the stage of maturity displayed by individuals in viewing the goals of life.

"Varnas stress human nature; Ashramas stress human nurture"

And, Lord Krishna advises "One's own duty, though done imperfectly is preferable to the duty of another even if well performed. Even death in doing one's own duty is blissful; doing another's duty is frightful".

So, everyone is advised to do his / her 'Dharma' according to one's Varna and Ashrama—and not to venture doing those outside one's own.

Every person has his Svabhava (natural being) fitting him for his Svadharma (natural function). We cannot change either our natural being or our natural function because nature cannot be forced into a change by our whims and fancies.

A Sadhu was rescuing a scorpion that had fallen into a pond. Every time he lifted it out of water, it stung him but he would not give up until it was saved. One of his disciples asked why he was persistent in saving the scorpion that stung him. The Sadhu replied: "The `Dharma' or nature of scorpion is to sting; the nature or Dharma of a Sadhu is to rescue a being from distress—and in this case sure death by drowning. So long as the scorpion does not give up its Dharma why should I give up mine and give up saving it?" The `Dharma' of fire is to burn, of water is to be cool, of wind is to blow. So, the Dharma of man is to be humane. This story emphasises how one should go on doing one's duty even if obstacles, impediments and difficulties intervene in discharging it.

The Dharma of a student is to study. If the student—neglects his studies he neglects his svadharma; if fire does not burn, it is not fire; When heated by fire (by external influence) water loses its nature (Svadharma) of being cool. When Svadharma is not practiced, there ensues an imbalance in the environment. This understanding and adherence to Svadharma is what distinguishes human beings from other beings.

Purusharthas

Purusha means human being and artha means object or objective. Purusharthas means objectives of man. According to Hindu way of life, a man should strive to achieve four chief objectives (Purusharthas) in his life. They are:

1. dharma (righteousness),
2. artha (material wealth),
3. kama (desire) and
4. moksha (salvation).

Every individual in a society is expected to achieve these four objectives and seek fulfilment in his life before departing from here. The concept of Purusharthas clearly establishes the fact that Hinduism does not advocate a life of self negation and hardship, but a life of balance, achievement and fulfilment.

Dharma: Dharma is a very complicated word, for which there is no equivalent word in any other language, including English. Dharma actually means that which upholds this entire creation. It is a Divine law that is inherent and invisible, but responsible for all existence. Dharma exists in all planes, in all aspects and at all levels of creation. In the context of human life, dharma consists of all that an individual undertakes in harmony with Divine expectations and his own inner spiritual aspirations, actions that would ensure order and harmony with in himself and in the environment in which he lives. Since this world is deluded, a human being may not know what is right and what is wrong or what is dharma and what is adharma. Hence he should rely upon the scriptures and adhere to the injunctions contained there in. In short, dharma for a human being means developing divine virtues and performing actions that are in harmony with the divine laws.

Dharma is considered to be the first cardinal aim because it is at the root of everything and upholds everything. For example see what happens when a person amasses wealth without observing dharma or indulges in sexual passion against the social norms or established moral values. Any action performed without observing dharma is bound to bring misery and suffering and delay ones salvation. Hinduism therefore considers it rightly as the first cardinal aim of life.

In ancient India dharmasastras (law books) provided guidance to people in their day to day lives and helped them to adhere to dharma. These law books were written for a particular time frame and are no more relevant to the modern world. The best way to know what is dharma and what is adharma, is to follow the religious scriptures such as the Bhagawad Gita and the Upanishads or any other scripture that contains the words of God.

Artha: Artha means wealth. Hinduism recognises the importance of material wealth for the overall happiness and well being of an individual. A house holder requires wealth, because he has to perform many duties to uphold dharma and ensure the welfare and progress of his family and society. A person may have the intention to uphold the dharma, but if he has no money he would not be able to perform his duties and fulfil his dharma. Hinduism therefore rightly places material wealth as the second most important objective in human life. Lord Vishnu is the best example for any householder who wants to lead a life of luxury and still be on the side of God doing his duties. As the preserver of the universe, Lord Vishnu lives in Vaikunth amid pomp and glory, with the goddess of wealth herself by his side and yet helps the poor and the needy, protects the weak, upholds the dharma and sometimes leaving everything aside rushes to the earth as an incarnation to uphold dharma.

Hinduism advocates austerity, simplicity and detachment, but does not glorify poverty. Hinduism also emphasises the need to observe dharma while amassing the wealth. Poverty has become a grotesque reality in present day Hindu society. Hindus have become so poverty conscious that if a saint or a sage leads a comfortable life, they scoff at him, saying that he is not a true yogi. They have to remind themselves of the simple fact that none of the Hindu gods and goddesses are really poor.

Hinduism believes that both spiritualism and materialism are important for the salvation of human beings. It is unfortunate that Hinduism came to be associated more with spiritualism, probably because of the influence of Buddhism, where as in truth Hinduism does not exclude either of them. As Swami Vivekananda rightly said religion is not for the empty stomachs. Religion is not for those whose main concern from morning till evening is how to make both ends meet. Poverty crushes the spirit of man and renders him an easy prey to wicked forces.

In ancient India Artha Shastras (scriptures on wealth) provided necessary guidance to people on the finer aspects of managing their wealth. Kautilya's Artha Shastra, which is probably a compilation of many independent works, gives us a glimpse of how money matters were handled in ancient India.

Kama: Kama in a wider sense means desire and in a narrow sense, sexual desire. Hinduism prescribes fulfilment of sexual passions for the householders and abstinence from it for the students and ascetics who are engaged in the study of the scriptures and in the pursuit of Brahman.

The Bhagawad Gita informs us that desire is an aspect of delusion and one has to be wary of its various movements and manifestations. The best way to deal with desires is to develop detachment and perform desireless actions without seeking the fruit of ones actions and making an offering of all the actions to God. This way our actions would not bind us to the cycle of births and deaths.

Hinduism permits sexual freedom so long as it is not in conflict with the first aim, *i.e.* dharma. Hindu scriptures emphasise that the purpose of sex is procreation and perpetuation of family and society, while the purpose of dharma is to ensure order in the institution of family and society. A householder has the permission to indulge in sex, but also has the responsibility to pursue it in accordance with the laws of dharma. Marriage is a recognised social institution and marriage with wife for the purpose of producing children is legitimate and in line with the aims of dharma.

One of the important sects of Hinduism is Tantricism. It recognises the importance of sexual freedom in the liberation of soul. The Tantrics accept sex as an important means to experience the blissful nature of God and the best way to experience God in physical form. They also refer to the concept of Purusharthas to justify their doctrines. They believe that sexual energy is divine energy and it can be transformed into spiritual energy through controlled expression of sex.

Just as the Dharmasastras were written for the sake of dharma, and Arthasastras for artha, Kamasastras were composed in ancient India for providing guidance in matters of sex. We have lost many of them because of the extreme secrecy and social disapproval associated with the subject.

Moksha: If dharma guides the life of a human being from below acting as the earth, showing him the way from above like a star studded mysterious sky is Moksha. Dharma constitutes the legs of a Purusha that walk upon the earth; both artha and kama constitute his two limbs active in the middle region; while Moksha constitutes the head that rests in the heaven.

Human life is very precious because of all the beings in all the worlds, only human beings have the best opportunity to realise the Higher self. It is also precious because it is attained after many hundreds and thousands of lives. Rightly, salvation should be its ultimate aim.

Moksha actually means absence of moha or delusion. Delusion is caused by the inter play of the triple gunas. When a person overcomes these gunas, he attains liberation. The gunas can be overcome by detachment, self control, surrender to god and offering ones actions to God.

If dharma is the centre of the wheel of human life, artha and kama are the two spokes and Moksha is its circumference. If dharma is at the centre of human life, beyond Moksha there is no human life, but only a life divine.

The four Purusharthas are also like the four wheels of a chariot called human life. They collectively uphold it and lead it. Each influences the movement of the other three, and in the absence of any one of them, the chariot comes to a halt.

The Four Yogas as Spiritual Discipline to follow the Dharma

Karman.yevaadhikaaras the' maa phalesuu kadaachana |

Maa karma-phala-hethur bhoor maa the sangosthv-akarmani || -II-47 || Chapter II-47

Thou hast a right to action or work alone, and never to its fruits;

let not the fruit of work be thy motive, let not thy attachment to inaction.

yoga-sthah: kuru karmaani sangam thyakthvaa dhananjaya |

siddhy-asiddhyoh: samo bhootvaa samathvam yoga uchyate' || -II-48 || Chapter II-48

Do thy work being steadfast in devotion and abandoning attachment, O Arjuna !

and being equal in success and failure. This evenness of mind is called Yoga

Doore'na hy avaram karma buddh'i-yogaadh dh'ananjaya |

buddh'au saranam annnviccha kr.panaah phala-hethavah: ||-II-49 || Chapter II-49 Bhagawad Gita

'O' Arjuna mere action performed with attachment is inferior to action performed with mind poised in evenness. Seek shelter in this state of unperturbed evenness in a desireless mind. Those who work for selfish gains are indeed pitiable..

The Spiritual Discipline and Teachings Applied for the Practice: The Philosophical teachings of Hinduism, like any scientific theory, are of no use to the common man unless it is applied for their daily practice. It has survived the test of time for many thousand years and still remains popular due to the sound principles on which its practice is based. It gives different rules of ethics and conducts for various categories of people. The Dharma Shastras and Smritis teach us of normal conduct in performing our work. Dharma, Artha, Kama and Moksha are the four Purusharthas that govern out activity. Dharma is the proper rules of one's duty, which literally means "that which holds" the universe and its beings. They are classified as Samanya Dharma or the general and universal rules and Visesha Dharma or specific personal rules for each individual. They give peace, joy, strength and tranquillity. Artha and Kama are the materialistic desire and passion, that also govern our actions. Unless one seeks the material benefits and pleasures within the scope of Dharma, it will cause grief with greed and lust. Moksha is the relief from pain and suffering and ultimate liberation that is the main reason for all our actions.

The Four Yogas as Spiritual Discipline: As rituals became popular and were being considered as the sole path for the eternal bliss, the soundness of its philosophy and ethics of practice were reestablished by the sages. The four Yogas give us the spiritual discipline of our conduct. Karma Yoga is the correct path of performing work without greed or desire and the action performed without looking for the fruits of benefit or loss. Raja Yoga is the discipline of control of our body and mind. It teaches concentration, meditation, breathing and physical exercise and a state of equanimity of the mind as a natural reaction to all activities. Bhakti Yoga is the spiritual discipline of absolute devotion and love of God. It teaches prayers and surrender to God at all times. It teaches to see and feel God in all people and all actions. Jnana Yoga is the path of obtaining Spiritual knowledge through action, study, meditation and devotion.

Three Gunas: Vedas describe three personality traits, Sathvika, Rajasika and Tamasika. Sathvika Gunas are present in the pious person who follows all teachings of the faith and Dharma. Compassion to all animals, Ahimsa and vegetarianism are advocated as Sathva Guna. The Rajasika Gunas are present in people who enjoyed some amount of worldly pleasures directed by desire and ego, which are Artha and Kama. Tamasika persons have no knowledge of the proper Dharma or they do not care for them. They are driven solely by Artha and Kama which are passion, greed and lust. These Gunas are present in all but one is dominant. The Yogas advocate the ways to follow the superior Sathva Guna and the ways to suppress the undesirable Artha and Kama without the proper Dharma. Performance of proper Dharma and all the Karma leads to a sense of peace and equanimity of mind and eternal bliss. The individual makeup of a person, his Guna and effects of his Karma determines the rebirth and ultimate liberation. Performance of one's duty without devotion to God is dry and empty. Performance of such duty should be without any attachment to its fruit but as a devotion to God. Hinduism gave us the four Vedas, the three Agamas, the six Dharsanas and the four Yogas.

Bhakti Yoga, the attainment of Divinity through worship.

Guru Brahmah Gurur Vishnuhuhu Guru Devoo Maheswaraha

Guru Sakshath Para Brahma Tasmai Sree Gurave' Namaha

Guru is Lord Brahma, Lord Vishnu and Lord Maheswara,

Guru is nothing but the Supreme Brahman devoid of attributes.

That is the reason why we bow to the Guru.

Bhakti Yoga, the methods of worship.

Various forms of Devotion and Sanskara

Hindu Religious Faith and practice are based on its strong philosophy and the ancient tradition. Most of the followers know about the Vedas and the Vedantha philosophy. Every one understands that there is one God who is worshipped in many forms. Most of them are familiar with the Advaita theory and Vedanta philosophy of oneness of the Divine and the human soul. However, the practice is much more closer to the Dvaita and Visista-advaita theories for the worship of the Divine. The paths of Karma yoga, Raja yoga, Bhakti yoga and Gnana yoga are taught as the spiritual disciplines for the practice. Some feel that Gnana or the path of wisdom is the ultimate while others consider that after performing duties without attachment as in Karma yoga, practicing meditation and controlling thoughts as in Raja yoga and gaining knowledge of Gnana path one will reach the state of ultimate surrender of Bhakti yoga.

Among all the paths of Hinduism, the most common and popular ones have been the ritualistic [Sanskara] path and the Devotional [Bhakti] paths of worship. The ritualistic path involves the practice of sanskaara which are performing the regular rituals for the formless Supreme Divine as prescribed in the Karma kanda and Upasana kanda portions of the Vedas. They are performed every day and for various events in one's life. These are practised and performed mostly by persons knowledgeable in the Vedas and the Hindu philosophy and those initiated to the practice of these rituals.

The Bhakti pathway is much easier to follow for everyone. It teaches a method of love and attachment towards a supreme God through one of His manifestations as in the Agamas and Puranas with devotional prayers and worship to various forms of Deities through poojas and bhajans. This form of Bhakti develops into various levels and degrees as an inner attitude of an attachment and feeling of love towards God, from a blind faith and devotion to God in one form to total surrender to the Supreme.

Bhakti Yoga-the Devotional Pathway: Para-Bhakti is the form of devotion with contemplation on the formless and unmanifested Brahmam. It is the highest form of Bhakti suitable only for few learned people, the Jnana Yogis, who have the true knowledge of God.

Apara-Bhakti or Gauni-Bhakti is the primal level of love and devotion to a manifested Iswara and prayers to one of His forms accepted as Ishta-Devatha or a personal God. There are many levels or grades in this, the most important being Bhaya-Bhakti, Anyaya-Bhakti and Ekantha-Bhakti.

Bhaya-Bhakti is the very external form of worship of a Deity as God. It is the adoration paid to a form of God outside ourselves. It is the most basic form of a faith, based on the unenlightened or Tamasika feeling that God is external to us and dwells in a particular locality like the prayer room or Temple. The pilgrimages, worship of several images of God, symbols and sacred books are examples of this. Most popular religions do not rise above this level.

Anyaya-Bhakti [meaning "not another"] is the exclusive and passionate, or the Rajasika, form of worship of one's Ishta-Devatha in the heart. It is an intense form of monotheism and gives a healthy direction to the spirit of devotion. But, it shall not give rise to bigotry and cruelty towards those who have different concept of God and different methods of approach. Among Hindus, it is well recognised that the gods whom others worship are only different forms of his own Ishta-devatha.

Ekantha-Bhakti is the purest and Sattvika form of devotion. Here, the devotee loves God for His own sake and not for His gifts. He learns to crave for his personal God alone, in prosperity as well as in adversity. He sees the presence of God, as his Ishta-devata, in all places, at all times.

Bhavas as an expression of Devotion and Love

1. *Santha Bhava:* [means calmness of mind] The mind of the devotee is filled with divine knowledge and is emotionless, always undisturbed, peaceful and tranquil. Only Yogis and Jnanis, like Bhishma, who are highly developed and have had direct experience of God will be able to practice Santha Bhava.
2. *Dasya Bhava:* The devotee considers himself as inferior to God. He takes God to be his Master and looks upon himself as just a humble servant. He considers it is his duty to worship and to love God. Hanuman is an example of Dasya Bhakti.
3. *Sakhya Bhava:* The devotee considers God to be a dear friend, the sole supreme companion, and as his equal in relation, with pure friendship not degenerating into familiarity. Arjuna is an example of Sakhya Bhaktha.
4. *Vatsalya Bhava:* The devotee considers God as his Child and the themselves as the mother giving and also getting the unconditional love of the Child. Mother Yashoda had Vatsalya Bhakti towards Child Krishna as her own child.
5. *Kantha Bhava:* This is the expression of devotion with a feeling like the one a wife gets and gives towards her husband, as in the case of devotion of Sita or Rukmini

towards Sri Rama and Sri Krishna, called Kantha Bhava.

6. *Madhurya Bhava:* This is the highest expression of Divine love. Here, the devotee takes the lord to be his beloved, with deep love, devotion and surrenders himself. When Gopikas like Radha develops Bhakti towards Sri Krishna, it is the romantic love and surrender of the self to the lover, without any sensuality but with pure devotion and surrender, called Madhurya Bhava.

Fundamental Disciplines needed for Bhakti Yoga

1. *Abhyasa:* Practice of constantly and continuously remembering God with a steady mind.
2. *Viveka:* Discrimination, the ability to choose between right and wrong.
3. *Vimoka:* Intense longing for God, rejecting everything that hinders our progress.
4. *Sathyam:* Truthfulness, to be always observed as a basic rule of spiritual ethics. We have to live a life of truth, think truth alone, speak truth and listen carefully to their own inner voice called conscience.
5. *Arjavam:* This is straightforwardness or honesty.
6. *Kriya:* Doing good to all beings, as the devotee will God in all forms.
7. *Kalyana:* This is wishing well of others with a loving heart, praying to the Lord for the well being of others, for the peace and welfare of the world.
8. *Dhaya:* Compassion, as God is love, mercy and compassion personified. As we seek to realise Him, we, too, must develop the same qualities.
9. *Ahimsa:* The practice of non-violence, non-injury to all creatures, by way of action, thought or word.
10. *Dhaana:* Abundant and spontaneous charity with a pure heart, for relieving the suffering of the distressed is a potent means of growing spiritually.

11. *Anavasada:* To be cheerful and hopeful is an essential quality of a devotee. One must always have faith and hope.

manmana bhava madh-bhakto madh-yaaji man namaskuru |

mam-e' vaishyasi sathyam the' prathijane' priyo'sime' | |

Bhagawad Gita Chapter XVIII-65

With your mind engrossed in Me, become My devotee, worship Me and salute Me.

I promise you that you will come to Me alone, as you are so dear to Me.

Etham Vibhoothim Yogam Cha; Mama Yo Ve'tthi Thatthvathah: |

So'vikalpena Yogena Yujyate'; Nathra Samsayah | |

Bhagawad Gita Chapter X-7.

He who knows about this manifestation of My divine majesties and my power unites with Me in steady and unfaltering communion. About this there is no doubt.

Cycles of time as recorded in the Vedas and Upanishads

Here are cycles of time as recorded in the Vedas and Upanishads.

Small Yuga: 2,000 years. The axis of the earth spends 2,000 years in an astrological sign and the moves on to the next sign, going backwards through the signs of the zodiac. Since we are finishing the Pisceaen cycle, we are ready to enter the Aquarian cycle for the next 2,000 years. We commonly refer to entering Aquarius as the "dawning of the age of Aquarius."

Complete Cycle of Small Yugas: 24,000 years. This is the amount of time needed for the earth to spend 2,000 years in each sign of the zodiac.

The Great Cycle: In addition to the earth's axis moving in an arc as it travels through the signs of the zodiac, there is another cycle. This is a cycle which involves the revolution of the entire solar system around the Central Sun of the Galaxy.

The orbit is elliptical rather than circular. To make the elliptical movement of the solar system around a great central point more understandable, the analogy of "seasons" is used. This is a useful analogy because changes in overall states of consciousness are represented as "seasons" through which the solar system passes on its journey.

When consciousness is in a high state, it is summer. At this time, 90 per cent of the inhabitants of the earth are enlightened. This is called Satya Yuga, or the Age of Truth. When Fall or Spring are in full swing, the numbers of enlightened beings drops to less than 10 per cent. When Winter comes, far less than 1 per cent of the people on earth are enlightened. However, there are trade offs.

First, it is easier to make progress in the "'winter of consciousness." The analogy is often used that if one tries to row one's boat in air, very little progress will be achieved. But when the oars are placed in water, much more rapid progress can be made. This is because compared to air, the resistance of water is much higher enabling the work of the oars to bear fruit. It is the resistance itself which provides a route to rapid progress. Similarly, in spiritual winter our efforts to achieve spiritual growth produce much faster results than they would in any other age of consciousness because of the great general resistance to things spiritual.

There is no disagreement among all the sages, pandits, gurus and swamis that Kali Yuga, the present spiritual winter, affords an opportunity for more rapid spiritual progress than any other age. Further, the medium for rapid growth is almost universally prescribed by these same classes of spiritual teachers as divine sound through the medium of mantra. Here are the various seasons and ages of the universe as measured in human years.

Winter (Kali Yuga): 432,000 years

The year 2001 is 5,093 years from the beginning of Kali Yuga of the long cycle. For the short cycle, winter is ending with the entrance of the planetary axis into Aquarius, which begins the season of Spring for the shorter, 24,000 year cycle.

Spring: (Treta Yuga) 1,296,000 years

Summer (Satya or Krita Yuga) 1,728,000 years

Autumn (Dwapara Yuga) 864,000 years

Total Time for One Cycle or Manvantara: 4,320,000,000 years

This is called "A Day of Brahma" and is followed by a night of equal length.

One complete day and night of Brahma: 8,640,000,000 years

360 of these days is called "One Year of Brahma": 3,110,400,000,000 years

100 of these years constitute the life of Brahma called a Maha Kalpa: 311,040,000,000,000 years

At the end of a "Maha Kalpa" or cycle of creation, Shiva manifests his destructive influence and the universe is dissolved. The ancient texts call this the cosmic dissolution. All the levels of the manifest universe disappear. After a great cosmic rest cycle, another creative cycle begins as a new Brahma emerges out of the navel of Narayana and the universe is created anew.

Another item of importance is that one who has achieved the highest level of conscious realisation is said to realise and become one with Brahman. At this point, all individuality as we know it disappears. The individual Jiva, Soul or Atman retums to its source from which it will not return of its own volition. However, for reasons known only to itself, certain souls may return for reasons understood only by Narayana.

Samskara

The ultimate goal of every Hindu is to attain Moksha. This can only come through atma-vidya, which is knowing one's self, through thought and introspection. To attain this, the scriptures give some guidelines. The first step is to master eight characteristics. These called atmagunas are:

1. Compassion (daya)
2. Forgiveness or patience (kshanti)

3. Absence of jealousy (anasuya)
4. Cleanliness (sauchyam)
5. Not feeling mental strain or doing work with effortless ease (anayasa)
6. Auspiciousness (mangala)
7. Non-miserliness (akarpanya)
8. Non-grasping or non-desiring nature (asprha).

Toward cultivation of these characteristics, the Vedas also give guidelines as to the rituals to be performed over one's lifetime. Sixteen such rituals are collectively called Shodasha Samskara.

Samskara denotes purification ritual. Starting from the time when the child is in the womb, these sixteen rituals end in the final journey of the body into the afterlife. They can be divided into those performed during five different stages of life, *i.e.* prenatal, childhood, student, adult life and old age or wisdom years. Forty rituals are discussed but sixteen are still in practice.

1. *Garbhadana Samskara:* Performed by a married couple when conceiving a child. This important samskara raises the act of conception to a sacred occasion, and is powerfully purifying and uplifting for the unborn child.
2. *Pumsavana Samskara:* Usually performed between the second and fourth month of pregnancy. Its purpose is, first, to promote the birth of a male child (for perpetuation of the family line and tradition); second, to insure the good health of the fetus and the proper formation of its organs, regardless of gender.
3. *Simantonoyana Samskara:* In the fourth or fifth month of pregnancy, the mind of the fetus begins to develop. This is when simantonoyana samskara is performed. Its purpose is to protect the fetus—especially its newly forming mind—from all negative influences, and also to stimulate the development of the unborn child's intellect.
4. *Jatakarma Samskara:* It is the ritual performed at the

birth of a child. It awakens the child's intellect, gives it strength and promotes long life for the child.

5. *Namakarana Samskara:* On the 11th day after the child's birth, namakarana samskara is performed. In this ceremony, the child receives its name.
6. *Nishkramana Samskara:* The baby's first outing into the world, beyond the confines of the home, is the occasion of nishkramana samskara.
7. *Annaprashana Samskara:* The first feeding of solid food to the baby, usually in the sixth month after birth, is the occasion of Annaprashana samskara.
8. *Karnavedha Samskara:* Usually performed in the sixth or seventh month after birth, consists of the piercing of the baby's ear lobes, so earrings may be worn.
9. *Chudakarana Samskara:* At the end of the first year, or during the third year, the child's hair is shaved—all but a tuft on the top of the head. This ritual shaving of hair, performed with ceremony, prayers and Vedic chanting is for both boys and girls.
10. *Vidyarambha Samskara:* This samskara begins a student's primary education by ceremonially introducing the child to the alphabet.
11. *Upanayana Samskara:* Initiates the formal study of the Vedas. It is one of the most important and esteemed of the samskaras. Upon performance of upanayana, a boy traditionally moves from home to live in the ashram of the Guru.
12. *Samavartana Samskara:* With samavartana samskara the disciple graduates from his Vedic studies and returns from the house of his Guru. Thereafter, the disciple will marry and raise a family, and so enter the stage of householder, grihasthaashrama.
13. *Vivaha Samskara:* The traditional Hindu wedding ceremony. It is considered by many to be the most important of all the samskaras.
14. *Panchamahayajna Samskara:* A married couple performs these five great sacrifices daily. In this

samskara, one honours, in turn, the rishis (ancient seers of Truth), the gods, the ancestors, humankind and all created beings.

15. *Vanaprastha Samskara:* According to the Vedic tradition, vanaprastha is the third stage of life, following brahmacharya (Vedic student/disciple) and grihastha (householder). Here, a man leaves behind his life in the world and retires to the forest (with or without his wife), to live an ascetic life devoted to study of the scriptures and to meditation.
16. *Antyeshti Samskara:* The final sacrament, the funeral rites.

Initiation or Upanayana: The initiation ceremony called the Upanayana or the second birth is a very ancient practice. The boy who undergoes the ceremony is said to be twice born or Dvija. He is also now considered an Aryan. The ritual consists of wearing a sacred thread called Yajnopavita with the utterance of the sacred mantra, which goes as follows:

"Om yajnopaveetam paramam pavitram prajapateryat sahajam purastaat.

Aayushyamagryam pratimuncha shubhram yajnopaveetam balamastu tejah."

"The sacred thread is great and pure.

It came to existence along with the birth of Brahma.

It is as old as He is.

May it, which is blessed by celestials, give us long life, strength and radiance."

The sacred thread is hung over the left shoulder and under the right arm. The cord is not to be removed once placed unless it is defiled by death or birth in the family. The cord was made of three threads, each of nine twisted strands made of cotton, hemp or wool, for Brahman, Kshatriya and Vaishya classes respectively. At this ceremony the boy (called Vatu) is taught the sacred Gayatri Mantra, whispered in his ear by his father and Guru (called Brahmopadesha). Only the higher classes can recite this mantra. It is as follows:

"Om Bhuh, Om Bhuvah, Om Suvah, Om Maha, Om Janah, Om Tapah, Om Satyam,

Om, Tat Savitur vareniam, Bhargo devasya dhimahi, Dhiyo yonah prachodayat."

"Om Earth, Om Sky, Om Heaven, Om Middle Region, Om Place of Births,

Om Mansion of the Blessed, Om Abode of Truth,

Let us think of the lovely splendor of God Savitur (Sun) that he may inspire our minds."

The Gayatri Mantra can also be translated as "That Eternal God or Creator, Independent Reality, the Worshipful, One who has no Beginning, Light of Wisdom and Truth. That Lord who manifests through the Sun (Savitur), propitiated by the highest Gods; One who bestows wisdom, bliss and everlasting life; we meditate on that Light. May that Light of God illuminate our intellect." A long time ago, most Kshatriyas and Vaishyas ceased to perform the initiation ceremony in its full form. The term 'twice born (dvija)' came to be applied more and more to the Brahman class.

Panch Mahayajna: Performance of numerous religious duties consists of proper following of one's Dharma. These are the bounden or obligatory karma of a Hindu. There are five great sacrifices (Pancha-mahayajna). These are to be performed thrice daily at sunrise, noon and sunset. They consist of:

- Brahmayajna, the worship of the Brahman the World Spirit, by reciting the Vedas:
- Pitryayajna, the worship of the ancestors, by libations of water and periodical Shraddha
- Devayajna, the worship of the gods, by pouring ghee on the sacred fire.
- Bhutayajna, the worship of all living things, by scattering grains and food for the animals and spirits.
- Purusayajna, the worship of men, by showing hospitality.

Kama was a legitimate branch of human activity and physical love was not disparaged. Though the term generally means desire, the word has definite sexual connotation. The Hindu literature, both religious and secular, is full of sexual allusions and symbolisms.

The temple carvings of the Middle Ages are full of couples in full embrace and sexual positions. Vatsyayana's Kamasutra is the most famous text dedicated to Kama. It is a remarkable work giving detailed instructions of erotic technique and aphrodisiac recipes and charms. There is emphasis on mutual gratification and foreplay. There are at least sixteen types of kisses detailed! In the historical perspective it gives a great insight into the life of Hindu upper class of the times.

It is important to remember the difference between similar sounding words. 'Brahman' is the Universal World Soul mentioned in the Vedas. 'Brahmanas' are the appendices to Upanishad where the sacrificial rituals are carefully delineated. 'Brahman' or 'Brahmana' is the priest class of Hindus, which is one of the four castes.

Bibliography

Agehananda Brarati, Swami : *The Light at the Center, Context and Pretext of Modern Mysticism*, Ross-Erikson, Santa Barbara. 1976.

Airi, Raghunath : *Concept of Sarasvati (in Vedic Literature)*, Munshiram Manoharlal Publishers Pvt. Ltd. Delhi, 1977.

Anant, S. S. : *Changing Caste Hindu Attitudes Towards Harijans: A Follow Up After Four Years*, New Delhi, Vikas, 1979.

Arnold E.V. : *Historical Vedic Grammar*, The American Oriental Society, New Haven, Connecticut, 1897

Atal, Yogesh : *The Changing Frontiers of Caste*, Delhi, National Publishing House, 1968.

Banerjee, Nitya Narayan: *Hindu Polity, Positive and Perverted*, Hindutva Publ., Delhi, 1985.

Benjamin, Joseph : *Scheduled Castes in Indian Politics and Society*, New Delhi, Ess Ess Publications, 1989.

Beteille, Andre. : *The Backward Classes and the New Social Order*, Oxford University Press, Delhi, 1981.

Bondurant, J. : *Harijan: A Journal of Applied Journalism, 1933-35*, Garland, New York, 1973.

Callewaert, Winand M. : *India, Betoverende Verscheidenheid*, Davidsfonds, Leuven, 1996.

Carroll, Lewis : *The Complete Illustrated Works of Lewis Carroll*, Chancellor Press, London, 1993.

Chatterji, Bankimchandra : *Essentials of Dharma*, Sanskrit Book Depot, Calcutta, 1979.

Dalit Panthers : *Dalit Panthers Manifesto*, London, Zed Books, 1973.

Devahuti : *Harsha, a Political Study*, Oxford University Press, Delhi 1983.

Dietrich, Gabriele : *Dalit Movements and Women's Movement*, Horizons India Books, New Delhi, 1992.

Diwan, Paras : *Modern Hindu Law*, Allahabad Law Agency, Allahabad, 1972.

Dubois, Abbe : *Hindu Manners, Customs and Ceremonies*, New Delhi, AES, 1983.

Durant, Will : *The Story of Civilization*, Our Oriental Heritage, New York, 1972.

Freeman, James M. : *Untouchable : An Indian Life History*, CA, Stanford University Press, 1979.

Gandhi, Mohandas Karamchand : *Truth Is God*, Navjivan Publ., Ahmedabad, 1955.

Ganesan, L. : *Relevance of Reservation*, Madras, Valentina Publications, 1991.

Goel, Sita Ram : *How I Became a Hindu*, Voice of India, Delhi, 1993.

Golwalkar, M.S. : *We, Our Nationhood Defined*, Bharat Prakashan, Nagpur, 1947.

Gopal, Ram : *The History and Principles of Vedic Interpretation*, Concept. New Delhi, 1983.

Gorhe, Neelam : *Social Development and Dalit Women*, Gyan Pub, House, New Delhi, 1995.

Gough, Kathleen : *Harijans in Thanjavur*, New York, Monthly Review Press, 1973.

Grimes, John : *A Concise Dictionary of Indian Philosophy*, Radhakrishnan Institute, University of Madras, 1988.

Gurukal, Rajan : *The Formation of Caste Society in Kerala*, Rawat Publications, New Delhi, 1994.

Gurumurthy, S. : *Hindu Heritage, Assimilative, Not Divisive*, Vigil, Madras 1993.

Hariharananda Giri, Swami : *Secrets and Significance of Idol Worship among the Hindus*, Karar Ashram, Puri, 1984.

Harsh Narain : *Myths of Composite Culture and Equality of Religions*, Voice of India, Delhi, 1991.

Indra Prakash : *Hindu Mahasabha, Its Contribution to Indian Politics*, Akhil Bharatiya Hindu Mahasabha, Delhi, 1966.

Jain, Girilal : *The Hindu Phenomenon*, UBSPD, Delhi, 1994.

Jordens, J. T. F.: *Gandhi's Religion: A Homespun Shawl*, St. Martin's Press; London, 1998.

Kakade, S. R. : *Scheduled Castes and National Integration: A Study of Marathwada*, New Delhi, Radiant Pub., 1990.

Kamble, N. D. : *Deprived Castes and their Struggle for Equality*, Ashish Publishing House, New Delhi, 1983.

Kane, P.V. : *History of Dharma-Shastra*, Bhandarkar Oriental Research Institute, Pune, 1990.

Karve, Irawati : *Hindu Society: An Interpretation*, Poona, Sangam Press, 1961.

Kavlekar, K.K. : *Non-Brahmin Movement in Southern India, 1873-1949,* Kolhapur, Shivaji University, 19790

Keith, A.B. : *Rigveda Brahmanas*, Harvard University Press, Cambridge, 1920.

Kishwar, Madhu : *Religion at the Service of Nationalism, and Other Essays*, OUP, Delhi, 1998.

Klostermaier, Klaus K. : *A Survey of Hinduism*, State University of New York Press, Albany, 1989.

Kooiman, Dick : *India: Mensen, Politiek, Economie, Cultuur*, Koninklijk Instituut voor de Tropen, Amsterdam, 1994.

Kosambi, D. D. : *The Culture and Civilisation of Ancient India in Historical Outline*, London, Routledge and Kegan Paul, 1956.

Kosambi, D.D. : *The Culture and Civilisation of Ancient India in Historical Outline*, Vikas Publ., Delhi, 1988.

Kshirsagar, R. K. : *Dalit Movement in India and its Leaders (1857-1956)*, New Delhi, MD Pub. Pvt. Ltd., 1994.

Kuiper, F.B.J. : *Aryans in the Rigveda*, Rodopi, Amsterdam, 1991.

Lakshmanna, C. : *Caste Dynamics in Village India*, Nachiketa Publications, Bombay, 1973.

Madhok, Balraj : *Indianisation*, Orient Paperbacks, Delhi, 1970.

Majumdar, D. N. : *Caste and Communication in an Indian Village*, Asia Publishing House, Bombay, 1958.

Majupuria, Trilok Chandra and Rohit Kumar : *Sadhus and Saints of India and Nepal*, Tecpress, Bangkok, 1996.

Marriott, McKim : *India through Hindu Categories*, Sage Publ., Delhi, 1989.

Mayer, A. : *Caste in an Indian Village: Change and Continuity 1954-1992*, Delhi, OUP, 1996.

Mckean, Lise : *Divine Enterprise, Gurus and the Hindu Nationalist Movement*, Chicago University Press, 1996.

Meadow, Richard : *Agricultural and herding in the early oasis settlements of the Oxus Civilization*, Antiquity, 1994.

Mesquita, Roque : *Madhva's Unknown Literary Sources – Some Observations*, Aditya Prakashan, New Delhi, 2000.

Mishra, J. : *Equality vs Justice, The Problem of Reservations for Backward Classes,* New Delhi, Deep & Deep, 1996.

Mitter, Sara S. : *Dharma's Daughters: Contemporary Indian Women and Hindu Culture,* NJ, Rutgers University Press, 1991.

Mohan, P.E. : *Scheduled Castes: History of Elevation, Tamil Nadu, 1900-1955*, Madras, New Era Pub., 1993.

Murugkar, Lata : *Dalit Panther Movement in Maharashtra: A Sociological Appraisal*, Popular Prakashan, Bombay, 1991.

Naidu, A. Nagaraja : *Caste and Land in Colonial South India*, Rawat Publications, New Delhi, 1994.

Nanda, B. R. : *Gandhi and His Critics*, Oxford University Press, Delhi, 1993.

Narayan, K. : *Storytellers, Saints, and Scoundrels*, Philadelphia, University of Pennsylvania Press, 1989.

Nath, Trilok : *Politics of the Depressed Classes*, Delhi, Deputy Publications, 1987.

Nehru, Jawaharlal : *Glimpses of World History*, Asia Publ., Delhi 1934.

Oddie, G.A. : *Hindu and Christian in South-East India*, London, Curzon Press, 1991.

Pangborn, Cyrus R. : *Zoroastrianism, A Beleaguered Faith*, Vikas Publ., Delhi 1982.

Patwardhan, Sunanda : *Change Among India's Harijans: Maharashtra a Case Study*, New Delhi, Orient Longmans, 1973.

Punekar, S.M. : *Harijan Contribution to Medieval Thought*, Prasaranga, Bangalore University, Bangalore, 1991.

Raja, C. Kunhan : *The Taittiriya Sarvanukramani of Yaska*, Madras, 1931.

Raulwing, Peter : *Horses, Chariots and Indo-Europeans*, Archaeolingua Foundation, Budapest, 2000.

Robb, Peter: *Dalit Movements and the Meanings of Labour in India*, New Delhi, Oxford University Press, 1993.

Roy Burman, B.K.: *Beyond Mandal and After Backward Classes in Perspective*, New Delhi, Mittal, 1992.

Sarkar, J. : *Caste, Occupation and Change*, Delhi, B. R. Publishing Co., 1984.

Sastri, P.S. : *Ananda K. Coomaraswamy*, Arnold-Heinemann Publ., Delhi 1974.

Savarkar, Vinayak Damodar : *The Indian War of Independence* 1857 Rajdhani Granthagar, Delhi, 1988.

Scheftelowitz, Isidor : *Die Kasmirische Rezension von Katyayanas Sarvanukramani,* Zeitschrift fur Indologie und Iranistik, 1922.

Sharma, K. L. : *Caste, Class and Social Movements*, Rawat Publications, Jaipur, 1986.

Singh, G. P. : *Early Indian Historical Tradition and Archaeology*, D. K. Printworld Pvt. Ltd. New Delhi, 1994.

Sri Aurobindo : *The Foundations of Indian Culture*, Sri Aurobindo Ashram, Pondicherry, 1984.

Staal, Frits : *Een Wijsgeer in het Oosten, Op Reis door Java en Kalimantan*, Meulenhoof, Amsterdam, 1988.

Talageri, Shrikant : *Aryan Invasion Theory and Indian Nationalism*, Voice of India, Delhi, 1993.

Tatachariar, Agnihotram Ramanuja : *Eternal Relevance of Vedas*, Tirumala Tirupati Devasthanams, Tirupati, 1985.

Tully, Mark : *No Full Stops in India*, Viking/Penguin, Delhi, 1992.

Upadhyaya, Baladeva : *Sanskrit Sahitya ka Itihasa*, Varanasi, 1968.

Van Lysebeth, Andre : *Tantra, le Culte de la Fesminite*, Flammarion, Fribourg, 1988.

Vedalankar, Pandit Nardev : *Basic Teachings of Hinduism*, Veda Niketan, Durban, 1978.

Venkateshwarlu, D. : *Harijan-Upper Class Conflicts*, Discovery, New Delhi, 1990.

Vivekananda, Swami : *Complete Works*, Advaita Ashram, Calcutta, 1992.

Waterstone, Richard : *De Wijsheid van India*, Kosmos, Utrecht, 1995.

Webster, John : *The Christian Dalits: A History,* Delhi, Indian Society for Promoting Christian Knowledge (ISPCK), 1994.

Winternitz, Maurice : *A History of Indian Literature*, Motilal Banarsidass, Delhi, 1987.

Zakaria, Rafiq : *Gandhi and the Break-up of India*, Bharatiya Vidya Bhavan, Mumbai, 1999.

Index

L

M

N

O

P

R

S

T

U

V

W

Y

❑❑❑